Liberation Theology
from Below

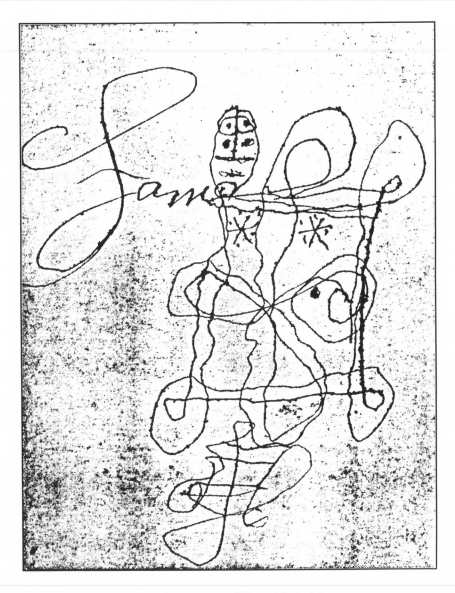

Hieroglyphic signature of Manuel Quintín Lame

This is an enlarged copy of Lame's signature. The last letter of his name is extended to form an intricate symbol, which is also found carefully drawn in all its details as a sort of authenticating stamp on every piece of his copious correspondence, including reports, petitions, complaints, and even receipts. It seems to allude to indigenous beliefs about the nature of the human psyche as it relates to history, to the past, present, and future, as well as to the cosmos. It certainly indicates Lame's own awareness of the complex nature of his own psyche, to which he often refers as "the image" of his mind and which caused his intellectual antagonists of the dominant society to affirm that "what the Indian Quintín Lame hides under his hair is a mystery" ("Los Pensamientos," par. 51).

Liberation Theology from Below

The Life and Thought of Manuel Quintín Lame

Gonzalo Castillo-Cárdenas

ORBIS BOOKS
Maryknoll, New York 10545

The Catholic Foreign Mission Society of America (Maryknoll) recruits and trains people for overseas missionary service. Through Orbis Books Maryknoll aims to foster the international dialogue that is essential to mission. The books published, however, reflect the opinions of their authors and are not meant to represent the official position of the society.

Manuscript editor: William E. Jerman

Library of Congress Cataloging-in-Publication Data

Castillo-Cárdenas, Gonzalo.
    Liberation theology from below.

    "English translation of Quintín Lame's manuscript, Los pensamientos del indio que se educó dentro de las selvas colombianas. The thoughts of the Indian educated in the Colombian forests": p.
    Bibliography: p.
    Includes index.
    1. Lame Chantre, Manuel Quintín, 1883-1967.
2. Liberation theology.   3. Indians of South America—Colombia—Government relations.   4. Indians, Treatment of—Colombia.   5. Páez Indians—Biography.   6. Indians of South America—Colombia—Biography.   I. Lame Chantre, Manuel Quintín, 1883-1967. Pensamientos del indio que se educó dentro de las selvas colombianas. English.   1987.   II. Title.
    F2270.1.G6C37   1987   230'.092'4   86-21812
    ISBN 0-88344-408-9 (pbk.)

Contents

Preface

On one level this book is intended to be a tribute of admiration to the struggling spirit and the creativity of the Indian peasants of Latin America and of the poor everywhere in the Third World. By focusing attention on a manuscript produced in the countryside, written in the rustic Spanish of the peasants by an Indian rooted in his cultural tradition, the book brings to light the intellectual activity of the poor and highlights the originality, vigor, and profundity of their thought.

On another level, my intention is to delve very deeply into the religious faith and spirituality of the poor. Many studies exist already about the popular religiosity—the ritual and devotional practices—of the masses of Latin America. Only a few, however, make a significant effort to grasp the intellectual content of this faith, much less its potential contribution to theology. It is by making that effort that my book may be helpful in opening some entry points into the rich archives kept in the collective memory of the oppressed and in their historical consciousness.

We find ourselves at a point in human history when the most significant event that is taking place in terms of hope for an alternative future for humanity may be the emergence of the power of Third World peoples. In Latin America we speak of "the rise of the poor"—that is, the colonized, the exploited, the marginalized—and we witness an assertion of the peoples, cultures, and classes that historically have been used as instruments for the implementation of various historical projects of conquistadores and dominators. Those emerging populations have something very important to say about nature and human life, history and society, work and struggle, art and poetry, and also about faith and works—about theology. *Liberation Theology from Below* is an example of this contribution, and it is on that presupposition that I have cast my interpretation of Lame's thought and work. This book may help readers from the United States to begin to listen to what Third World peoples existing in their midst have been saying for a long time in lanugage similar to Lame's. It may also be a challenge to the academic theologians from the United States as well as from Latin America to learn, as Dietrich Bonhoeffer did, "to see the great events of world history *from below*, from the perspective of the outcasts, the suspects, the maltreated, the powerless, the oppresed, the reviled, in short, from the perspective of those who suffer . . . " (*Letters and Papers from Prison* [New York: Macmillan, 1971], p. 17).

Before ending this preface I want to express my profound debt and gratitude to the Indian Council of Ortega-Chapparral, in the Tolima Department of Colombia, for having preserved Lame's manuscript and for having helped me understand its contents and significance.

GONZALO CASTILLO CÁRDENAS

CHAPTER I

The Legacy and Its Challenge

ENCOUNTER WITH THE SUBJECT

In October 1970 I had the opportunity to participate in a pilgrimage to the grave of the Indian leader Manuel Quintín Lame Chantre. He is buried in a small Indian cemetery called Monserrate, at the top of a hill on the Ortega River, just outside the old town of Ortega, Tolima, nearly two hundred kilometers south of Bogotá, Colombia.

The march had been organized by the Cabildo Indígena ("indigenous council") of Ortega, a group of ten Indian peasants who had been militants in the "Lamista movement" in years past and who still continued — three years after the death of their leader — to keep alive the memory of his teachings and example. Most of the participants were Indian peasants of the area: men, women, and children, some fifty to seventy in all.

Once on the site, the "pilgrims" gathered around a tall black wooden cross and deposited on the grave flowers and branches plucked from surrounding fields. Abel Tique, the elderly and dignified president of the *cabildo,* holding a straw hat in his hand, explained to the group that the purpose of the meeting was "to render honors and to pay homage to the memory of General Lame."[1]

Then Gabriel Yaima, one of the younger members of the inner group and the secretary of the *cabildo,* read several pages filled with metaphors and poetic images, sprinkled here and there with poignant statements about "God the Supreme Judge of every human conscience," "the rights of the aboriginal race," "the destiny of the Indian people," and ending with a call to continue the struggle against "land grabbers" *(acaparadores),* "multimillionaires," "aristocrats," and "oligarchs," and to remember Quintín Lame's "doctrine and discipline."

Following the speech the members of the *cabildo* formed a circle around Lame's tomb and raised their right arms, signifying a commitment not articulated in words. After the short ceremony, the "old fighters" sat on the ground reminiscing about their "sufferings" while the younger ones

1

showered them with admiration. All of them had experienced insults, yellings, humiliation, harassment, expropriation, eviction, prosecutions, jail, shootings, the death of relatives, and, above all, hunger. They spoke of their movement as "the indigenist cause" *(la causa indigenista),* and always referred to Quintín Lame with awe and admiration. On the cross over his grave they had written:

> Here sleeps the Indian Manuel Quintín Lame Chantre, October 7, 1967. He was the man who did not bow his head before injustice.

Later I learned that this was a short summary of the epitaph that Lame himself had helped to write in anticipation of his death. Its full text reads:

> Here sleeps the Indian chief Manuel Quintín Lame Chantre who did not let himself be humiliated by departmental, judicial, or municipal authorities, or by the rich land grabbers, multimillionaires, oligarchs, and aristocrats who offered him sums of money to give up his litigation in behalf of the Indian *resguardo* ["protectorate"] of Ortega, to which he answered: "I am an advocate under the sun, and before God and men, of the Indian tribes and hosts of the Guananí land: a race that is depleted, expropriated, weak, ignorant, illiterate, abandoned sadly and pitifully by civilization."[2]

On the way back from the cemetery the small crowd quickly disbanded, and the Lamista peasants resumed their weekly routine of a market day.

That afternoon in Ortega I visited with Eduardo Lozano, whose name had been given to me as a reference by a friend in Bogotá. Lozano belonged to the inner circle of the townsmen, having been mayor of the town some years before. He took me to the "club" where landowners and small businessmen usually met to drink and chat on Sunday afternoons. They were apprehensive and cautious in talking to a stranger. The word had gone around that I was asking questions about Quintín Lame. After a few drinks, a relative of Lozano who owned a hacienda in the area exploded: "I don't know why you people from Bogotá are interested in that brute Indian *(indio bruto).* Lame was an ignorant Indian like all the rest!" In the drinking atmosphere that followed, many anecdotes were told about Lame, some about his natural cunning *(malicia indígena)* and fanaticism, but all with contempt and hate.

For me the entire experience in Ortega became something of a challenge to discover the intriguing personality of an Indian who, three years after his death, still elicited such strong reactions among followers and foes. Besides, the statements made at the cemetery had triggered in my mind the suspicion that subsequent visits and lengthier conversations would fully confirm that the "Lamista" peasants were in possession of a common body of teaching, which they referred to as "the doctrine and discipline," taught by Lame. Was it an oral tradition or perhaps a written document?

For the following six months my empathy with the group increased; I found myself identifying with their ideals and sharing their emotional commitment to "the Indian cause." I took their messages to Bogotá, reported their complaints to the press, and put them in touch with resource persons in the area. All of this built up their trust. One Sunday they produced before my eyes a handwritten document, half destroyed by time and moths, authored by Manuel Quintín Lame.

It was this discovery that led me to the decision to delve into the life and thought of this Indian leader, a knowledge that eventually convinced me of the academic interest and value of the subject, and of the need to turn it into a serious project of investigation.

LAME'S MANUSCRIPT

Lame's work, "Los Pensamientos del Indio que se Educó dentro de las Selvas Colombianas" ["The Thoughts of the Indian Educated in the Colombian Forests"], in its original form is 118 pages long.[3] It is written in rustic Spanish, the work of "a mountaineer who received his inspiration on the mountain, educated himself on the mountain, and learned to think how to think on the mountain," according to Lame's self-description.[4] In fact, Lame had had no access to any school except to the school of suffering and struggle that filled his life. In the Prologue to his work he wrote:

> I am making my work known to the Colombian public. However, it is not with proper or learned language, but with the experience of some years of suffering that I have been putting together little by little the present book.[5]

The style is rustic but the message is clear, revealing a human experience of remarkable depth and expressing a religious conviction and a moral protest from within a distinctive cultural perspective, a social experience of oppression, and a keen sense of historic solidarity with what he calls "the Indian race."

The structure of the manuscript is simple. The Prologue lays out the major themes that shall be developed: Lame's messianic calling, his moral indignation because of injustice done to him personally and to the Indian people, and his boldness in trying to emulate white intellectuals by producing his book. The rest of the material is organized in two "books," the first one with eleven chapters and the second with nine, under the following headings:

BOOK ONE

1. the indigene who learns lessons from nature
2. the image of my thought

3. the virtue of the Indian reared by the loving care of nature in the mother forest

4. the prehistory of the Indian race before October 12, 1492

5. the experience

6. the passing of time and of humanity

7. the judicial lesson

8. the prosecution, humbug, and deceit against the Indian on trial

9. the condition of the indigene in darkness

10. the harem of justice

11. the mist in the thought of the Indian educated in the mother forest

BOOK TWO

1. the pollen of humanity

2. the palace of wisdom

3. on marriage and passion

4. the unjust trial of the Indian who came down from the mountain to the valley of civilization

5. spiritual manna

6. man's friend

7. the spirit of the poor little Indian who writes this book

8. the birth of the fountain in darkness

9. the three mansions that support the bird of human immortality

Under these cryptic headings three kinds of material are found:

1) A body of *religious reflection* that Lame's followers call "the doctrine and the discipline." It is a prophetic theology[6] that can be summarized as follows: the present conditions of the Indian people under white civilization originally introduced on October 12, 1492, by the Spanish conquest, shall be radically reversed one day when the Indian shall reclaim his throne, and "the white man shall become the tenant of the Indian."[7] This expectation is grounded in a mystical experience. But it is also related to belief in a principle of justice that is inherent in nature and also operates in human history, a principle that Lame calls "the law of compensation." Although Jesus Christ ("the Liberator of humanity"), the Virgin Mary, and various Christian saints play a major supporting role in relation to the believer's struggle and hope, the radical reversal of conditions shall take place only with the participation and activism of the Indians themselves, through education, self-reliance, and "patriotism" (i.e., commitment to the struggle for justice). In this major transformation Lame himself shall play a decisive role, for which he has been providentially chosen and endowed by God.

This line of thought predominates throughout the manuscript, expressing a religious faith in struggle and hope with theological, ideological, moral, and ethical dimensions.[8]

2) *Memories* of the peak moments of Lame's life, particularly his spiritual experiences, his juridical battles, and his social confrontations with representatives of the national society (landowners, governors, mayors, priests) in the Colombian departments ("states") of Cauca, Tolima, and Huila, covering three decades, from 1910 through 1939.

3) *Denunciations* of specific crimes and abuses committed by regional authorities and by other representatives of the national society whom Lame sometimes mentions by name, as well as more general denunciations of the racial prejudice, the ethnic discrimination, and the social and economic abuse to which the Indian people are subjected in Colombia. This kind of material is scattered throughout every page of Lame's manuscript.

If not the work of a "learned man," "Los Pensamientos" is the work of a natural philosopher, a careful observer of the natural kingdom and of society. It is also the expression of a religious temperament in whose soul flowed powerful mystical currents that caused him to see visions,[9] to enjoy the consolation of the "mysterious image,"[10] and to feel supported in moments of crisis by a powerful force that he called "the image" of his mind.[11] Above all, "Los Pensamientos" is the spiritual testament of an Indian prophet who bequeaths his revelation and his exhortation to future Indian generations for their historical struggles and final liberation. At the end of his work Lame realized that "the thought of a mountaineer" had come out "limping";[12] nevertheless, he never doubted the transcendental role that his book was destined to fulfill. "This book," he said "will serve as a horizon in the midst of darkness for [future] Indian generations."[13]

PROBLEM AND PURPOSE

The problem addressed by this study is, in the first place, the nature of Manuel Quintín Lame's religious thought as expressed in his manuscript "Los Pensamientos" and, in the second place, a critical interpretation of it in terms of its significance as an expression of a popular theology — that is, a reflection on faith arising from conditions of oppression and marginalization, as articulated by the oppressed themselves.

This definition of the problem requires that attention be focused particularly on the following aspects of the question:

1) The relation of Lame's religious faith to the human condition of the Indian communities of southwestern Colombia, especially of the area known as *Cauca Indígena*.

2) The religious and ideological connection of Lame's thought to the traditional worldview and spirituality of the Colombian Andes.

3) The extent to which Lame's religious thought as articulated in his manuscript represents a meaningful theological response (in terms of appropriation, adaptation, or transformation) to the christianization process carried out in the past by Catholic missions in the area.

4) The extent to which Lame's prophetic theology may be said to

express a critical awareness of, and a social protest against, the historical conditions originally imposed by conquest and colonization, and to raise significant issues and challenges for contemporary theological activity in Latin America.

Thus stated, the problem and research objectives of this study presuppose that both Christianity and the indigenous traditions of the New World are alive among the people and can be transformed and developed as they are appropriated by real human beings like Manuel Quintín Lame and become an integral part of their existential struggle for life.

Hence, in stating that the purpose of this study is to determine the significance of Lame's thought as an expression of a "popular theology," it is clear that the concept of theology is endowed here with a conceptual value different from the traditional one, but without implying a derogatory innuendo from the perspective of any established "orthodoxy."[14] Rather, my statement of the problem and purpose presupposes that a genuine theology may indeed arise and develop among the poor and illiterate, as it has also arisen and become systematized among the more affluent and the literate. The question here has to do with the nature and significance of this form of theology as a reinterpretation of the faith that takes place in conditions of oppression and domination.

In other words, the present approach to Lame's manuscript strives to avoid the perspective of cultural or religious "purisms" that would hope to find the constitutive elements of a purely Indian perspective that would serve as testimony or example of a *past* reality. Many such efforts have often been concentrated on the task of finding elements of tradition or some kind of documents expressing a purely *natural* worldview, a pre-Columbian perspective with no traces of Indian encounters with the West.[15] This attitude betrays the fundamental assumption — seldom stated in writing — that Indian culture and experience is static, frozen in some remote past, lacking in dynamism and resilience, with no capacity for evolution through adaptation or conflict, incorporation or transformation.[16] In making these assumptions, naturalists and cultural purists concur with the dominant segments of the national societies in denying the humanity of the native populations of the Americas, because it is precisely the very qualities they expect *not* to find in Indian documents that are the most characteristic of *human* history.

A similar attitude is taken by many missionaries and religious purists who would write off the pre-Columbian Indian experience as belonging to an ahistorical age of darkness, a subhuman stage of existence with no valid knowledge of historical reality, and only vague and distorted visions of transcendental realities. Implicit in this attitude is the assumption that the "hominization" of the Indians began to take place only with the arrival and work of the missionary, a process that is considered more successful the more it involves the total eradication of traces or remnants of the "pagan" past. From this wrong perspective, the value of any oral tradition or written text coming from native populations of the New World, such as Lame's manuscript, would reside in the degree to which it repeats the Christian formulas, beliefs, and accounts taught to them by missionaries. Any pre-Columbian beliefs or spiritual values are seen as impurities carried over from the "pagan" past.[17]

My study approaches "Pensamientos" from a different perspective, one that takes full cognizance of the existential social matrix out of which the document arises and then goes on to ask the question, How does this document represent a creative theological response to the pressures and dilemmas raised by historical reality? The social matrix of Lame's manuscript is one of conflict and struggle in which both accommodation and resistance are not only existential alternatives but most of the time the condition for survival. This means that there is no a priori reason to believe that the reflective activity of an indigenous intellectual such as Lame would have no imaginative response to the restrictive situations imposed on him and on his people by their historical conditions of life. Rather, one might expect that because of his involvement in the struggle for survival, his work would show a greater adaptability and creativity than would the reflection of an academic theologian of the Western tradition. It is from this perspective that Lame's thought reveals its full significance. In it Christianity appears as a living factor inside the social structure, being in many ways an entirely new phenomenon resulting from the reinterpretation of Western religious ideas by one who appropriated them as his own.

THE QUESTION OF METHOD

The attempt to understand the prophetic personality of Manuel Quintín Lame and to interpret his unique manuscript "Pensamientos" presents difficult methodological problems to the student.[18] How is it possible for a "Western" scholar — a philosopher or theologian — to understand the word of the illiterate, the oppressed, the one whose humanity has been historically denied and continues to be denied in practice, often by scholars themselves?

Recognizing the wide gulf between the world of the dominator and that of the dominated, how is it possible to establish between the two a common ground for communication? What is the conceptual framework in which such communication is more likely to take place, and interpretation and humanizing activity are possible? It is suggested here that such a possibility rests on three premises. In the first place, it is necessary that the attempt to hear and understand the voice of the oppressed be grounded on a critical attitude towards the conceptual domination exerted by the Western intellectual tradition. This premise recognizes the totalitarian tendencies inherent in the rational *logos* and calls for a hermeneutical model that is open to "revelations" from outside the totality of Western rationalistic tradition.[19]

In the second place, it is necessary to develop an attitude of openness to the word of the oppressed in the many forms in which it is expressed, recognizing it as a voice coming from "the outside," expressed by "the other," the one who is by definition to some extent beyond my comprehension and grasp. This attitude is characterized by openness to the "otherness" of others, to their novelty.

The third premise is ethical in nature: it recognizes that the placing of "the same" and "the other" face to face is not enough and makes the specific demand that the interpreter (the scholar, philosopher, or theologian) be placed at the service of the other. Once established, this ethical foundation becomes the catalyst of a kind of praxis that is humanizing and liberating, one that goes beyond the ontological order and advances further as "service in justice."[20] In this conceptual framework the scholar is able to listen, interpret, and serve, even though only imperfectly, because "the other" is in fact "other."

In the Latin American context this perspective needs to be grounded historically in the colonial experience. Here, Latin America was born precisely as the bipolar *other*, conquered and oppressed by European conquistadores and colonizers who attempted to involve it within the European totality. Europe then became the point of reference for "Latin American" self-identity; its assimilation within the European historical undertaking became the condition for Latin American existence. The "otherness" of the people of the New World was thus denied as newly discovered continents were considered only a "new setting" for the European experience.

This same fate was assigned to the indigenous populations whose existence was made contingent upon their incorporation within the newly born "Latin America" and its system of domination. The Indian, therefore, became in the colonial context the prime example and paradigm of "the other" whose "otherness" was denied in the most radical way by the European totality, now expanded in the creole oligarchies and their systems of domination.

DOMINATION AND LIBERATION AS THEOLOGICAL THEMES

The question, whether the inhabitants of the New World were human beings or not, was hotly debated in the intellectual and theological circles of the sixteenth century. The famous debate between Bartolomé de Las Casas, the "apostle to the Indians," and Ginés de Sepúlveda, the ideologist of European supremacy, summed up the ideological terms of the confrontation.[21] The papal bull *Sublimis Deus* solemnly declared in 1537 that the Indians were "authentic human beings." In practice, however, the historical dynamics of the period were such that the indigenous population was either massacred or subjugated to forms of economic slavery, political oppression, and social discrimination and marginalization, which meant that Indians were in fact treated as less than human, and forced into a condition of increasing dehumanization. In such a situation both the dominated and the dominators, although in different forms and for different reasons, are reduced to a level of existence less than human.

Throughout history all systems of domination have denied human dignity to all those who are either the oppressed within the system or those who are considered to be "barbarians," "enemies," "irrational," the goyim, outside the system.[22] Such a condition implies a relationship that is unidirectional and asymmetric, in which some human beings (the dominators) relate to other human beings (the dominated) as if the latter were mere objects or "things," in a process in which only the former are the subjects and protagonists of history.[23]

In the case of the Colombian Andes the human condition of the Indian population has its roots in the colonial past of the country. Its genesis is found in the violent invasion and conquest of pre-Columbian native societies beginning in the sixteenth century and in the social stratification that it generated.

The Indian population that survived the initial massacres, plunder, and despoliation was to remain in conditions of subjugation and dependence, in the various forms of *encomiendas, repartimientos, peonías,* and other varieties of Indian slavery. Thus, the nature of the imposed social relations was one in which the value of the Indian was measured in terms of usefulness to the conqueror and the colonizer. Despite the fact that among the conquistadores themselves there developed drastic inequalities, their global relation to the Indians became one of radical superiority and domination, in which the very humanity of the Indian was de facto denied, both in the conscience as well as in the actual practice and behavior of the colonizer.

The foundations were thus laid for the construction of stereotypes, mental images, beliefs, myths, and ideologies intended to explain, interpret, and justify the kind of relations and institutions that had already been established de facto.[24] Thus, since the earliest colonial times, the denial of the identity of the dominated — that is, the negation of their humanity — becomes a precondition for the maintenance and preservation of the kind of relations and institutions in terms of which dominators define their own humanity. This dialectical relation in which the non-humanity of one is necessary for the humanity of the other is the most basic characteristic of the "Indian peasant areas" of the Andes, even when the first contact with isolated Indian groups did not take place in the early colonial period but after independence or in more recent times.[25]

Against this background it becomes quite clear that every historical development that changes this kind of relation for one of freedom and equity becomes objectively a process of anthropogenesis — that is, a social "creation" of human beings, a historical process in which both oppressors and oppressed are liberated from their mutual condition and are able to relate to each other as full persons. In this light history can be understood from two perspectives: on the one hand, it can be seen as a process of dehumanization, when peoples relate to each other in conditions of domination and subjugation, which are less than human; and on the other hand, it can be seen as an ongoing project of liberation from dehumanizing conditions, in which the dehumanized stand up against those conditions, reclaim their humanity, and become aware of what they are intended to be — fully human beings.

Ideologically, reflection about God becomes a theology of domination when it articulates in a theoretical way arguments derived from the interests and preconceptions of a dominant society, or of a dominant group that practices oppression in that society. When this happens the system of domination is made into a totality and is endowed with special qualities supposed to be acceptable to the divinity, if not directly bestowed by God. The system of domination thus becomes sacred, a fetish, an idol, the absolute and only criterion to measure value, dignity, and status. In such theology of domination every form of existence residing outside the limits of the system, or every form of existence inside its own limits that resists total integration and assimilation, become ipso facto the enemy of the totality of value, and therefore God's enemy. In other words, in a theology of domination "the other" is accorded only a relative existence — insofar as it is related to the system — with no intrinsic value or dignity or status before God. Thus, within the ideological universe of the system there is no place for "the other," except as the epitome of evil or as a manipulable and usable instrument: there is no *humanity* outside the system of domination.

Essential to the system of domination is the repression of "the other's" voice, either because it has nothing to say, inasmuch as its existence does not reach the level of humanity, or because what it has to say is deemed by its very nature wrong or beastlike; or else because it is considered totally unintelligible. Hence, in the course of time there develops what has been called "the culture of silence."[26]

In sharp contrast with a theology of domination stands the prophetic tradition of the Bible. There, in spite of several indications that the ancient Israelites also developed at several levels totalitarian ideologies of domination, there developed a stronger reflection about God that challenged those developments and established a radically different theological perspective.[27] At the very core of this prophetic tradition there is an understanding of the nature of God as freedom and justice, sometimes equated with God's "holiness," which makes it impossible for any religious or political system or establishment to claim God for itself since on the contrary God is the one who sets the standards to all the peoples of the earth, including Israel, based on justice (*hesed*). This same prophetic theology involves a doctrine of human nature founded on the belief that all human beings have their origin ultimately in God and belong therefore to the same human family, regardless of ethnic or social origins.

For this reason, a major feature of prophetic social ethics is concern for those who are considered without dignity in society, the most vulnerable and most likely to be abused and oppressed: they might be slaves (*ebed*), foreign immigrants (*gher*), mean or wretched (*misken* and *jelka*), men of whom one is ashamed (*ras*), weak (*dal*), poor or oppressed (*ebyon*) or those who can only answer yes to their master (*ani*). According to Enzo Bianchi:

> All of these find a figure which represents them all in the state of being without dignity and who does so perfectly: the *ebed* IHWH: the servant Messiah, who is simultaneously historical and prophetic; and who at the same time is also an individual in the history of salvation and a collective figure.[28]

In this prophetic tradition the denial of the human "right" is tantamount to the attempt to destroy God's very image, or at least the remnants of it, and the agents of such attempt become the protagonists of a process of dehumanization that is the epitome of sin. This is precisely the basis of all prophetic indictments of the social order: the prophets see humankind becoming inhuman wherever it denies its fellow human beings recognition, justice, and dignity.[29] Hence, in this prophetic tradition of the Bible, particularly in its eschatological and messianic dimensions, the denial of the humanity of the goyim is reversed and God's activity is seen as oriented towards the liberation of "the nations" (i.e., the pagans, those who were thought to be outside the borders of the system of salvation).[30]

Thus, contrary to a theology of domination that sets frontiers outside which there is no salvation, the prophetic tradition goes beyond the limits of the system and sees "the other" as the object of God's liberating activity, through which it becomes an equal, a brother, a sister, a member of the eschatological community, a full human being.[31]

In the sixteenth century Bartolomé de Las Casas represented this prophetic tradition in Latin America when he interpreted the events that were going on before his eyes during the early decades of the conquest of the New World. In his *Brevísima Relación* (1552) he charged that what was taking place was the extermination of a great segment of humanity through large-scale genocide, forms of torture and atrocities, and several forms of slavery, in which the wretched Indians "died little by little." He also interpreted the Indians' resistance as a sign of their humanity ("their right"), and considered that in them Jesus Christ was incarnated, experiencing in history human suffering, affliction, and death, "not once but thousands of times." This seminal insight is the core of a theology of history in which Jesus Christ, God's revelation, reveals himself in the Indians — that is, in those treated as less than human beings, the "barbarians" who are pushed outside the borders of humanity by a system of domination. In this perspective the oppressed become an anthropological epiphany as well as

God's own epiphany: the locus where God's intentions are revealed.[32]

It is this prophetic tradition that Quintin Lame appropriates for himself and for the Indians who are de facto excluded from the human family and treated "with the greatest contempt." Lame's religious thought adumbrates a prophetic theology that espouses the emphatic affirmation of Indian humanity, arising from historical conditions in which it was consistently denied — an affirmation that carries with it the explicit refusal to accept the decision of the dominator who pretends that the only way for the Indian to acquire human worth and dignity is through disappearance *as an Indian* and assimilation *as a peasant* into the structure of domination imposed by the national society. This is the basis of the prophetic tone of so many passages of Lame's "Pensamientos," and the profound meaning of his religious experience, which, in his own words, transformed "the head of the wild wolf into that of a man," and awakened his conscience "to combat injustice."

CHAPTER II

Cauca Indígena
at the Turn of the Century

Under this heading the community that "produced" the Indian leader Manuel Quintín Lame will be described: his social and cultural base. Beginning with the natural setting in which such community belongs, the chapter will then go on to identify the ecological, social, and cultural forces that have determined the human situation in the area, with special attention to the struggle for the land and to the religious situation, particularly since the dawn of the twentieth century.

THE NATURAL SETTING

Geographers divide the territory of Colombia into five natural regions: the Caribbean plains, the Pacific coast, the Andean region, the eastern plains, and the southeastern forests or Colombian "Amazonia."[1] The Andean region, though not the most extensive in territory, is the most important in the role its population has played in the history of the nation. It runs for twelve hundred kilometers south to north, forming the geographical spine of the country. Its width varies from 150 to 500 kilometers, divided into three *cordilleras* (mountain ranges) by the Magdalena and Cauca rivers and their tropical valleys. In one of the *altiplanos* of the eastern *cordillera* lies Bogotá, the capital of the country. West of the Magdalena River runs the western *cordillera,* lower than the others but high enough to block off the Cauca River valley from the winds of the Pacific Ocean. In the middle rises the central *cordillera,* the highest of the three, which is the continuation of the majestic eastern *cordillera* of Ecuador.

In the central *cordillera* towards the southwestern corner of the country is found the area known as Cauca Indígena. It stretches over the steep slopes and high plateaus east of Popayán, the aristocratic capital of the department ("state") of Cauca, covering approximately four thousand square kilometers. Geographically, the area is cuddled within an imposing cluster of high peaks and volcanoes — the Pan de Azúcar, the Puracé, the

13

Sotará. To the north it spreads on both sides of the central *cordillera*, reaching up to the rocky peaks that pierce the sky with altitudes well above the perennial snow line. The highest of these, the famous Nevado del Huila, 5,700 meters high, is the region's natural frontier on the northeast. Even though the Cauca Indígena includes lands spreading over all the four temperature zones *(pisos térmicos)*, the Indian population is restricted today mostly to the *tierra fría* and the *páramos.* Only a few Indian communities still cling to their traditional lands in the more valuable temperate zones.[2]

Deep inside the Cauca Indígena region, bordering with and penetrating at some points the adjacent departments ("states") of Huila and Tolima, lies Tierradentro, an ecological niche of approximately nineteen hundred square kilometers, formed by steep slopes, profound precipices, and small inter-Andean valleys along the powerful waters of the Páez River and its tributaries, the Ullucos, the Moras, El Escaño, and San Andrés. These hinterlands, shrouded in mist and legend, are the inner core of the Cauca Indígena region, and the ancestral home of two ethnic groups, the Páez or Paeces and the Guanaca Indians. Together they constitute the largest single concentration of Indians in Colombian territory, an Indian enclave that once created a highly developed culture and whose population has never been fully incorporated into the national society.[3]

Although concentrated in Tierradentro, around the market towns of

Belalcázar and Inzá, the Páez and other Indian peasants of the Cauca Indígena region have been slowly migrating to neighboring areas, particularly since the last quarter of the nineteenth century, due to the social pressure on the land. As will be shown later, this pressure intensified not only because of the natural growth of the indigenous population but as the result of illegal encroachment and colonization of Indian lands by white and mestizo settlers, a process that may be traced back to colonial times but which became more acute after independence. At the turn of the century there were Indians from Tierradentro scattered all over the western slopes of the central *cordillera,* north of the municipality of Silvia, as well as in the east along the high waters of the Saldaña River, deep inside the department of Tolima. Besides Páez at least four other Indian languages were spoken at the beginning of the century in the Cauca Indígena area: Paniquitá, Guambiano, Totoró, and Polindara, of which only the first three were spoken by any sizeable number.[4] There were also descendants of other linguistic families, such as the Guanacas, who had completely forgotten their ancestral language. The language of trade is Spanish, which has become with time the lingua franca of the area.

STRUGGLE FOR THE LAND

The land question in Cauca Indígena revolved around the legal rights granted to Indian communities by the Spanish crown in the form of *resguardos* — that is, lands set aside since early colonial times by royal decrees exclusively for Indian use and beyond the claim of settlers and *encomenderos.*[5] The original intention of the *resguardo* institution seems to have been that of fixing the residence of Indians in order to facilitate their control and indoctrination. But when the vicious treatment of the Indian population, which involved all kinds of excesses aimed at extracting with their labor the greatest possible wealth in the shortest possible time, threatened to annihilate all the native labor force in the colonies, the *resguardos* served as a protective shield against the blows of irrational colonial practices. The "protection" came right on time when, by the end of the sixteenth century, the decline of the native population had already reached catastrophic proportions.[6]

In time, the *resguardo* institution came to serve still another purpose in the larger list of concerns which beset the Spanish colonial authorities: the attempt to check the expansionist spirit of the *encomenderos,* whose greed for new lands seemed to recognize no limits. By establishing new *resguardos* the crown created the legal fiction of protection of Indian lands where the natives could carry on their communal style of life in conditions more likely to assure their survival. Thus, labor would be guaranteed for the future, if restraint could be achieved in the meantime. The *criollos,*[7] however, scorned this legal protection and took advantage of every pretext to enlarge their estates by taking over *resguardo* lands.[8] There is evidence that this process of encroachment, invasion, and expropriation was carried on in the Cauca Indígena region through the seventeenth and eighteenth centuries, becoming one of the sources of permanent tension between *criollo* landlords and royal investigators when Indian complaints managed to reach the ears of Spanish authorities.[9]

After the wars of independence and with the birth of the new republic, the pressure on Indian lands intensified. Revolutionary "heroes" turned to Indian lands with a greedy eye as a source of wealth for themselves and their political and military allies. Ideologically, they attacked the *resguardo* as a vestige of colonial rule, a traditionalist, conservative, if not retrograde institution, standing in the way of progress.[10] Determination to extinguish the *resguardos* was reiterated time and again by all legislators during the nineteenth century and its enforcement was quicker in areas where the value of land increased rapidly because of its proximity to population centers. By 1850 most of the *resguardos* of the central highlands (Boyacá and Cundinamarca departments) had been dissolved,[11] and pressure to dissolve those of the southwest (Cauca and Nariño departments), where the surviving Indian population was the largest in the country, was strong.[12] At least thirteen *resguardos* in existence in colonial times around the city of Popayán, in the plateau known as the Pubenza Valley, were with time either formally or de facto dissolved.[13]

In the Cauca Indígena region the Indian communities succeeded in preserving their *resguardos* throughout the turbulent nineteenth century. Their exact number and the extension of their lands, however, is difficult to ascertain. On July 12, 1898, the legislative assembly of the department of Cauca authorized the governor to appoint a commission with Indian participation to travel to Tierradentro and "trace the limits of the Indian *resguardos,* according to the documents and data provided by the Indian governors of the *resguardos*."[14] But there is no record of the implementation of this *ordenanza.*

The earliest official list of *resguardos* (called *parcialidades*) appears in an ordinance of the Cauca Assembly dated March 20, 1922, enjoining the Indian communities to take the steps prescribed by law for the speedy division and dissolution of their *resguardos.*[15] The list includes a total of 59 *resguardos,* as follows:

Province	*District*	*Resguardos*
Popayán	Cajibío	Ortega
	Morales	Chimborazo
	Puracé	Puracé
		Coconuco
	Timbío	Rioblanco
		Timbío

Province	*District*	*Resguardos*
	El Tambo	Alto del Rey
		Pandiguando
		La Laguna
		Chapa
		Piagua
		Achintes
	Popayán	Calibío
		Poblazón
		Julumito
		Peulenje
		Santa Bárbara
		Yanaconas
Camilo Torres	Toribío	San Francisco
		Tacueyó
		Toribío
Silvia	Silvia	Pitayó
		Guambía
		Quichaya
		Quisgó
	Tunía	Tunía
	Inzá	Guanacas (Inzá)
		Turminá
		La Laguna
		Topa
		Santa Rosa
		San Andrés
		Pedregal
	Páez	Ricaurte
		Cohetando
		Araújo
		Belalcázar
		Mosoco
		Tóez
		Huila
		Tálaga
		Vitoncó
		San José
	Totoró	Totoró
		Polindara
		Paniquitá
Caldas	Almaguer	Caquiona
	La Vega	Guachicono
		Pancitará

Province	District	Resguardos
	San Sebastían	San Sebastían
		Santiago
	Santa Rosa	Descanse
		Yunguillo
	Bolívar	San Juan
Santander	Caldono	Caldono
		Pueblonuevo
		La Aguada
		Pioyá
	Jambaló	Jambaló

It may be assumed that at least the same number of *resguardos* existed at the beginning of the century, with some additional ones that were unable to escape the governmental order to partition and allocate their lands to commoners.[16] The information that has been gathered concerning the rise of Manuel Quintín Lame and the early stages of his movement provides sufficient indications that the entire Cauca Indígena region at the beginning of the century was passing through one of the most intense crises of its history, centered precisely on the Indian struggle to preserve *resguardo* lands, upon which depended their spiritual and physical survival.

Three aspects of the land problem were particularly threatening to the Indian communities: (1) the intense pressure exerted upon their communal holdings by non-Indian settlers, expansionist hacienda owners, and rural entrepreneurs of the dominant society; (2) the pressure exerted by regional and national authorities whose policy was to divide all communal lands and distribute them individually to Indians; and (3) the frustrating labor conditions of *terrazguero* Indians, often subjected to humiliating and harsh treatment and always exploited as cheap labor in conditions that would ensure their continuing poverty.[17] A better understanding of these three aspects will clarify the objective conditions out of which Manuel Quintín Lame rose to leadership, as well as the content of his prophetic call to fight back at the national society on the way towards a better future for Colombian Indians.

1. Social Pressures

The Indian communities had always lived a precarious existence, surrounded as they were by inimical neighbors (*vecinos*).[18] But these conditions became more critical at the beginning of the present century because of a number of national and regional developments affecting the entire fabric of Colombian society. One of these was the Thousand Days War, from 1899 to 1902, the longest and most costly of all Colombian civil wars. The background issues were ideological and economic between liberals (who stood for free trade, with emphasis on cash crops for export, and favored in politics greater decentralization and a strong stand against clericalism) and conservatives (more favorable to state monopoly of key resources, more committed to a rural power base, inclined more towards protectionism, strongly centralist in internal politics and, with regard to religion, deeply committed to granting special privileges to the church).

The immediate issues of the war had to do with the crisis of the coffee industry in 1896 and its political repercussions. They affected particularly the landholding class and the export-import elites. The latter group, which headed the revolt under the banner of the Liberal Party, blamed the entrenched nationalist government formed by the conservatives for financial, fiscal, and political measures leading to their ruin.[19]

The Indians were not involved in the fight but were manipulated and drafted by the leaders of both parties, whose sons or relatives soon became "generals" and "colonels" in the war. The result was that by the end of the protracted conflict many lands that had always belonged to Indian communities as *tierras de resguardo* were claimed as their own by victorious "generals," who also hoped to incorporate the Indian population into their haciendas as *terrazgueros*. This was especially the case in the departments of Cauca and Tolima, whence some of the most prominent liberal and conservative leaders emerged.

Another important development of an economic nature that came to impinge indirectly upon the integrity of the *resguardo* lands was the expansion of international trade that the country began to experience at the turn of the century and picked up momentum in the decades that followed. The demand for coffee increased significantly in the world market in 1890, opening up unexpected possibilities for enrichment to those holding lands in temperate zones, who could mobilize the intense labor force required by the coffee industry.[20] The long-awaited construction of the Cali-Buenaventura railroad, opening the fertile Cauca Valley and the entire department of Cauca to the great sea lanes of the world, was being completed successfully, thanks to the combination of Colombian and U.S. engineering and capital, as well as to the political support of the dynamic and entrepreneurial president of the country, General Rafael Reyes.[21] With the opening of the Panama Canal considered imminent, any small infrastructural improvement on the Colombian Pacific coast acquired a much larger strategic importance.

These promising prospects spurred many ambitious members of the landholding class of western Colombia to turn their haciendas into productive enterprises. Among this emerging elite can be counted many family names from the department of Cauca — Mosquera, Valencia, Angulo, Arboleda, Muñoz, and others.[22] One prominent example of this new type of rural entrepreneur, marking the early stages of modern capitalism in Colombia, was Don Ignacio Muñoz, the owner of the hacienda San Isidro, forty kilometers east of Popayán, where Manuel Quintín Lame's parents lived and worked as *terrazgueros* for most of their lives and where Manuel Quintín himself was born:

Even though Don Ignacio had had only three years of schooling, he became the richest man in the entire Cauca department. He owned farms as far north as Pance and Tierra Grande in the northernmost corner of Cauca. To the east his estates encroached deeply into the Cauca Indígena, reaching the high points of the *cordillera central*. His properties were scattered all over the area. He came to own over 30,000 head of cattle on good cattle-raising lands.[23]

Don Ignacio's *terrazgueros* chopped down eleven thousand hectares of forest in the Puracé region, not far from Lame's birthplace. His considerable wealth was well invested in trade and other economic ventures including road and railroad construction under contract with the political administration of the department of Cauca and the national government. Several Cauca fortunes can be traced back to Don Ignacio's original accumulation.

The chief obstacle encountered by men like Don Ignacio was the scarcity of cheap labor. Some of them turned their eyes to the Indian communities for field hands. For Indians to become field hands, however, was almost as difficult as for hacienda owners to become Indians, and the only way to force them out of their subsistence economy into the labor market was to dissolve their *resguardos* by breaking them up into individual tracts.[24] It was in this period that the *resguardo* institution, which traditionally had guaranteed the stability of Indian communities, was subjected to the most concerted attack by all "progressive" representatives of the national society.

3) One aspect of this thrust against the integrity of the *resguardos* was the practice of declaring public lands (*áreas de población*) the areas surrounding newly-formed towns. As settlers moved into a region and became tenants, field hands, traders, or public employees, villages and small towns began to appear. They were given *áreas de población* substracted from lands belonging to Indian *resguardos*. Thus, for example, the district of Inzá was divided in two in 1907, giving birth to the district of Páez. Subsequently the following towns were established throughout Cauca Indígena: El Pedregal, Turminá, San Andrés, Topa, Yaquiva, Santa Rosa de Capisisco, Calderas, Togoima, and Viborá. In the newly-formed district of Páez there arose the towns of Belalcázar, Ricaurte, Coetando, Araujo, Irlanda, Vitoncó, San José, Mosoco, Lame, Suin, and Chinas. All these towns were located in Tierradentro, and each one of them claimed its right to an *área de población* that extended from ten to seventy hectares and that was substracted from the communal lands of the Indians.[25]

2. Judicial Pressures

The social process of encroachment and colonization of the Cauca Indígena region was supported at the political level by legal pressures intended to accelerate the demise of the *resguardo* institution. Since the end of the nineteenth century the legal basis of the *resguardo* had been defined in Law 89 of 1890. The purpose of the legislator had been to set this controversial institution, inherited from colonial times, within the framework of the legal mechanisms of the republic, and take steps for its final demise. Although the product of a paternalistic and racist philosophy, as indicated in its very title,[26] this legal statute had the merit of providing a clear juridical base for the *resguardo* as an operating institution. It defined its internal organization, its objectives, and its relation to local and regional authorities. To this day the forty-two articles of this law continue to be the backbone of Colombia's voluminous corpus of "special legislation concerning Indians" produced in the course of over one and a half centuries of republican life.[27] Central to Law 89 are the following principles:

1) The authority of each *resguardo* is vested in the *pequeño cabildo* (small council), to be elected annually by the *comuneros* (Indians belonging to the *parcialidad*) in the presence of the civil magistrate (*alcalde*) or his delegate (Article 3).

2) The principal function of the *pequeño cabildo* is that of allocating plots of land inside of the *resguardo* to each Indian family, and supervising all matters related to land tenure within the confines of the *resguardo* (Articles 5ff.).

3) Inside each *resguardo* individual Indian families enjoy the use of the land, not its ownership, which belongs to the community (*tierras de comunidad*).

4) Indians are not allowed to sell or lease their communal land. In this respect Indians are classified as *minors* before the law, regardless of their age, and consequently they must ask legal permission from the courts to do any transaction with the land. Land can be sold only by public auction (Article 40).

5) Detailed provisions are made for the eventual extinction of the *resguardos* through parceling of the land and its distribution in fee simple to *comuneros* (Articles 30-39).

6) Regional authorities (*gobernadores de Departamento*) are empowered to determine the appropriate procedures for the implementation of this law in their jurisdictions, as well as to fill in the gaps (*los vacíos*) that might exist in the law, provided that such additions do not run contrary to the law itself (Article 41).

The conceptual framework of this legislation sees Indians as persons in transition from a "savage" state to a "civilized life," a process that involves leaving behind the communal organization of the *resguardos* and becoming individual citizens of the republic, which in practice meant entering into the life of general society as individual *terrazgueros,* rural workers in haciendas, plantation hands, maids, servants, and so on. As long as Indians remained in their *parcialidades* or *resguardos* they were clearly set on the margin of the general law of the republic, subject to "special legislation."[28] In practice this special status meant, on the one hand, being placed under the tutorship of the Catholic Church, because it was "through missions" that the transition from a "savage" state to a "civilized life" was to be achieved.[29] On the other hand, and most significantly, the special status accorded to *resguardo* Indians meant also that the *resguardo* institution was sentenced to disappear, because the same law that guaranteed the legal existence of the *resguardo* also prescribed its extinction as the expected goal. This explains why a substantial part of Law 89 was devoted to setting down the procedures to "dissolve" a *resguardo,* a matter to which both national and regional authorities were to grant special attention.

In the department of Cauca a voluminous "complementary legislation" was soon passed beginning with Decree 74 of 1898 consisting of 178 articles intended to speed up the extinction of the existing *resguardos* starting with those that could be considered "vacant" — that is, where the Indian population was thinning out and their lands were considered to be "too large" for the remaining commoners. In these cases Indians were pressed to take a census *(padrón)* of their constituents and request partition of the land. It was very seldom that Indians wanted to do this by their own will and new legislation was necessary to force the issue.

During the presidency of General Rafael Reyes, a man of similar qualities to those of Don Ignacio Muñoz, Law 55 of April 20, 1905, was passed. It not only legalized explicitly the practice of segregating lands from the *parcialidades* for *áreas de población* (Article 2) but also opened the door for the authorities themselves to take the initiative, ordering the partition of *resguardos* by executive decrees *(decretos del ejecutivo)* whenever regional authorities deemed a given *resguardo* underpopulated. In such cases the land was to be sold by public auction and titles acquired in this fashion were to be recognized as legal titles to the property.[30] Article 4 set definite deadlines before which Indians living in underpopulated *parcialidades* were required to show proof of possession of their plots and to register their *resguardo* titles in a public notary lest their lands be declared "abandoned" and sold in public auction.

3. Terrazgueros *Indians*

The net result of all this official pressure brought to bear on the *resguardo* institution as well as the social pressure from encroaching *hacendados* and settlers was one and the same: the creation of a floating Indian population, ever greater in size, formed by indigenes whose *resguardos* had been declared extinct, or who had lost their individual plots through indebtedness or fraud, or who could not be accommodated in their shrinking *parcialidades,* or who had fled because of the violence involved in the social conflict for the land. Many Indians thus alienated from their *resguardos* became beggars, personal servants, maids, or in most cases *terrazgueros* — that is, landless Indians who were allowed to till a plot of land or to raise a few head of cattle for the subsistence of their family on a hacienda, and build their huts there, in exchange for which they had to pay a kind of rent called *terraje* in the form of several days of labor every week for the hacienda owner. Reference has already been made to the fact that by the turn of the century most of the communities around the city of Popayán had been dissolved, and their population converted into *terrazgueros*. The same process was taking place on the slopes of the *cordillera*.

Scattered around in nuclear families, living at a subsistence level on haciendas, their life depending on the good will of the hacienda owners, without organization that would keep them in contact, the *terrazgueros* were the most exposed of all Indians to pressure for acculturation to the dominant society, as well as the most vulnerable to the exploitation of their labor. A descendant of the Lame family, interviewed in 1971, still remembered his own experience as a *terrazguero* during his youth:

> One had to pay sometimes up to twenty days of *terraje* for the right to raise several head of cattle out there in the grazing lands. That was every month. There were *hacendados* who charged only three days a week. And the *patrones* said that any Indian who would not go out to work their *terraje* would be evicted from the hacienda. Some Indians had as their obligation [*obligación* in this context is synonymous with *terraje*] to carry to Popayán a sack of potatoes weighing five *arrobas* on their backs! The sick also had to pay *terraje* once they started to get well ... and if anyone opposed any resistance then they would cut the wire of his fence, push cattle through his garden or even set his *rancho* [hut] on fire![31]

The bitter experience of the *terrazguero* Indians stood before everybody's eyes as a warning (*voz de alerta*) to those commoners who still enjoyed the communal lands of the *resguardos* and who still maintained the minimal organization offered by the Indian councils or *cabildos*. It was also one of the reasons why so many of them were ready to sympathize with and follow any leader who understood their predicament and proposed a way to stop the dominant society from further encroaching into their ancestral lands. For the Indians of Cauca Indígena it was a matter of survival.

THE RELIGIOUS SITUATION

The christianization of the Indians was carried out in the Cauca Indígena region by Franciscans and Jesuits with little success during the seventeenth and eighteenth centuries.[32] The most distinguished of them, Father Eugenio Del Castillo I Orozco, lived for over twenty years in Tierradentro, beginning in 1735. He not only learned to communicate with the Indians in their own language, but also produced the only vocabulary of the Páez language rendered into Spanish.[33]

Reports and studies on the religious life of the Indian communities to which Quintín Lame belonged call attention to the Indians' staunch resistance to give up their traditional religion in exchange for that of the missionaries.

As early as the seventeenth century, the Jesuit Manuel Rodríguez, who was the first missionary in the area, expressed his frustration because of a most peculiar way in which the Indians reacted to Christian preaching: "The devil has them accustomed to laugh at everything, and to burst into loud noises as if mocking at anything that is being said, unless it is that because of their incapacity they can only respond with a loud laugh to what they don't understand."[34] Father Rodríguez's suggestion that the Indians' peculiar response to Christian preaching was due to "their incapacity" was in fact a basic conviction on his part:

> They are the most barbarian and incapable people of those dis-
> covered in America, to the point that *there are grounds to doubt
> their rationality;* their best known inclination is to idleness and
> drunkenness. . . . It is not known that they recognize any deities,
> *unable as they are to grasp a Supreme Being,* the first cause of all.[35]

Father Del Castillo I Orozco, in the eighteenth century, left equally negative judgments about the Páez Indians who, according to him, demonstrated "an innate hostility to learn Christian doctrine."[36] More recent writers concerned with the religious life of the Páez communities conclude that pre-Columbian religious practices predominate in spite of the efforts of missionaries. Carlos Cuervo Márquez, for example, who visited the area at the end of the last century, wrote:

> Today the Páez Indians find themselves in the same degree of social
> and religious backwardness as they were four hundred years ago.
> The most educated in religion among them, who are relatively few,
> only know that they need to pay tithes and offer first fruits, and
> their religious knowledge is limited to the recitation of fragments of
> incomplete prayers; regarding ceremonies, they neither practice
> nor understand them and hardly have a confused and crude idea of
> the existence of a Being superior to man, whom they still imagine to
> inhabit the deserts and *páramos,* or else in the depth of forests or
> presiding over storms and tempests.[37]

However, because the christianization efforts persisted albeit sporadically over a long period of time, the religious life of the Indian communities became mixed, through the accumulation of traditions both pre-Columbian and Christian in origin, which were sometimes superimposed in an eclectic fashion, sometimes integrated in a syncretistic manner. Thus, a mixture of spiritualities and religious traditions became the most characteristic feature of the religious life of the Cauca indigenes. The resulting form of religiosity includes beliefs in supernatural beings both beneficent and malignant; in spiritual powers that reside in particular geographical sites such as lakes, rivers, volcanoes, and high peaks; in souls that hover around the house after death and need to be attended to; religious practices such as sorcery and spiritual healing through the intervention of shamans; and intense drinking sessions on special occasions.[38] All these aspects of native religious life have been supplemented by Catholic beliefs and practices introduced by missionaries sporadically over a long period of time, including a particular conception of God as a judge, faith in the Virgin Mary as spiritual advocate, and cult of the saints. Special importance is accorded to the festivals of the saints and to the celebration of Christmas and Holy Week, which have become the most important social events of the year, providing an opportunity for spiritual expression and social distinction.[39]

The concept of God as a judge who is angry because of evil human actions, and who, therefore, needs to be appeased or placated by good works and other acts of devotion, has its roots both in the indigenous religiosity of the Andes as well as in the early work of the Christian missionaries. In effect, pre-Columbian religious traditions of the area testify to a profound belief in the destructive power of nature spirits, as well as in the hostility of the disembodied spirits of the dead, whom the living must assiduously propitiate.[40]

The "angry God" theology can also be traced back to the early stages of missionization about which, however, there is not much specific information. Mention has already been made of the *Vocabulario* that Father Castillo I Orozco prepared in the middle of the eighteenth century and to which he attached some valuable catechetical material, including the full text of two meditations (*pláticas*) and a commentary on the Ten Commandments, all of this in the Páez language with Spanish translation. Thanks to these materials it is possible to have an idea of the kind of Christian preaching and teaching that the Jesuits spread among the Indians in the early period of catechization.

The *pláticas* are fiery rhetorical pieces on such subjects as God's wrath and God's impending punishment, with detailed descriptions of heaven and hell:

> With God's help I want to preach about hell . . . because you should know for sure that there is hell for those who do not keep God's law. And if you die without asking God's pardon, without the confession of all your sins, without repentance, you shall go to hell without escape, whence there is no return as long as God is God!
>
> Hell is a very large cave in the center of the earth, closed on all sides, very dark, where no air comes in, nor even a ray of

light. Nothing can be heard there except the yelling of demons as they torture the souls of the damned. These cry and curse, yelling (*aullando*) like mad dogs, trembling and cracking their teeth.[41]

This short sermon ends with a double exhortation — to love the Virgin Mary so that she may intercede before her son and thus spare the Indians "from the dungeons of hell";[42] and to confess everyting to the priest "without hiding from him even one single sin" because "God is watching everything."[43]

The second meditation or *plática* describes "the glory and the things that God has in store to reward the good."[44] Heaven is defined in terms of "happiness," absence of hunger, of thirst, of sleep, of night, or of lack of clothing; but above all it is the place where the blessed ones shall be freed "from all fear, even fear of the devil."[45]

Following the two *pláticas* Father Castillo I Orozco includes his explication of the Ten Commandments, addressing them personally to the Indians with very specific applications, such as: "not to believe in *brujos* [shamans] or birds or snakes or dreams" (first commandment); "to obey the priests and the elderly" (fourth); "not to get drunk with *chicha,* to the point of losing consciousness" (fifth); and "not to be sad because others are rich, but rather to be very content with whatever God has given us, even if it is very little."[46]

Father Del Castillo does not dwell on the commandments of the church (as supplementary to the commandments of God) but summarizes them all in one: to obey the supreme pontiff (*Sumo Pontifice*), whom Christians of the entire world obey, whether they be "kings, bishops, priests, governors, mayors, all white men and Indians; all Indian chiefs and their seconds in authority (*mandantes*)."[47]

Thus, taking Father Del Castillo's doctrines as an example, it would seem that the major thrust of early missionary teaching was directed towards shaping the character of the Indian along three major ethical lines: (1) fear of divine punishment and the promise of being spared from punishment if correct conduct was observed; (2) the rejection of negative indigenous practices, such as sorcery and drinking sessions; and (3) complete obedience to the church (the pope, ultimately, but more immediately, the priest, from whom "no sin should be hidden").

This ideological contribution became in the course of time an integral part of the religious world of the area, but in an ambiguous way: on the one hand, it reinforced the preexisting religious worldview, which was always conceived in dualistic terms (hostile and beneficial powers); and on the other hand, it set up a new religious system around the church and the priest, intended to extricate the Indians from their ancestral culture and to introduce them into the culture of the dominant society. This tension is reflected in the two major characteristics of the religious situation of the area, which can be summarized as follows:

(1) the staunch persistence of certain forms of religiosity relative to death ✓ ᵃ and to the spirits of the dead in continuity with the ancestral spirituality of the indigenous population; and (2) the explicit social function of the ✓ *b* church in terms of deculturization of, and social control over, the native population.

All existent studies of the religious life of the area testify to the fact that beliefs in malignant nature spirits and in hostile spirits of the dead resulted *a* in widespread fear of sudden death or painful sickness caused by evil spirits.⁴⁸ To deal with these difficult problems Indians have developed since time immemorial a complex religious system in which the shamans (*Te-eu*), and various kinds of witchcraft and sorcery, together with appropriate rituals of appeasement and propitiation, have played a major role.⁴⁹ Christian missionization and its "angry God" theology, far from liberating the Indians from religious fear, resulted rather in Indian adoption of a new set of religious resources to deal with the same spiritual problems. These resources have included, above all, a special veneration of the Virgin Mary as heavenly advocate, and the cult of the saints, who now become beneficial spirits who aid believers in their battle against inimical spirits. In this context the function of the priest and the entire sacramental system of the church (Mass, confession, penitence, etc.) find their place side by side with the traditional resources of indigenous spirituality.

The missionary's intention, however, as well as the role assigned him by the national society, has been quite different — to bring the Indians out of *b* their "primitive" and "savage" state, under the guidance and tutorial care of the church, into the civilization of the national society. It is this avowed purpose which the church has failed to accomplish completely.

According to Father David González, himself a missionary for over thirty years, from 1922 on, under the jurisdiction of the apostolic prefecture of Tierradentro, this partial failure has been due in part to the Indians' racial and cultural inferiority, and also in part to the failure of the national government to be more aggressive in the division and distribution of Indian lands:

> The government has tolerated the absurdity that the Indians believe and act as if they were the owners of immense plots of land. . . . For this reason [the governments] left the Páez race abandoned to their natural indolence, to their racial laziness, to vegetate in their lack of feelings of dignity, and in the absence of any desire for self-improvement, since it is a fact that the Indians by their natural inclination wish to remain in their primitive state.⁵⁰

Father González further laments that in spite of the church, and schooling, and work on the haciendas, the Indians of Tierradentro have not shown an inclination "to progress," as with the white population, through the acquisition of wealth, education, and higher levels of life, but rather, after experiencing all these forms of contact with civilization, "the Indians turn back to their lands where they go on with the same life of their ancestors."[51] Father González's blatant racism, which echoes the judgment of the first missionary to the region who had charged the Indians with inherent "incapacity," is also characteristic of the attitude of the Colombian intellectual elites and upper classes towards the Indians.[52]

To the extent that these attitudes were reflected in the way in which the missionaries related to the indigenous population, they were probably one of the reasons for the limited success achieved by the church in bringing the natives into "civilization." Father González rightly registers a major fact: that the church has failed to a large extent in fulfilling the role which the dominant society assigned it — that of ushering the Indian communities into "civilization."

To the extent, however, that the missionary enterprise was able to accomplish its goal, the church became de facto an effective agent of social control over the indigenous population, as has also been the case in other areas of the Colombian countryside.[53]

At the turn of the century this prescribed role of the missions received decisive political support with the signing of the Concordat and its supplementary Missions Agreement, concluded between the Holy See and the republic of Colombia in 1887 and 1888.[54] By these documents the Catholic Church received the exclusive right to the evangelization and acculturation of unbelieving Indians living in Colombian territory. Indian regions became "mission territories" (called vicariates or apostolic prefectures), the actual administration of which, both civil and ecclesiastical, largely remained in the hands of missionaries.[55] Subsequent legislation reinforced the special status of the missions. On the one hand, it was declared that "the general legislation of the republic *shall not apply* to the savages who are being brought to civilized life by means of missions."[56] On the other, the state delegated to the missions "extraordinary powers to exercise civil, penal, and judicial authority over catechumens.... Until leaving the savage state, in the judgment of the government the Indians are ... to be governed by missions."[57]

Around the time of Lame's emergence as an indigenous rebel (early in the twentieth century), missionary work was in the process of being reorganized and intensified under the leadership of a new missionary agency, the Lazarist Mission, which took formal charge of the religious administration of Tierradentro in 1905.[58] The mission was elevated to the rank of apostolic prefecture in 1924, and since then has continued to be in charge of the christianization of the area to the present.[59]

The Lazarist missionaries are generally credited with having "pacified" or "subjugated" the Páez (or Páeces), a goal that the Spanish conquistadores had failed to achieve in earlier times through military means.[60]

The religious and spiritual strain that Christian missionization and Western penetration of Cauca Indígena has produced in the Indian

communities is indicated in part by a number of pseudo-Catholic cults
with strong nativistic features which have appeared at various times in
the area.[61]

The first was founded by an Indian named Francisco Imbachí or Undachí,
in 1706, from the town of San Andrés de Pisimbalá. The Indian, who
claimed to have seen God and spoken to God in his native Páez language,
developed a large following. He took from the church religious para-
phernalia and religious images, and withdrew to the upper reaches of the
Cuevas River, where he built a chapel. When the news of a new cult came
to the attention of the ecclesiastical and civil authorities of Popayán and
La Plata, a commission was dispatched, and Imbachí was apprehended,
tried, and sentenced.[62]

Over a century later, in 1833, some fifty years before Quintín Lame's
birth, another nativistic religious cult emerged in Tierradentro. According
to the oral tradition of the area a supernatural being appeared first to a
principal elder of the community of Suin, in Tierradentro, and later to
the entire community gathered outside the parish church, and told them
to destroy all the Catholic symbols, crosses, and statues of the saints. The
Indians not only obeyed but went even further: the women took orna-
ments of the church and the cloths of the altar and dressed themselves
with them. The sacred cup was used to drink *guarapo* (fermented cane
juice) and thus they celebrated the occasion. On the same day they filled
the niches of the saints with villagers: in place of the Virgin they put a girl
of fifteen years, the most beautiful whom they found, and in place of St.
Anthony and St. Michael they placed Indian boys of the same age:

> Thus, everybody worshipped them. In the evenings they were carried
> outside on stands, decorated with lights and with flowers from the
> fields, and thus they paraded them around the fields surrounded by
> many.[63]

In this case too, the authorities, after two months, succeeded in cap-
turing the leaders of the movement: one of them was shot to death in
downtown La Plata, the others were tortured and placed in jail.[64]

Against the background of this lively religious history characterized by
strong indigenous traditions and punctuated by subversive messianic
movements in sharp tension with the goals of Christian missionary work,
it is not surprising that Lame's emergence as a nativistic leader, early
in the twentieth century, encountered the immediate opposition of the
Lazarist missionaries who would play an important part in Lame's apprehension and in the eventual suppression of his movement.

CHAPTER III

Manuel Quintín Lame:
The "Cry of a Race
Hated by Civilization"

BIOGRAPHICAL PROFILE[1]

The Formative Years

Manuel Quintín Lame was born on the hacienda San Isidro, about fifty kilometers east of Popayán, on October 31, 1883.[2] His father belonged to the Páez Indians, an indigenous ethnic group historically known for its staunch resistance to outsiders, especially conquistadores and settlers, against whom they have carried on an age-old struggle to preserve their communal lands and their ancestral culture. However, the acculturation process of the Lame family to the national society was well advanced at the time of Quintín's birth. His great-grandfather, Jacobo Estrella Cayapú, had been uprooted from the Indian hamlet of Lame in the remote hinterlands of Tierradentro, almost a century before, due to some kind of confrontation with the communal authorities.[3] Having migrated westwards he had come to the Indian town of Silvia where he was given the name "Lame" as an identification of his place of origin. He settled as a *terrazguero* in one of the haciendas near Popayán where Mariano Lame, Quintín's father, was born. His mother belonged to a local Indian family of the Guambiano group. She had lived all her life in close contact with mestizo society.[4] Thus, neither of Quintín's parents belonged to an Indian community in the sense of working their own communal lands within the organization and authority of the *resguardo* institution, as was the case with most of the Indians of Cauca Indígena at the turn of the century. The Lames were not *indios de parcialidad* but *terrazgueros*, working for the landlords of haciendas.

According to his own account, Quintín taught himself to read and write in the solitude of the forests against the will of his father who had reacted very strongly against his desire to go to school.[5] In his adult years, Lame offered several romanticized accounts of the ways in which he learned by himself, without the benefit of a teacher. According to one version he learned by "observing the worms make their scribblings on the leaves of trees";[6] or else, "using for pencil a piece of wooden coal, for slateboard a flat piece of the same wood."[7] But there are few independent accounts of his intellectual development as a youth, besides his own testimony about a powerful "enthusiasm" for learning.[8]

An early influence on Quintín's life was without a doubt the profound ✔ religiosity of his family. Internal evidence from Lame's manuscript as well as independent testimony indicate that both parents were practicing Catholics who cooperated in various forms with organized religion, particularly with the Comunidad de Padres Redentoristas, a Catholic missionary society that had initiated catechetical work in the region around 1899.[9] The hacienda owners themselves made it a point of patronizing religious activities both for their own religious needs as well as for the Indians. Ignacio Muñoz, for example, the *patrón* of the Lame family, donated land to the church and had a chapel built on his own hacienda of San Isidro. Religious campaigns were carried out there several times a year, especially during Holy Week, which all *terrazgueros* were supposed to attend.[10] This early religious influence will show later in Quintín's life, developing to the point of permeating all his thought, blended in an intricate way with the ancestral spirituality of the Páez Indians, particularly in connection with his rebellion against injustice.[11]

Another important formative influence on the young Lame was his ✔ participation in several military activities. According to a reference in "Los Pensamientos," he took part as a corporal in the Thousand Days War (*La Guerra de los Mil Dias*).[12]

Lame refers to another trip, this time to Panama, also as a soldier, drafted by General Carlos Albán, provincial governor.[13] Both of these military experiences must have acquainted the young Páez Indian with the use of weapons, the basis of military discipline and tactics, and above all with different places to the south and north of Cauca. The patriotic rhetoric to which he was exposed in these experiences is easily discernible in his future verbal confrontations with representatives of the national society. Around 1903, when the country began to count its casualties, to ponder its misery, and to suffer its international humiliation, Quintín returned to his mountains where his fellow *terrazgueros* saw around him the halo of a traveled man, one who had had first-hand knowledge of the white man's world. Now in his twenties, Quintín must have enjoyed this popularity, and it is likely that he even indulged in fantasies about his "military" achievements, for very soon his fellow Indians started referring to him as "General Lame."[14]

Two distinct stages divide Lame's public activity as an Indian leader. The first is his earlier campaign concentrated in the Cauca Indígena region from 1910 to 1921, which some of his original followers will later refer to as "La Quintinada."[15] The second stage, from 1922 to 1939, is concentrated almost entirely in the department of Tolima, northeast of Cauca Indígena. It will be referred to as "the Tolima Campaign."

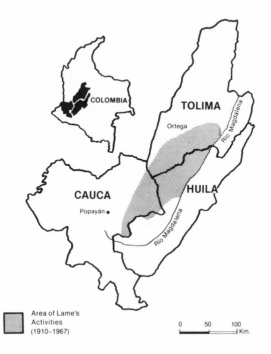

The Cauca Campaign: "La Quintinada" (1910-1921)

During this period Manuel Quintín Lame rises as a nativistic rebel who becomes the catalyst of Indian resentment, and the vehicle for their protest against white-mestizo domination. The movement that emerges with him is to a large extent spontaneous and anarchistic, with strong racial and ethnic overtones. Lame's personal development as a leader can be traced along the following sequence of events.

According to his own information, he was "elected" in 1910 by the Indian *cabildos* (councils) of Cauca as "their Chief, Representative, and Advocate General."[16]

In the years that followed his "election," Lame devoted himself entirely to an agitational campaign throughout the entire region.[17] In its more general form it was a campaign to incite and mobilize the Indian population against the "dissolution" of the *resguardos*, to defend their communal lands.[18]

However, in its more specific aspects Lame's rebellion was "nativistic" in nature, as expressed, for example, in his staunch opposition to what he understood as "civilization,"[19] which led him to stand against the white "aristocrats" who ruled from Popayán, the hacienda owners, the white-mestizo settlers who encroached upon *resguardo* lands, the urban centers established in the midst of Indian communities, the traders' business practices, and above all against the generalized "contempt" that characterized white and mestizo attitudes towards Indians. These stands had widespread resonance throughout the Cauca Indígena region, whose indigenous population began to regard him as a kind of Indian messiah, with awe and admiration.[20]

The rise of Quintín Lame seems to have boosted the will to resist oppressive conditions among the Indian population, judging from the complaints voiced by white and mestizo power holders. Hacienda owners accused the Indians of a wide variety of crimes including cattle stealing, slaughtering of cattle for domestic consumption without the payment of taxes, clandestine distilling of liquor, refusal to pay *terraje,* collecting dues for the "Lamista" movement, punishment of Indians who did not collaborate, and the establishment of a general climate of harassment and intimidation of the mestizo and white population. Of particular concern to the authorities was the practice of *boleteo* — that is, personal threats to the life of *hacendados* and their rural foremen (*mayordomos*) with the intention of forcing them out of the area.[21]

As a consequence of these threatening developments, the civil and political authorities, the hacienda owners, the priests, and the entire non-Indian population joined ranks against the common enemy. A massive hunt of the "wild ass"[22] was set in motion. As early as 1911 hacienda owners had been authorized to arm their *mayordomos* and peons, to register them as rural policemen, "and to organize them in squads for the repression of cattle stealing."[23] Thus, the political authorities had hoped that the movement could be put down by private initiative of the hacienda owners. As insecurity increased, however, the regional authorities began to assume the coordination of a strategy of repression of which the governor of Cauca himself, Don Antonio Paredes, became the central figure. He started by singling out Lame as the one person responsible for the "climate of violence" prevailing in the area. The governor accused Lame of being a "subversive," an "arsonist," and "the instigator of a racial war."[24] Then the governor went on to authorize the mayors of all towns of Cauca Indígena to organize "commissions" to search and capture Lame.[25]

The priests and missionaries of the region also closed ranks with the rest of white-mestizo society against the Indian rebel and his movement, which was perceived (in spite of Lame's profession of Catholicism) as one more attempt on the part of the Indians to revert to paganism.[26]

The capture of the Indian leader did not prove easy. The search operations lasted several years (1914 to 1917) during which period the Lamista movement picked up momentum among the Indian populace. The governor became convinced that Quintín Lame "had followers and accomplices throughout the entire province," and that, in fact, the Indian movement "was widespread" (*el movimiento indígena es general*).[27]

The final stage of "La Quintinada" is marked by the stepped-up repression of the movement, and the continuous danger and insecurity of the Indian leader. In March 1915 he was surprised by troops in the chapel of the hacienda San Isidro where he was participating in religious exercises in preparation for Holy Week, at the invitation of the priest, Gonzalo Vidal.[28] There was a bloody confrontation inside the chapel between the troops and Lame's followers. Lame was taken prisoner to Puracé for about a month and then released for lack of formal charges. Two months later he was captured again "because of treason" near the El Cofre River. He is said to have been dragged down the mountain to Popayán tied by the neck to the tail of a horse. This time he was put in jail for an entire year, his legs chained "to an iron bar of twenty-eight pounds."[29]

It was during this year of solitude and physical hardship in the jail of Popayán that Lame claims to have experienced a profound and transforming spiritual encounter with "a mysterious image," which he describes in "Los Pensamientos" in sublime religious terms.[30] According to Lame's own testimony, this encounter with the numinous led him to discover the potentialities of his mind, to reconsider the nature of his role, which he will define from that time on as one of "an advocate and apostle" of the Indian race.

Soon after his release, however, Lame resumed his agitational activities with renewed boldness and apparently with much greater prestige and a larger following among the Indian populace.[31] According to the secretary of government of Cauca, "sedition was at its peak!"[32] In November 1916, in effect, a most serious confrontation took place in the town of Inzá, capital of Tierradentro. The secretary of government reported it to the governor in sharp terms: "The fears of the inhabitants of Inzá have been realized: Lame attacked the town with his followers; there were dead and wounded!"[33] Lame, however, reported the events in quite a different light. According to him he had entered the town to have a number of Indian children baptized in the church, and during the ceremony police squads fell on Lame's group by surprise. Seven Indians were killed and eighteen wounded, including women and children.[34] Lame accused the priests and held them directly responsible for the massacre:

> One of the priests led the militia units which had been after us, and incited them to kill Indians, since Indians were not Christians. [Later on] the same priest had the Indians who fell prisoners hanged from trees to make them confess my whereabouts.[35]

The bloody events of Inzá achieved the desired effect for which the governor had been pressing for a long time: the central government agreed to send national troops to eradicate definitely the Lamista threat.[36] Lame was apprehended in June 1917, together with most of his assistants, and kept in jail for at least four years.[37]

After Lame's apprehension, the secretary of government reported to the Assembly of the department of Cauca the reasons for the success of the authorities:

The governor secured the cooperation of Don Pio Collo, a prestigious Indian from Tierradentro who did not support Lame, to help regain tranquility and order, and to induce the Indians to respect and obey the authorities. The same cooperation was secured from the Missionary Fathers of those regions.[38]

Thus, according to the political authorities it was the offering of rewards to disaffected Indian leaders (Pio Collo, the Indian governor of Julumito, and others), as well as the open collaboration of Catholic priests, that finally achieved the goal that the armed squads of the landowners and the militia units of the police had proved unable to achieve.

The Tolima Campaign (1922-1939)[39]

Lame was released from his Popayán prison some time towards the end of 1921. We know this from the fact that early in 1922 he abandoned the Cauca Indígena region and moved to the southern Tolima area, which became the theater of his activities until his death in 1967. He settled in the vicinity of Ortega, making the hamlet of Llanogrande his new center of activities.[40]

At the time of Lame's arrival in the area, the social condition of the Indian population was in several respects worse than it had been in Cauca two decades earlier, chiefly because in Tolima the civil and political authorities considered that the Indian descendants were in fact not "Indians" but peasants, fully integrated into Colombian society.[41] This contention was partially true on several counts. In the first place, Indians did not enjoy in Tolima even the precarious security of the *resguardo* institution, because the old reservations had been declared "dissolved" and the land divided and distributed among commoners since the middle of the nineteenth century. As a consequence, Indian descendants, unprotected by the "special legislation" which applied only to *resguardo* Indians (Law 89 of 1890), had fallen victims of land grabbers and settlers with expansionist and enterprising outlook who dispossessed the majority of them of their plots. The Indian families that had succeeded in preserving their traditional inheritance were now under the continual threat of losing it through fraud or violence or by official confiscation and sale by public auction for nonpayment of taxes. In the second place, there was the problem of cultural identity, inasmuch as the Indian had lost not only the measure of control of their own lives implicit in the *resguardo*, but also their own language and communal style of life which had been the matrix of the traditional values associated with Indian communities.[42]

This condition of the Indian peasant population in Tolima was a part of the total social phenomenon associated with the development of rural capitalism (what Lame will call "civilization") which had already achieved a more advanced stage in southern Tolima than in Cauca. One of the reasons for this was the growth of the coffee economy which had increased significantly the demand for rural labor and at the same time raised the value of the land, particularly in the eastern slopes of the central *cordillera*. Another reason was the development of cash crops such as rice, tobacco, and cotton in the fertile valleys of the Magdelana and Saldaña rivers. Both of these economic developments signified a more intense pressure upon the small landholdings inherited by Indian families through the division of old *resguardo* lands which were increasingly considered inefficient and unproductive; the same developments intensified the social conflict between the floating labor (*peones*) and the large hacienda owners who were intent on preventing, by all means, *peones* from settling on their haciendas as squatters (*colonos*).[43]

When Lame settled in Tolima, competing ideologies were already developing in the area claiming to respond to the various segments of the rural economy: the socialist-communist ideology that followed the intellectual orientation of María Cano, Ignacio Torres Giraldo, and Eutiquio Timoté; the socialist-liberal tendency which had developed on the left wing of the traditional liberal party and which would become organized as an independent free party under the leadership of Jorge Eliecer Gaitan and his militant UNIR (Unión Nacional de Izquierda Revolucionaria); and the conservative ideology represented by large landowners and rural entrepreneurs who eventually became organized in APEN and SAC.[44]

In these conflictive conditions, Lame became the catalyst of a new ideological force, an indigenous ideology which could be called "Lamista," nurtured by a strong religious faith with prophetic and millenarian characteristics which emphasized racial-ethnic identity and set as the immediate objective of the native population the reconquest of ancestral lands and the revitalization of the *resguardo* institution as a kind of mystical entity represented by the Indian Council (*Cabildo Indígena*) with socio-political and religious functions.[45]

The nature of Lame's activities,[46] and the effects of his ideas and personality in the southern Tolima area, are indicated by the following social facts.

In 1924, ninety Indian families of the Ortega-Chaparral area formally appointed Lame and his assistant, José Gonzalo Sánchez, as their legal representatives and advocates in matters regarding land rights as well as in every other respect related to the social conflict of the area.[47] Lame and Sánchez took their assignment very seriously. From 1924 to 1931 Llanogrande (which Lame renamed San José de Indias) became the spiritual and religious center of the new movement as well as the headquarters for agitation and organization centered on the goal of reactivating the *resguardo* and eventually reclaiming the ancestral lands.

Llanogrande, or San José de Indias, is remembered by Lamista informants above all as a religious and cultural center. In effect, one of the five houses built there functioned as a church, where Father Heliodoro Perdomo, a priest who sympathized with Lame's ideas, said Mass every

Sunday.[48] Lame himself is said to have had the custom of praying every day before dawn in the chapel. The traditional religious holidays of "folk Catholicism," particularly Corpus Christi, Sts. Peter and Paul, All Saints, and the Immaculate Conception, were celebrated with dances and live representations of ancestral legends about Indian chiefs and "kings."[49]

One more indication of the influence of Lame's ideas among the Indian populace is provided by the document "El Derecho de la Mujer Indígena en Colombia," which appeared as a broadside on May 18, 1927, carrying the signature of thousands of Indian women of the southern Tolima area.[50] It is an impassioned justification of the participation of Indian women in the Lamista movement based on the following ideas: (1) "The son of an Indian woman shall sit on the throne" (no further details about this expectation which, however, confirms the millenarian nature of Lame's ideology); (2) two sons of Indian women (presumably Lame and Sánchez) shall play decisive messianic roles, but Lame alone is singled out as "the man who has never even clouded the mirror of truth"; (3) national laws demanding the partition of Indian lands and the payment of taxes on Indian plots are called "subversive laws of the government"; and (4) Indians are enjoined to stay out of national elections as a protest against "the deceit" of the traditional parties.

All of this ideological agitation expressed itself in mass rallies, particularly in Ortega, which raised real or imagined threats to the non-Indian population of the area, especially to hacienda owners.[51] This climate of confrontation and tension filled the entire decade of the 1920s throughout the countryside around Ortega and culminated in the violent repression of the movement and the destruction of San José de Indias, on February 1, 1931.[52] Lame himself was captured some weeks later and subjected to abuse and humiliation in the jail of Ortega.[53]

Despite the repression, Lame and his followers regrouped and continued their movement in a more secretive and clandestine way into the 1930s. Finally, in a general assembly held in the locality of Palomá-Peralonso, District of Ortega, on December 31, 1938, Lame's followers declared the *resguardo* reconstituted.[54] Lame himself was elected "governor," and twelve Indians were elected to the *cabildo* (council).[55] The first act of the *cabildo* was to initiate an official registry (*el Libro Padrón*), which would remain open for three years to allow all family heads to register themselves as "Indians," thus claiming their "right" to the lands of the old *resguardo*.[56] Lame declared December 31, 1938, the date of his "triumph" and the culmination of his messianic career. In his book, which he concluded a year later, the event is recorded with millennial overtones, stating the conviction that a new day had already dawned for the Indians of Colombia who needed only to follow his example. He wrote:

Indians who can interpret . . . this book shall be able to rise with the greatest aplomb to confront the Colombian Colossus, and to reconquer their territories, in the same way that I also took back the Indian *resguardos* of Ortega and parts of Chaparral in Tolima. . . . I

began officially as Governor to defend the domains which had been
reclaimed ... *a victory achieved with my pen and my example.*[57]

In the years that followed the reconstitution of the *resguardo,* the
newly formed *cabildo* took Lame's ideas very seriously. Its activities pol-
arized the rural population of the area, especially around Ortega.[58] True
believers regarded Lame with awe and admiration, as a savior or messiah.[59]
His antagonists, whether Indian peasants, white landowners, or civil
authorities, hated him bitterly. Soon, however, it would become clear that
Lame, his movement and ideology, was but one expression of a larger and
deeper historical conflict inherent in Colombian society, having to do
with the issues of national integration and the socio-economic development of the countryside in which all sectors of the national society were
involved. The conflict erupted during the 1940s and 50s with the force of
a cataclysm, so much so that many popular minds associated it with "the
end of the world." It is known in Colombia as "La Violencia."[60] The Indian
peasants of Tolima refer to it as "the war" when all legal norms broke
down. Taking advantage of the confused situation, landowners and civil
authorities unleashed a devastating wave of repression throughout the
zone, particularly against the popular organizations, including the Lamista
Indians. The weakness of Lame's movement then became apparent. The
intense ideological motivation had not run parallel with an effective
organization capable of standing up against repression. Consequently,
countless Indian peasants were evicted from the land and went into "exile."
The base collapsed and the *cabildo* was left floating in a void.[61]

During the 1950s and 60s, though the Indian movement was already
broken, Lame continued a desperate, almost supplicant struggle, through
purely legal means, of which his letter to the Ministry of Agriculture on
March 2, 1967 (the year of his death), is an example:

Weighed down in body by hunger and nakedness, we address ourselves to you, distinguished doctor ... requesting you to protect us,
to give us guarantees, so that we may be able to enter our gardens
and harvest our crops, which are held retained by the rich, by the
judges, by the mayor, by the chairman of the city council, by the
procurator, for all are making a mockery of us.[62]

However, "the cry of a race hated by civilization", according to Lame's
self-description, was not to be silenced either by repression or indifference. A few years after his death the banners of the Páez leader would
be picked up once again with renewed strength by new Indian organizations
firmly grounded on the best tradition of Lame's "doctrine and discipline."[63]

Lame's Religious Development

Lame's religious thought is in many respects a reflection of the religious
life of the Indian communities of the Colombian Andes. As has been

shown, this was characterized by a lively syncretism between the ancestral spirituality of the indigenous people and the teachings of the Catholic missionaries active in the area. It was also marked by the concerted attempt on the part of the church to become an effective agent of social control over the Indians. Both of these characteristics are clearly reflected in "Los Pensamientos." However, at several crucial points Lame's religious ideas represent also a transformation of popular religiosity in the context of his own experience of struggle and the conditions of his contact with the dominant national society. Hence, both continuity and transformation characterize Lame's religious development.

One of the features of the syncretistic spirituality of the Indian communities that occupies a prominent place in Lame's religion is the belief in an "angry God," and the concern with supernatural punishment and judgment which resulted in fear with the concomitant need for an appropriate religious system to deal with it. A major dimension of this kind of religiosity revolves around the concern with death, particularly with untimely and painful death, which evil spirits were able to inflict on the living when they were not properly guarded and protected.

This preoccupation involved not only concern with approaching the termination of physical life, but mainly with the possible meaning of physical death as an indication of a moral judgment cast by the divinity upon a person's life, and the consequent fear of spiritual punishment after death. For example, Lame shares the popular belief that the conditions of a person's death are indicative of the moral quality of that person's life and the anticipation of his or her destiny beyond death: "if a man is good he will undergo a good death, because as is a man's life so is his death, and according to his death so is eternity."[64]

The unexpectedness of death is part of its mystery, as well as the incentive for constancy in living the appropriate kind of life and in performing the right kind of religious activities so as to be prepared for the arrival of "that 'tomorrow' which was not tomorrow any longer, but today!"[65] Hence, for Lame, fear of death was important as a restraining factor in human behavior. He says, for example, that the mother who abuses her child should remember "that tomorrow she will have to render accounts before the frightful Supreme Judge," and that this applies not only to the poor and the ignorant but also to the powerful and the wise ("Who do not know the palace of wisdom" — i.e., natural knowledge).[66] Therefore, Lame concludes:

> Man should work as if he were going to live one hundred years, and should live as if he were going to die at this very moment, because the righteous man thinks about life, but even much more about death.[67]

When man least expects it, "death jumps on him!"[68]

A related dimension of this religious fear of death and of supernatural punishment has to do with the appropriate system of religious practices that can provide the individual human soul a measure of spiritual assurance and protection. In Lame's thought this "system" revolves not around sorcery, as is the case in traditional indigenous religiosity, but around "good works." To the question, "What are good works?," Lame answers, "They are faith and charity which rise like incense to the throne of our Celestial Father to placate the wrath of his justice."[69] In a related passage, Lame is more specific, explaining that the practices that have the power of appeasing God's anger are works "such as charity, prayer, fasting, confession rightly made, and the practice of penance."[70] Here Lame's spirituality is profoundly marked by popular beliefs about the individual human soul and its need of purification in order to reach immortality. He explains:

> It is the human soul which builds the Palace for the happiness of the immortal soul when she leaves the body. And how does she come out of the body? In the same way that the warrior's sword comes out of its sheath. . . . But if the warrior allows his sword to get rusty, so that when he needs to present it to his higher in command it is stained, he is not considered a good warrior. Likewise with man's spiritual soul: if stained, it cannot be presented before the Court of Divine Justice![71]

To the question, "How to get rid of that stain?," Lame answers: "By doing penance by means of true faith," which includes such purification practices as self-inflicted suffering which God "immediately assuages,"[72] as well as bearing the burdens imposed by the human condition, like "St. Isidro, the tiller of the land, and many other cultivators who now enjoy the fruits of their humility in the Palace of immortality."[73]

A related feature of popular religiosity that appears also in Lame's manuscript has to do with the decisive role of the Virgin Mary in the system of religious salvation. She is not only an intermediary between the divine judge and the believers,[74] but also the most effective one, because, according to Lame, "the most corrupt man . . . if he is devout to the Virgin, she will lead him to the mansion of bliss."[75] Besides, the Virgin is the very key to understand the nature of God inasmuch as she is "conceived without sin" and in her dwells "the mystery of the Trinity."[76] For Lame, the Virgin is a fascinating aspect of the numinous:

> The Empress of the heavenly court, more beautiful than the sunrise, brighter than the sun, prettier than all the gardens of nature.[77]

In comparison with the fear of death, eternal punishment, and the role of the Virgin Mary, the veneration of the saints plays a less decisive role in Lame's religiosity. In "Los Pensamientos" he refers to many saints, not as intermediaries but as examples of virtue:

> Consider the patriotism of Saint Rita de Cacia, for whose faith she received the name of Saint Rita of the Impossible; and also Saint

Rosalia de Palermo, as well as the name and charity of Saint Isidro the Farmer; of Saint Roque the medicine man (*médico yerbatero*), and so on and so forth.[78]

Saints, for Lame, are important examples whose role is related to practical matters: they assist persons in their daily struggle, not so much in their final destiny.

Many of these features characteristic of popular religiosity sink their roots in the pre-Columbian religiosity of the Andes, not without significant parallels in the religion of the Old Testament, and have become inextricably intertwined with similar systems of religiosity carried over from Europe into the Indian communities through Catholic missions.[79] Lame is aware of this continuity when he writes about "the sacrifices ... that were offered by the ancient Christians to placate God's wrath."[80] However, in spite of these continuities with ancestral features of popular religiosity, Lame suggests the ideological elements of a religious reinterpretation and transformation which he developed in the context of his embattled experience as an Indian rebel. One of these elements has to do with his concept of "the man of faith" (or, "the man of high faith"); the other, with the fundamental doctrine of "good works," as necessary for salvation.

Lame's religious piety is summarized in his concepts of "faith and good works." In "Los Pensamientos" Chapter 3 of book I begins explaining to the reader that "this chapter is dedicated solely to demonstrate the value of virtue when accompanied by faith, because faith that is not accompanied by good works is dead"; but then he goes on to explain that "he who fears God does right, and he who seeks justice, will possess it," thus making the all-important connection between piety and "seeking justice."[81] It is therefore in the context of the search for justice that one is able to understand the religious categories of faith and good works. In effect, in the rest of the same chapter Lame goes on to recall the sufferings of the Indian ancestors at the time of the conquest, and to call attention to the fact that "the indigenous race here in Colombia has been hated by all capitalism."[82] Against this background of oppression Lame makes the momentous announcement that "justice shall arrive and the Colombian Indian shall regain his throne, etc., etc.,"[83] a transformation in which the Indians shall be directly involved as protagonists of their future.[84]

Throughout "Los Pensamientos" Lame insists on referring to himself as "the man of faith," or "the man of high faith."[85] In his description of his vision in the jail of Popayán,[86] where he is said to have discovered his humanity and his intellectual potential ("the image of my thought"), he adds:

That image which I had regarded in rapture with a faith higher than that of Moses the leader (*caudillo*) of the people of Israel,... gave me the assurance that I was destined to overcome those men who had studied fifteen or twenty years, and make them bow their heads.[87]

Here Lame links his faith with the struggle to overcome the enemies of the Indians, thus transforming the religious faith of the sacramental system of protection from death and punishment, and the salvation of the soul, into a historical trust that God is on his side in the struggle for justice: "He told me: through your faith God has given you your life; in the midst of your affliction and your struggle God has consoled you."[88] Henceforth, Lame sets himself in line with ancient religious heroes such as Moses, Noah, Daniel, and the three young men thrown to the lions by King Nabuchadnezzar, "because through faith accompanied with good works the human being is very great, both on earth and also before the tribunal of God's justice."[89]

In all these references Lame clearly implies that "the man of faith," or "the man of high faith," is the one who — like himself and the prophetic figures of the Old Testament — has refused to accept injustice. This explains his rebellion:

> Because I regarded it a heroic and sacred thing not to submit to injustice and inequity, even when it carried the signature of the most frightful Colombian judge.[90]

A similar suggestion is present in Lame's thought in regard to the concept of "good works," which sometimes he uses in the traditional sense of acts of religious piety and other times in quite a different sense. In effect, throughout "Los Pensamientos" there appears to develop in Lame's thought a movement away from the traditional concept towards a more activistic conception of "good works," in terms of Lame's fundamental struggle for justice. In this second, more dynamic sense, "good works" become associated with "patriotism" — that is, perseverance and constancy in the Indian struggle against the dominant society.[91]

Thus, "faith and works" become the criteria to discern true piety and religious integrity, because "faith without good works is dead."[92] This theological background explains in part Lame's confrontation with the Catholic priests both in Cauca Indígena and in Tolima.

As a faithful Catholic, Lame is careful not to condemn the church as a whole. Nor does he ever imply that Christianity is responsible for the kind of "civilization" that is intent on destroying the Indians. He frequently recalls Bartolomé de Las Casas, who "observed the misery and injustice" inflicted upon the native population and who became the "Protector" of the Indians.[93] However, Lame does have very definite complaints about the church's ministers. He laments, for example, that "very few priests" have spoken in defense of the Indian, "because their thoughts have been far removed from the ideas of . . . Bartolomé de Las Casas."[94] He believed that one of the reasons for this failure was that "there have not been priests [ordained] from our own race."[95] Another general complaint had to do with the church's alliance with the state. Lame argued ✓ that the church does not need the defense of political power:

> The Church is defended by God; the Church falls into the hands of her enemies for the little faith and misbehavior of her children, as when the tablets of the law which were in the Ark fell... into the hands of the enemies... but it was God's punishment for [Israel's] disorder.[96]

Lame's major criticism is based on his understanding of "faith and ✗ works" and of their relation to the struggle for justice. In this respect Lame found priests most of the time on the wrong side of the struggle, for "very few" follow Christ's commandments:

> Because there are many priests who hate the Indian and obey the white man, not realizing that... God taught the apostles... "blessed are the poor in spirit because theirs is the Kingdom of heaven"; but he did not say "blessed are the rich, the white, the lawyers, the intelligent, etc."[97]

Thus, it is with the criterion of *practice* that Lame judges the priests: "Because Jesus... called to himself the children, healed the sick, gave life to the dead, food to the hungry," and ordered Christians to fulfill his commandments:

> But many priests baptize first the child of the white man, and a long time afterwards the child of the Indian... [and] many priests say, "I belong to the company of Jesus," but it is only words.[98]

Lame did add, "I do not accuse all the priests of Colombia, only some who are weak."[99] However, his denunciation of those who were "weak" was bitter, on the following grounds: (1) "some priests... have hated [my] campaigns"[100] or were "enemies of my campaigns";[101] (2) many priests allowed themselves to be "tied up" to the interests of corrupt judges and greedy commercial firms;[102] and (3) the priests of Cauca Indígena "led the militia squads" and incited them "to kill Indians" because they were not Christians![103]

During his Tolima campaign Lame seemed to have been labeled "the Antichrist" by at least one priest who is said to have put religious pressure upon the Indians "to stop making petitions to the authorities, and to abandon Quintín Lame."[104]

Thus, a major transformation has taken place in Lame's religious life and thought in the context of his experience as an indigenous rebel. On the one hand, there are in his religious thought clear indications of ideological change through new insights into the meaning of "faith and works" — that is to say, into the meaning of the system of religious salvation as believed and practiced among the Indian communities; and on the other hand, a new religious situation has been created between Lame as a Catholic believer and the institutional church represented by the missionaries and priests who were active in Cauca and Tolima. The extent and depth of these developments is best seen in the analysis of Lame's prophetic theology, which is the major ideological contribution of the Indian rebel and to which I now turn.

LAME'S PROPHETIC THEOLOGY

The Numinous Experience

> The mystery of light transformed the head of the wild wolf into that of a man.
> — "Los Pensamientos," par. 120

Throughout "Los Pensamientos" Lame refers to several spiritual experiences of a very special nature which he underwent at some points of his life, bearing all the distinctive characteristics of encounters with "the numinous."[105] According to his testimony, these experiences involving rapture or ecstasy (*embeleso*) happened to him at least twice,[106] and were of such a powerful nature that they produced a profound effect in his mind, indeed a transformation of his whole life.

One of these "two times" occurred in the solitude of his cell in the jail of Popayán "after eleven months of having been held incommunicado."[107] Lame's account is vivid and emotive:

> Twice I met the image of thought, and I met it in rapture in spite of having passed swiftly, as when lightning tears the majestic mantle that the gods wear in the late hours of the night. Suddenly the wayfarer sees through lightning the blue garment that nature wears. In the same way I also met the image mentioned before after eleven months of being held incommunicado in one of the dungeons of Popayán...the image which I had regarded in rapture with a higher faith than that of Moses, the leader of the people of Israel...because my faith of being saved began in God and ended in God, the Supreme Judge of the human conscience.[108]

This account provides a number of details that surrounded his experience: the rapture took place in conditions of intense psychological and physical stress; the experience is compared to the vision of the firmament which a wayfarer catches in the midst of a storm, thanks to the lightning that tears open "the majestic mantle that the gods wear in the late hours of the night." The experience is further described as an encounter with a reality not clearly defined: Lame affirms to have met "the image of thought," or "the image of my thought," which he refers to elsewhere as "the mysterious image" that "talked to me in the interior of my spirit."[109] Lame's response was one of "faith" in God, a faith that he considered "higher than that of Moses."

The second time to which Lame alludes in the passage above is not clearly indicated, but seems to refer to a later experience in some remote hideout in the mountains, when escaping from the persecution of the authorities and preparing his own defense to be presented before the courts. He refers in the third person to this experience in the following terms:

> The man who on the top of high cliffs did his writing accompanied by that mirror that never loses its luster, *because he was carried in the arms of that mysterious image, the same that accompanied me in the dungeon,* and which helped me carry the iron bar between my ankles, and which was an agent that talked to me in the interior of my spirit, pointing to me the present and announcing the future. And it said to me: "Blessed the man who thinks in the things of tomorrow, and who foresees them, interpreting their spirit; and cursed be the man that cares only about the present!"[110]

In both descriptions Lame conveys quite forcefully the elements of mystery and majesty, and the feelings of awe and reverence, caused by the overpowering presence of the numinous reality, which years later he shall call "the mysterious shadow of Jehovah."[111]

The intricate mixture of cultural traditions and the intertwining of religious mythologies that are apparent in the above descriptions will be examined in greater detail later in this study. However, from the very outset it is important to note the effects of such experiences, which according to Lame's own testimony were at least four:

1) The most immediate consequence was a sense of inner peace through the assuaging of the anxiety and fear produced by his condition of an outlaw who had fallen in the hands of his enemies. "He [Lame] was carried in the arms of that mysterious image, the same that accompanied me in the dungeon, and helped me carry the iron bar"; it was "an agent that talked to me in the interior of my spirit."[112]

2) The second and most profound effect was a deep awareness of his humanity, which Lame describes as a transition from an animal state to that of a human being. Throughout his manuscript Lame surprises the non-Indian reader with the interpretation of his numinous experience as a "mystery" through which his head was transformed from that of a "wild wolf" into that a "a man."[113] Towards the end of his book he refers again to the same experience as the momentous realization of having passed from the animal state to the human condition:

> The mysterious shadow of Jehovah was transformed into a ray of light . . . making me understand that savagery and ineptitude did not

exist anymore, *and that I was not any longer the wild ass, but the devoted Indian (el indio aficionado)* who would come to know the human destinies.[114]

③   3) Equally important, according to Lame, was his discovery of the potentialities of his intellect, which he called very often "the Giant of my mind,"[115] or "the eagle of my thought";[116] and he affirms that it was the "mysterious image" that "showed me where to find the perfumed garden of the logic of Nature"[117] — that is, to discover natural wisdom. The same "image" pierced his mind, which was like piercing "a sardonyx rock," thus creating a fountain of ideas, especially when he had to appear before law courts contending with men "who had refined their language in the colleges of Colombia and Europe."[118]

④   4) Still another consequence of his numinous experience was a compelling sense of vocation. Lame explained that "when it woke up my thought, I too was awakened, socially and morally, to be able to combat injustice."[119] Thus, the Indian rebel who had been possessed by anger and indignation at the cruelty and injustice committed against his father, his brother, and other friends, and who had reacted spontaneously and violently against the perpetrators of oppression,[120] a course of action that led him to the dungeons of Popayán, interprets the vision that he experienced there in terms of divine support, approval, and even predestination:

> He told me: "Your name is written in the book of the predestined of the Lord. Through your faith God has given you your life; in the midst of your affliction and your struggle, God has consoled you."[121]

Awareness of Injustice

> *The remnants of my race, which live today in this Colombian land since October 12 of 1492, |are| hated, deceived, persecuted, trampled underfoot, and robbed by non-Indians of Colombia.*
> — "Los Pensamientos," par. 118

One of the major ideological features of "Los Pensamientos" is the vehement denunciation of injustice, as the comprehensive concept of the evil afflicting the Indian people, and the correlative affirmation of justice, as the moral criterion for human action.

Even though Lame uses in some passages of his manuscript the concept of justice in an objective sense, as *legal justice*,[122] and despite the fact that he spent much of his life fighting legal battles, especially when he discovered that the existing Colombian legislation could be used as a shield against white-mestizo encroachments on communal lands (*resguardos*), and that he encouraged Indians to study and to learn how to handle the law in their own defense, it is still remarkable that "Los Pensamientos" hardly refers to any specific legal rights of the Indian, such as protection from the state, voting rights, free education, or even land rights whose defense and affirmation were so close to the center of his campaigns. This absence calls attention to the fact that Lame's major concern was not to obtain the redress of particular grievances, or to find a path towards Indian integration into the white-mestizo social order, but rather the moral denunciation of a pervasive social ethos that denied the humanity of the Indian.

Lame's concept of justice has philosophical and moral connotations, clearly indicated in this statement that "Justice is the right that every person has."[123] Philosophically, Lame sees justice firmly rooted in God — that is, in the natural law of the universe — and therefore as the source and foundation of Indian hope in spite of present defeat and powerlessness. Lame explains that this understanding came to him for the first time as a consequence of his numinous experience, because it was then that his thought was awakened "to combat injustice."[124]

Morally, Lame's understanding of justice as "the right that every man has" provides the criterion for analyzing and interpreting his human condition, as well as the condition of the Indian population. And even though he did not develop that statement in the form of a theory, it is possible nevertheless to perceive a great deal of what he has in mind by examining some of the specific forms of injustice that dominated his attention and provoked his indignation and action. They are related to the human dignity and to the self-determination of the Indian, which he sees violated and denied by the white-mestizo society.

The concern with human dignity was the result of Lame's own experience as well as the product of his acute observation of the Indian condition. About his own experience he wrote:

Until this day non-Indians have regarded me and still regard me with the greatest contempt! (*con el mayor desprecio!*).[125]

In a related passage he complains that the intellectuals of Popayán regarded him as a "wild wolf," and that they had "embalmed [my] reason through a thousand slanders."[126] They had laughed at him when he had refused to accept a white attorney, deciding instead to take up his own defense at his trial in Popayán. Lame implies that resentment at this kind of "contempt" was one of the major forces which set him on the road to rebellion in the struggle for justice. Lame's account of the immediate cause that motivated his first uprising in Cauca Indígena, when he found his father, his brother, and two other Indian tenants "hanging by their wrists from the ceiling" for failing to pay land rent to the hacendado, clearly shows his concern with the violation of the human dignity of his kin.[127] There is substantial evidence which suggests that the tremendous effort required to produce "Los Pensamientos" was prompted in part by the need to refute the notion, deeply entrenched in the minds of the non-Indian elites, that Indians are intellectually worthless, a prejudice that Lame did not expect to change with his writing but one which dogged him to the very last sentence of his manuscript, when he pondered on the reaction of white intellectuals to his achievement. He wrote:

> The white man will say about my book, "these are beastlike things (*bestialidades*) of the Indian Quintín Lame; because the white man has hated and still hates me to death; has slandered me,... and made a mockery of me, making faces of hate as the devil does when he is unable to snatch away a man's soul.[128]

His own experience helped Lame understand and interpret the condition of his fellow Indians, as well as their psychological outlook. He observed that, if the Indian is poor, the white man looks at him "as he would look at a rotten dog lying on the street."[129] Lame warned Indians to watch out when the white or mestizo sought their friendship:

> Outwardly [the white man's] lips are full of smiles but his intention is to humiliate [the Indian].[130]

Lame believed that this was the social root of Indian resentment and rebelliousness:

> The Indian... never forgets the white man who struck a physical blow at his father and insulted him with words, or his brother or his wife. The Indian does not say a word but in his interior he nurtures the thought of the fighting cock.[131]

The themes of "contempt," "scorn," and "humiliation" run through the entire manuscript, making it clear that for Lame justice was the right that everyone has to be respected as a human being, and to have his inherent worth recognized.

Besides, Lame's concern for justice was prompted by his own experience of being a captive under white-mestizo domination. He felt that Indians are denied justice because they cannot determine their own lives:

> The Indian is always under the white man's boot like a slave, and the Indian who defends his right is persecuted like a fugitive robber (*ladrón fascineroso*).[132]

According to this denunciation, "the Indian's right" is the right to freedom, liberation from "the white man's boot."

It is against this ideological background that Lame's indictment of the national society is best understood. "Los Pensamientos" portrays a picture of Colombia as a society afflicted by a profound rift between Indians and non-Indians, the latter sometimes further defined as "the white and mestizo race."[133] These are the basic categories of Lame's rudimentary sociology which he applies not only to Colombia but in some passages to the entire fabric of humanity.[134] According to Lame, the relations between these two social groups are characterized by attitudes of domination, contempt, and hate, on the part of the white-mestizo society. The Indians are always referred to as victims: "the proscribed and abandoned race,"[135] "the proscribed race," or simply "the wretched poor" (*los pobres infelices*).[136]

In Lame's ideology this dichotomy refers to the radical polarization that he sees between the white and the mestizo on the one hand, and the Indians on the other. This is a profound and pervasive division that cuts across all other interests and loyalties, such as those represented by social classes, political parties, professional or religious affiliations. It is tantamount to a division between "humans" and "nonhumans."

Lame's "interpretation" of this social dualism includes on the one hand a description-denunciation of the Indian experience, and on the other an analysis of the motivations and causes that have produced it.

Lame's description-denunciation of the Indian experience develops along the following lines:

1) The Spanish conquest introduced a system of violence aimed at the physical and cultural annihilation of the Indian people. October 12, 1492, marks the date when Indian suffering started, because Christopher Columbus and the other conquistadores were sent by the nations of Europe "to persecute and murder us like rapacious wolves."[137] They did not come "to civilize the Indian," but "to place them under their boots, to plunder their possession, and to murder cowardly and villainously my ancestors."[138] The remnants (*los restos*) of the Indian race which survive today are still the victims of whites and mestizos who deal with the Indians as "birds of prey"[139] and "tigers."[140]

High on the list of Lame's denunciations is the white man's appropriation of Indian lands and natural resources ("our wealth"), an act with no moral justification whatsoever. It was sheer robbery:

> These lands are the exclusive property which the Omnipotent Judge gave to our original ancestors... and who would have said, except out of insanity, that some greedy guests would one day take away by force our most beautiful gardens![141]

The Indians were robbed of their culture and their material possessions:

> Those who arrived on October 12 of 1492 and seized our wealth, our laws and customs, as well as our religion.[142]

Lame's complaint that the whites had seized Indian "laws, customs, and religion" is not incidental. Throughout "Los Pensamientos" he refers with warm admiration to the culture and spiritual heritage of the Indian people before the conquest. Beliefs in the nature of the divinity, in the various forms of its manifestation according to traditions and legends such as those associated with Sinviora, Muschcate, Bochica, the Sun, the Moon, the holy places such as lakes and ponds, "the god of the rivers," and "the monarchs" of nature, the "old woman Ocllo," and many other myths and "legends" are mentioned by Lame with respect and appreciation. He refers with pride to the great creations of Indian culture "carved with extraordinary beauty": works of art, carvings, monuments, and inscriptions, "which the wrath of centuries has not been able to destroy."[143] Nowhere did Lame make an explicit call to his fellow Indians to revitalize old beliefs, or to return to the old ways, but there is in his denunciation a deep sense of loss and a moral outrage at the insensitivity and malicious destructiveness of the white man's civilization with respect to Indian culture.

2) Under white domination the relations between Indians and non-Indians are like those between "the working bees and the loafer drones": the latter (the non-Indians) "want to eat without working."[144] The economic abuse introduced by the conquest continues today, because "the Spanish treated us like beasts of burden, and *still continue to do so.*"[145] This abusive treatment falsifies all human relations between the two groups because even when the white man acts outwardly like a friend, his intention is to cash in this friendship by asking the Indian to lower the price of his produce.[146]

3) Another aspect of Lame's denunciation has to do with the corrosive nature of social discrimination and racial prejudice characteristic of the white-mestizo treatment of the Indian:

> The Indian cannot go with a white man to a coffee house, to a hotel, or sit at the table as his guest, no matter how dressed up he might be, because the white man degrades himself before his own and looks down on him with arrogance.[147]

Lame detected a close link connecting discrimination with economic exploitation, because, according to him, it was only when the Indian had possessions ("cattle, coffee farm, wheat farm") that the white man came close to him saying "you are my friend, my pal." But when the Indian was poor and had to live from his daily labor, then:

> The white man looks on the wretched poor as he would look at a rotten dog lying on the street; he tightens his nose and says: "Those Indians smell like hell."[148]

4) Lame vehemently denounced the Colombian system of "justice" which, according to him, was in the hands of "false lawyers" and "frightful and vindictive judges."[149] Lame's interpretation of the immoral con-

duct of lawyers, which he bequeathed to future Indian generations, is given in a dramatized form:

> The white lawyer says to the Indian (who has a legitimate complaint against a white man): "Your lawsuit does not look good at all, it is very difficult, but if you pay me 800 pesos, putting down half of it in advance, in a week your case shall be won." The Indian answers: "I have only 200 pesos with me." The white man says: "No, no, only if you give me 400!" The Indian answers: "In two weeks I'll bring them." Says the white man: "No! Bring them in a week" (and he promises and swears that the lawsuit will be won in favor of the Indian). The Indian brings the 400 pesos, and two months later comes back to ask: "How is my case going, Mr. Lawyer?" But the lawyer who is a loafer and a liar says: "I have done everything possible! The outcome lies almost entirely in my hands, but today I am broke. Give me 100 pesos, which I will appreciate as if it were a present!" The Indian says: "Today I have nothing, but in a week I'll bring the 100 pesos, or at least fifty." Five months later, failing to hear from the lawyer again, the Indian asks the secretary of the Court about it, and she says: "It is already two months since your lawyer presented a brief, but he never came back again!" "But he told me that the case was practically won!" says the Indian. The secretary answers: "That man is really swindling you. Find yourself a good, honest lawyer who at least shows up at the office!" But by this time the Indian's money has run out, he sinks in misery, and the lawsuit is won by the other side. The lawyer of the poor Indian is now happy because secretly he was in cahoots with the defendant![150]

The dishonesty of lawyers is compounded by the venality of judges whose racial allegiance to their white companions is stronger than their oath to do justice. Thus, "the white man steals the little farm from the Indian by making him drunk, having him sign documents of debt without owing anything, dragging him to the courts to legalize the despoil, and the judge cooperates by saying to the Indian: 'It is better for you to pay.'"[151] Lame's experience throughout his life led him to see in judges "terrible," "vindictive," and "frightful" figures,[152] and he takes pride in having been the Indian who had the courage "to stand up against the most frightful Colombian judge."[153]

How to explain this irrational behavior on the part of white-mestizo society? Lame's interpretation points in several directions. Sometimes he stresses the economic motive as being the predominant one ("the white man hates the Indian who does not sell cheap").[154] Other times Lame suggests psychological motivations and political stakes. Often his explanation follows racial or ethnic lines.

On the psychological level Lame believes non-Indian persons are inherently tainted by evil tendencies expressed in "envy," "pride," "arrogance," "contempt," and "hate" towards the Indian. Non-Indians, especially those who stand up as their leaders, are possessed by "evil intelligences."[155] Over and over again Lame states that the white man "hates the Indian to death."[156] After the expression "the white man" Lame almost invariably adds "the enemy of the Indian," to identify what he perceives to be the chief characteristic of non-Indians,[157] and to impress in the mind of his followers the unsurmountable barrier that stands between the two groups. It is "a Satanic hate" that makes the non-Indian wage constant war against the Indian.[158]

However, besides this evil cant of the white man's mind, Lame also sees a more specific and "rational" political motive: the white man is determined to stamp out any Indian attempt to shake his domination. It is as if non-Indians could be proud of themselves *only* by asserting over and over again their domination of Indians — that is, as if their identity depended entirely on the nonidentity of the Indian. Hence, according to Lame, any attempt to affirm the Indian's intrinsic worth had the effect of turning the non-Indian into "a tiger," consumed by insecurity and hate.

Sometimes, however, Lame's interpretation of white hostility towards the Indian follows racial and ethnic lines.

The white elites of Colombia, particularly those of the department of Cauca, repeatedly accused Lame of "instigating a racist war" because they detected an element of racism in Lame's agitational activities long before the Indian leader put his ideas in writing.[159] There is in fact a racial emphasis in Lame's ideology, which runs through his "Los Pensamientos" as well as in all his other shorter writings or public statements. He took pride in being "a legitimate Indian" because, as he said, "through my veins does not as yet run Spanish blood, thanks be to God!"[160] Conversely, he decried those who were not "pure" Indians, whom in principle he excluded from the purpose of his campaigns. This purpose was to defend "the true right which Indians of Colombia have," but he explained to whom he was referring:

> The legitimate Indians, not those in whose veins already runs Spanish blood stained with envy, selfishness, and pride ... whose conscience comes down from generation to generation stained with sprinkles of Indian bloodshed.[161]

Thus, there is in fact a racial emphasis in Lame's ideology. However, his conception of Indian identity is mostly ethnic rather than racial in nature. This points towards another major theme in Lame's thought to which I must now turn.

Indian Superiority

Nature has taught her harmonious songs to those whom she has educated for generations.

— "Los Pensamientos," par. 112

Belief in Indian superiority is one of the most consistent features of Lame's ideology. Lame believed, for example, that "Indian intelligence surpasses, and shall surpass extraordinarily that of the white";[162] that the Indian is endowed with a "better memory," and that "his inspiration is faster than lightning."[163] For Lame, "the poor little Indian" (*el indiecito*), despised by the dominant society, is nevertheless richly endowed by God with natural wisdom and is able to "stroll with greater poise and faster than the bee over all the flowers of the garden of science."[164] Lame saw this superiority corroborated by the greatness of Indian history before the Spanish conquest. This high regard for the achievements of his race is extended to include not only his own Páez family of Tierradentro and all the Indians of Colombia, but in fact all nonwhite cultures (what today is known as the Third World), which Lame lumps together under the category of "Indians":

> The Indian naively has given everything to the white man without realizing the superiority of Indian intelligence. Consider the history of the Veda Indians, of the Egyptian Indians, of the Japanese Indians; the pagodas of India reveal a knowledge that the white doctor does not and will not possess.[165]

Indian superiority over the white man is not only racial, but also cultural, and both blend and reinforce each other in Lame's mind. His explanation, for example, of the greater Indian longevity as compared with that of the whites, is in the first instance racial:

> The Indian lives up to one hundred years, and the white reaches only forty or sixty at the most; after sixty he becomes bent (*encorvado*), because his blood is degenerated.[166]

However, immediately afterwards he suggests that Indian longevity is due to the Indian knowledge of certain "secrets of nature" which the mythological woman Ocllo taught them, and which Indians never revealed to the whites.[167]

The concept of civilization elicited strong emotional and moral reactions in Lame's mind. Morally he considered civilization a negative phenomenon inextricably linked to "the civilization that arrived on October 12 of 1492 to murder cowardly and villainously my ancestors."[168] Consequently, for Lame, civilization was a process led by "evil intelligences" dominated by the irrational tendency to destroy and humiliate Indians. As a rustic philosopher and sociologist, Lame saw civilization as a way of life that was self-destructive and frustrating to the whites themselves: a social order that simply did not work. The negative nature of "white civilization" is shown more clearly when it is compared with the Indian way of life. Thus, Lame contrasts "white poverty" with "Indian poverty":

> The poverty of the white man is sad, painful, shameful, because of his envy and bad faith towards the poor Indian, due to our ignorance, simplicity and illiteracy...[whereas] the poverty of the Indian is not seen (*no se conoce*) because the Indian dresses badly, eats badly, works under the sun all day long, with the help of the cocoa vice or tabacco; if he gets a crop, he is satisfied; if not, he is also satisfied; if he has money, he is satisfied; if not, he is also satisfied; if he has salt, he eats his food with salt; if not, he eats without it; *whereas the white man, if he does not have all of this, detests and curses his lot* and becomes like the rotten trunk of a tree thrown out in the garden, eaten by worms.[169]

Perceptively, Lame locates the root cause of the problem that plagues civilization in the white compulsion to have things and to achieve greater comfort, generating in his mind anxieties and frustrations alien to Indian culture.

The same perception leads Lame to extol the Indian home and the Indian marriage, "where one finds humility, peace, tranquility; [even though] the children go around naked and work naked outdoors until they themselves earn for their own clothes."[170] Lame is not explicit about the point of comparison with the white home, but he adds cryptically: "In the white man's marriage I have seen extraordinary happenings which have served me for information!"[171]

What is the reason for the higher quality of the Indian way of life when compared with that of the white man? Besides pointing out the virtues that he perceives in the Indians (simplicity, humility, peace, tranquility) Lame offers in several passages of "Los Pensamientos" a more basic explanation: Indian culture has developed in close interaction with nature so that the Indian receives lessons from nature, the only source of true knowledge. Nature, for Lame, is "The Book of God,"[172] or rather, a series of books, a library that contains all wisdom: true philosophy, true poetry, true love relations.[173] The beauty, order, and wisdom of nature never cease to amaze Lame:

> One finds the condor's nest so neatly prepared, the little houses of sundry birds so well built, the beehive with its guardian at the door, and likewise everything so harmoniously arranged.[174]

Indians who live all their life in close contact with these marvelous processes cannot help but learn from them. Nature is the true educator of the Indian. Whites, on the contrary, have no natural knowledge,[175] and therefore, wisdom is hidden from them. This is particularly true of those white intellectuals "who have burnt their eyelashes in schools and universities."[176] Not only do they lack direct and physical contact with nature, but their attitude and intention prevent them from learning from it. "God's garden," says Lame, "is hidden from the sight and from the idea of those great men."[177] Lame's interpretation of the white man's "idea" in relation to nature is stated quite plainly:

> Nature has taught her harmonious songs to those whom she has educated for generations, not like the white man, the enemy of the Indian, who has learned to read and write through teachers; *and the same nature possesses her own reserves which predators* (tunantes) *squeeze with their lips, stealing her perfumes and fruits,* while the wind which owns them, passes by.... [the] evil mind, on the contrary, distills poisonous fumes against the ignorant Indian.[178]

Lame seems to be saying that whites relate to nature as predator and to the Indian as enemy, and for these reasons true knowledge is hidden from them. Indians, on the contrary, have received their wisdom as a gift: "Science has a very large garden and few are the [white] men who have seen it, even from afar. But the poor little Indian has seen it from very near!"[179]

Lame thought of himself as an example of this superiority because, as he said:

> Nature educated me under her shade.... She taught me to think how to think. She pointed out to me my desk in the desert.[180]

The fact that today white civilization is in power, and Indians are proscribed and persecuted, is not a true reflection of its inherent value but accidental to it: it has to do with money! Lame realized, therefore, the illusory nature of white prosperity and happiness not based on virtue:

> The white man is today full of bread, full of praise and visits, because he has money.[181]

Thus, in conclusion, Lame's interpretation is clear: the world is upside down and "evil intelligences" are in power: but this is an abnormal situation, not reflecting the true reality of things. This reality is that the Indian race is inherently superior to the white-mestizo race, and that the Indian way of life is preferable to white civilization.

Eschatological Hope

The Law of Compensation is drawing near.
— "Los Pensamientos," par. 96

A major feature of Lame's theology is his belief in a radical change that is bound to take place in the existing order of the world, particularly in regard to the wretched condition of the Indian under white-mestizo domination. This conviction, partially expressed or hinted at throughout the main body of "Los Pensamientos," is explicitly stated in the very last page of Lame's manuscript, where the Indian leader reveals in the sharpest possible terms his expectations for the future:

> The day shall come when a handful of Indians shall form a column to reclaim their rights as God reclaimed humanity, that is, as God rescued it from the tyranny of the devil; in the same way the Indian race shall rescue its rights in Colombia, and the white man shall become the tenant of the Indian, of those Indians who are still asleep in the mind of God.[182]

Two points in this proclamation deserve special attention: first, that the present condition of Indian captivity shall be radically reversed, particularly in regard to the crucial issues of land tenure and Indian rights; and secondly, that this transformation, which Lame compares to God's redemption of humanity from the tyranny of the devil, is going to take place through the initiative of Indians. The first of these two points, having to do with the nature of Lame's eschatological hope, shall be considered now in greater detail; the second one, concerning the means of achieving the expected transformation of society, will be analyzed later in connection with Lame's own messianic consciousness and the role to which he believed he had been specially called by God.

Lame did not describe in detail the various aspects of the announced transformation of the world, but he did point out its general nature. Early in "Los Pensamientos," he made the emphatic statement that "Justice shall arrive and the Colombian Indian shall regain his throne."[183] This announcement, although not elaborated, provides a clear indication that the restoration of Indian sovereignty is part of Lame's vision of the future. This political dimension is further emphasized by his comparison of Indian liberation with God's redemption of humanity "from the tyranny of the devil," which implies that the present condition of Indians is in fact "a tyranny" destined to be overcome by "justice." In this context, Lame's insistence on the restoration of "the Indian right" is better understood: the time shall come when the liberty and sovereignty of the Indian shall become a reality. Lame's eschatology, therefore, involves the expectation of a future reversal of the present power relations, a doctrine intended to keep alive the hope of liberation in Indian consciousness.

Still another aspect of Lame's eschatological hope is his belief in the symmetrical reversal of social conditions expressed in his assertion that "the white man shall become the tenant of the Indian."[184] Lame did not elaborate on this millenarian announcement. Neither did he suggest the probable time when such a radical transformation was going to occur, or the signs that would accompany it. Lame simply announces the eschatological event for an indeterminate future, sometimes referred to as a rather remote occurrence, for the Indian generations that shall experience it "are still asleep in the mind of God."[185]

Other times, however, the millennial future is indeterminate but not remote, as when Lame writes that "the law of compensation shall come very soon,"[186] and warns that even though whites and mestizos do not know it, the settling of accounts is in fact "drawing near!"[187]

As conceived by Lame, "the law of compensation"[188] is an expression of the moral order of the universe, an integral part of divine nature. It is also a "law" that is at work in human history, taking the form of a corrective and punitive principle that vindicates "justice" and denies final victory to human evil actions. For Lame, the Spanish conquest introduced into the world an evil rule:

> The law of fatalism, the law of pride, the law of envy, the law of lies, the law of hate, the law of slander, the law of contempt, the law of threats, the law of bribes and deceit (*superchería*).[189]

This evil rule is responsible for the present miserable condition of Indian peoples, having caused immense human loss and suffering for Indians, who have been proscribed, hated, and persecuted. However, this moral disorder shall come to an end "very soon" because a more permanent and powerful rule is also active in history in spite of man's actions and "above man's head." This more powerful rule is "the law of compensation," which operates naturally, with the passing of time, invisibly and ineluctably. It is not, however, impersonal or impartial, but punitive and vindictive towards the oppressor of the Indian, and lenient and compensatory towards "the wretched poor," who have faith and hope.

Therefore, it was possible for Lame to see justice prevailing despite the intentions of the enemies of his cause, even in times of rejection, persecution, and unjust punishment. His reflection on one of his most painful experiences, when he was held incommunicado for an entire year in the dungeon of Popayán, is typical:

> Justice emanates from God: that image, which always accompanies me, kept saying to me: "You are free, You are free." Therefore, I knew that Justice had already taken away the keys from the jailer (*carcelero*) to set free the poor little Indian, Manuel Quintín Lame.[190]

This belief in a moral principle that overrules evil human actions was a conviction that inspired the Indian leader during his long struggle for justice. It was an important feature of his religious thought, a source of hope in the final vindication of the Indians. Lame finds a wealth of examples to illustrate his belief:

> The captain conquistador who discovered our possession ... died in the city of Valladolid in the arms of misery and hunger. *And everyone who has committed ruinous actions against the Indian race has been attacked by misery, together with natural death.* ... Because it was for the sake of the wretched poor that the Liberator of Humanity came into the world.[191]

And again:

> Time wears a glove wherein man's evil actions are kept, and slowly punishes him, bending his body like the bow of an arrow, and taking away his riches in those moments when man sinks in material or civil calamity: the ruler dethroned, the warrior defeated, and the wise man comes near the shadow of the Tower of Babel; *but he who believes that God loves him, and has hope in God the creator and regulator of time, is never defeated.*[192]

The statement that "everyone who has committed ruinous actions against the Indian race has been attacked by misery" is further illustrated by what happens to lawyers without conscience, of whom Lame has so much to say throughout his manuscript. The law of compensation catches up with them because "in their house there is hunger, there is misery, there is ruin."[193] Thus, the punitive hand of "the law of compensation" reaches the evildoer on *this side* of the grave, the form and conditions of death itself being part of the punishment.

Lame's eschatology includes a "final judgment," "the day when we all shall appear together at the Josaphat Valley, the Court where the sheep shall be separated from the goats,"[194] but he lays the emphasis on what happens to persons *during this life* when Indians and non-Indians are on their way toward the ultimate court. In spite of his wretched condition, it is not the Indian who should be pitied, but the white man because even though he seems to be enjoying this life ("the white man is full of bread, full of flattery, full of visits"), his situation is really tragic:

> He is unaware of his enemy, which is tenacious, powerful, and invisible. And what is it? It is time, because time ... gathers in its glove all of man's remains and counts one by one the steps remaining to reach the point when it will execute the Law of Compensation![195]

Lame did not ask himself the question that dogged the ancient Hebrews: "Why, Lord, does the evildoer prosper?" (Jer. 12:1). Cauca and Tolima did not lack in "evildoers" who prospered and increased in power every day. Lame, however, did not ask the question of theodicy. One reason could have been that for Lame the law of compensation did not ensure *material* rewards to the Indian, the man of faith and hope. Lame did not see "prosperity" as a sign of divine approval, nor as a reward for righteous behavior, as the Hebrews seem to have believed. On the contrary, when Lame refers to riches, to money, to human greatness, he does so with suspicion, as if these were illusions and even traps which make whites unaware of their tragic condition.

What, then, is the rewarding and compensatory side of the "law of compensation"? Lame does not give specific examples or signs of divine approval, at least not in the same specific way in which he illustrates the calamities which "the law of compensation" inflicts on evildoers. He limits himself to affirm the hope in an impending victory with a faith that defies empirical reality: the messianic announcement that present conditions will be symmetrically reversed and that "he who believes...and hopes...is never defeated."[196]

Messianic Consciousness

I am not a prophet, but I have been and I am the apostle of my race.
— "Los Pensamientos," par. 33

A major component of Lame's ideology is his own "messianic" consciousness — that is, awareness of having received a transcendental mission to fulfill in behalf of the Indian people. This awareness, which first developed as a result of his numinous experience, is forcefully expressed throughout "Los Pensamientos" in three ways: (1) the way he saw himself related to the history and traditions of his own Indian tribe, the Páez; (2) the way he understood his vocation, against the background of the "sacred history" of the West; and (3) the way he understood the magnitude and importance of his role as a leader in relation to the future of the Indians.

1) In one passage of "Los Pensamientos" Lame explains that his great-grandfather's name was Jacobo Estrella y Cayapu (Estrella on his father's side and Cayapu on his mother's), but that having migrated westwards from the hinterlands of Tierradentro and settled in the town of Silvia not far from Popayán, the Indian chief of that community, belonging to a different Indian family and speaking a different language, could not communicate with him and gave him the name of his place of birth, Lame, an Indian hamlet situated in the very heart of Páez territory.[197]

The importance of this biographical detail is revealed in another passage dealing with what Lame calls "the prehistory of the Indian race."[198] In this passage Lame recalls an Indian legend about pre-Columbian Indian "sages" who had predicted one hundred years before October 12, 1492, the captivity of the Indian race under "Guagaz," the white man. Lame brings to memory other mythological heroes, created by "the Sun God," who taught Indians the arts and sciences, and to Bochica, the divine messenger of the Chibcha mythology, who had broken with his "magical" staff the rocks of the eastern *cordillera* creating the Tequendama Falls, thus draining the waters of the flood from the Bogotá plateau, and saving the Indians from certain death. After recalling this sacred "prehistory" of his people, Lame introduces himself, saying:

> But 447 years having passed, one of the descendants of the Indian race [came forward], the grandson of Juan Tama de Estrella.[199]

Who was Juan Tama de Estrella? Ethnohistorians of the Cauca Indígena region mention his name.[200] He was a historical figure living before the eighteenth century who became a powerful chief (*cacique*) of his people and who achieved the goal of uniting under his leadership most of the Indian *parcialidades* of Cauca Indígena, on both sides of the *cordillera*. He received titles of ownership of his lands in behalf of the natives from the hands of an old Spanish *encomendero*, Don Cristóbal Mosquera y Figueroa, on June 19, 1708. Juan Tama distinguished himself as a jealous defender of Indian land titles and rights against encroaching white settlers.[201]

After his death, Juan Tama became a legendary figure. Oral traditions endowed him with fabulous attributes, enshrouded his name in myth, and transformed him into the greatest culture hero of the Páez Indians. The mythological elements which have persisted in the collective memory of the Indian communities around this famous personage can be summarized as follows: Juan Tama is a son of the stars, or the son of a star (*de Estrella*), born in a lake and gathered from the rushing waters of the Lucero River; he was reared first at the breasts of chosen women, who died, and later on the milk of vigorous cows, who also died, until he could nourish himself with the fruits of the land. Above all, Juan Tama became the legislator of his people, establishing three important laws: (1) the Páez shall be an unvanquished people; (2) the land must belong only to the Páez; and (3) the Páez must not blend their blood with that of other peoples.

Juan Tama disappeared in the lake where he had been born, Pataló. For this reason the Indian councils used to go there to cleanse their staffs, beg pardon for their faults in office, and make offerings of silver coins.[202]

By thus tracing his genealogy to Juan Tama de Estrella, Quintín Lame is making a statement about himself: he belongs to the sacred tradition of the Indian people and he intends to continue the main lines of struggle of his mythological ancestor.

2) Another indication of Lame's messianic consciousness is provided by the kind of parallels that he draws between his own identity, vocation, and experience, and those of famous prophetic figures of the biblical tradition. Twice he compares his "call" to that of Moses, "the *caudillo* of the people of Israel" destined to dominate the enemies of his people.[203] Lame finds a parallel of his own experience in that of the prophet Daniel and his three Jewish friends who were thrown in the lions' den by King

Nabuchadnezzar. "Likewise," says Lame, "since my tender youth I have fallen in the den of the experts of envy."[204] In another passage Lame compares himself with Noah, sailing in the ark of God's protection "on the sea of slander."[205]

Lame more often finds a parallel to his experience in the sufferings of the Christian messiah. Lame's account of the many sufferings that he underwent in the fulfillment of his transcendental destiny — having to follow "a road full of thorns and thistle," and to cross two rivers, "one of tears and the other of blood,"[206] because of the hate and envy of the enemies of the Indians — runs parallel to the story of the suffering messiah of the Bible. Both Lame and the biblical messiah are vindicated by God who gives them full assurance of the rightness of their cause. In both cases their mission opened the way for the final liberation of the man of faith. Just as the gates of hell did not prevail against "the Lamb of God":

> Who was destined to be sacrificed on the cross in defense of humanity...and was tempted by the devil.... the sea of slander could not drown the poor little Indian... with my hands tied with handcuffs... thrown on the ground like a pig for the slaughter.[207]

Three times Lame indicates specific parallels between his own experience and that of Jesus: (1) he was contemplating "the valley of civilization," whither he was to descend, just as "Jesus was contemplating the city of Jerusalem, where he was going to die";[208] (2) he was betrayed by a close friend for four hundred pesos "paid by the government," like Jesus who was betrayed by Judas Iscariot;[209] and (3) he was deprived of all recognition by his enemies who deliberately tried to hide his merits from the people, "like the Jews who requested the Roman authorities to erase the *INRI* from the cross."[210]

Thus, Lame considered himself not only specially linked to the sacred tradition of his own Indian ancestry, but also providentially related to the messianic tradition of the Christian faith, entrusted with a historic mission that only he could perform. Because of that high calling, Lame believed that he enjoyed special providential protection, for his leadership was to be decisive for the liberation, or salvation, of the Indian people.

3) Nothing conveys better the nature of Lame's messianic consciousness than his own view of the role that he was destined to play in shaping the future of the Indians.

It has been pointed out already that Lame's experience of the numinous issued in a sense of vocation to become "the apostle" of the Indians, which Lame interpreted in terms of becoming an activist determined "to combat injustice."[211]

In his mature years as an Indian leader, Lame projected the birth of his messianic consciousness to his very childhood when "at the age of six" he has a vision to which he refers several times in "Los Pensamientos." His description of the experience is poetic and full of symbols:

> There was an oak tree, old and robust, cultivated by nature.... Climbing on that tree at the age of six I was able to contemplate another tree top, even taller, proud and haughty, that crowned over the virgin forests which had witnessed my birth and that of my ancestors.... A thought came to me that as high as that tree would be placed my ideas in the Colombian nation, when I should come down from the Mountain to the Valley to take up the defense of my Indian race.[212]

This vision or myth which Lame uses to express his messianic consciousness reveals quite clearly that he thought of himself as an indigenous intellectual whose "ideas" were destined to "crown over" the Colombian nation as part of his transcendental mission for which he had come down "from the mountain to the valley." That mission was "the defense of the Indian race."

Thus, Lame assigned himself a combination of roles in which three forms of leadership seem to compete as images of his messianic identity: (1) he sees himself as a defender of the Indian people — that is, a combatant engaged in constant struggle against the enemies of the Indians; (2) he envisages himself as an indigenous intellectual especially endowed by nature with natural wisdom, who has descended to the valley of civilization and become literate in legal and judicial procedures so as to be able to face the intellectual leaders of the dominant society; and (3) he depicts himself as a millennial prophet who has been granted a vision of the future of the Indian,[213] which Lame conceived in terms of a final liberation, when the Indian would reclaim his throne and the present condition of oppression and humiliation would be turned around. These three dimensions of his messianic role were in different ways and with various degrees of intensity expressed in Lame's actual performance as an indigenous leader, but not without ambiguity and even contradiction, which is apparent in his various courses of action.

Activistic Orientation

> God said: "Help yourself and I shall help you."
> — "Los Pensamientos," par. 147[214]

Despite the dire condition of the Colombian Indians, there was no trace of fatalism or resignation in Lame's attitude to life. He charged that "the law of fatalism"[215] was the law that the dominant society wanted to impose so that "when the Indian hurts, [he] does not complain."[216] Lame refused to abide by this "law" and instead he complained, protested, denounced, agitated, organized, argued in court, and mobilized his people all the time.

Lame was well aware that taking upon himself the role of "advocate" and "apostle" of his proscribed people would bring upon him the ire of its enemies. In "Los Pensamientos" he expresses his belief that the systematic persecution which put him in jail 108 times stemmed from the fact that he was "the advocate of the Indian":[217]

Because the Indian who defends his right is persecuted like a fugitive robber (*ladrón fascineroso*).[218]

The intensity of persecution which he underwent in Cauca and Tolima corresponded, according to Lame, to the same logic: not because he was breaking the law ("not because of being a sinner"), but "because I gathered with my people and helped to shape the good in the heart of the Indian."[219] Thus, Lame realized fully that it was his agitational and educational activities that brought upon him the reprisal of his enemies. Persecution, however, did not deter the Indian leader from assuming the role for which he felt uniquely endowed by divine nature.

Lame's activism was grounded upon his criterion of justice,[220] which provided him with three general guidelines for action:

1) Justice is the criterion by which civil authority is to be measured, and the moral basis for challenging unjust laws. He wrote:

I regarded it a heroic and sacred thing not to submit to injustice and inequity, even when it carried the signature of the most frightful Colombian judge.[221]

2) Justice is the principal virtue of a leader:

Man establishes the criterion which will allow him to see realities with the clarity of truth, and his will [will be] the perfect example of uprightness and honesty when he determines to direct all his actions towards justice.[222]

And Lame added: "Justice shall call upon the historian to point out where to find the deposit of my actions."[223]

3) Justice requires of the Indian leader the openness to recognize the existence of seekers of justice within the non-Indian camp. This understanding produced in Lame a kind of "double consciousness" in regard to white-mestizo society: on the one hand, a strong ethnic identity which prescribed the total rejection of its spirit and its intention, and on the other, an identification with its "moral consciousness" which struggled for justice. As the advocate and apostle of his people, Lame asserts all the time his unswerving allegiance to the Indian "race," and takes pride in being "a legitimate Indian," with not even one drop of "Spanish blood," thus setting himself squarely outside white society. But his criterion of justice widens the horizon of his concern and leaves the door open to possible forms of cooperation and alliance.

Lame recognizes, for example, that the central authorities of the country and particularly the supreme court had acted justly on a number of occasions, invalidating biased decisions of lower regional authorities. He interpreted this fact as one more indication of the overruling power of justice, as a superior norm that stood above historical actions.[224]

In book I, chapters 10 and 11 of "Los Pensamientos," Lame portrays himself not only as the apostle of the Indians, but also as the guardian and defender of "the national conscience," which he saw as a temporary refuge for the Indian. He even takes pride in affirming his loyalty to the national society and lists various instances of national crisis when the territorial integrity of the country was threatened and he had offered the unreserved support of Indians in the field of battle against foreign invaders.[225]

"The national conscience" is not, however, identical with white civilization or with the Colombian nation, but rather the adherence to a moral principle that has expressed itself through history in outstanding moral figures who have come out in open defense of Indian rights. Lame mentions at random a number of personalities from all centuries, including popes, presidents, and priests, and affirms that it was because of this "national conscience" that he has pledged allegiance not only to the Indians but also to Colombia as "the motherland."[226] Thus, Lame sees himself as a citizen of two worlds: on the one hand, he is first and foremost the apostle and advocate of the Indians, and on the other, he is bound in loyalty to the national society based on the moral bond of "justice."

However, besides this rather vague criterion of "justice," which Lame borrowed from the moral ideology of the dominant society,[227] there were many other considerations, ideological and strategic in nature, which motivated Lame's activism at various points of his embattled life. Lame believed that Indians needed to become literate and to be mobilized for their own good. He set in sharp contrast two kinds of human beings: on the one hand, "man in a state of foolishness," whom he compared to the "wild ass," the powerless victim of physical or environmental limitations, captive in the claws of civilization, whom he also called children of ignorance; and on the other hand, the human being "who has found the image of his mind"[228] — that is, who has become aware of his inherent worth and potentialities.

This latter kind of human being is what Indians need to become. Literacy became for Lame almost an obsession. As a mature Indian leader, at the time when he was writing "Los Pensamientos," he remembered with joy his own development. Metaphors and images came easily to his mind when he wanted to describe the indescribable experience of learning to speak for the first time in the Spanish language, and thus being able to communicate with the wider society, an ability which he associated with the inspiration received in his encounter with "the numinous":

Because the image of my thought was transformed through a mysterious dream under the forests of ignorance and illiteracy in the time when I used to greet others, saying *auchimgá*, and it was not *auchimgá* but *buenos dias*; and I used to say to my grandfather *cuscachí*, and it was not *cuscachí* but *hasta mañana*! Because my language was transformed, as had happened to my thought, which today is transformed into ideas.[229]

As has been noted before, Lame considered his "enthusiasm" for learning to read and write a divine gift, received at the time of his numinous experience, a part of his vocation to become "the apostle" of the Indian race, a task that he assumed in spite of opposition from his very father:

Because when I asked my father . . . to send me to school, he gave me instead a shovel, an ax, a machete, and a sickle, and sent me with my seven brothers to clear the forest. *However, with that overpowering enthusiasm which I felt inside me, I thought that I should instead learn to write.*[230]

To inspire in the Indians this same enthusiasm for learning, and to implement it, became one of the goals of Lame's activism. The establishment of separate schools for Indian children during his Tolima campaign in the 1920s and 30s prepared the road for the reconstruction in 1939 of the already "extinguished" *resguardo* of Ortega-Chaparral. It also became one of the aspects of Indian activism which triggered anger and repression from the white-mestizo population of the area.

Lame also intended to develop in the Indian populace an ethnic consciousness, even a racial pride, as part of the ideological platform necessary if Indians were to become a social and political force able "to reconquer their domains."

Colombian authorities seemed to have feared this aspect of Lame's activity the most. They accused Lame of inciting a racial war,[231] which they saw implicit in his conscientizing activities — for example, in his teaching that "very soon" the Indians would rise "to confront the Colombian Colossus."[232]

Lame also taught a line of ideological separation from the white social order, coupled with a cautious and intentional participation in it for the purpose of defending the rights of the Indian. In all relations with white-mestizo society, Lame recommends caution and critical judgment. In some respects his advice is very specific:

1) Never to trust white-mestizo friends:

We Indians ought to abandon and refuse the gifts of the whites, the bluffing mouthful (*pendantezco palabrerío*) that says: "I care for you as one of my own family, as a true friend, and it is because of

this love that I ask you to sell me your produce at a lower price."...
Beware of white or mestizo friends!...The white man accepts
the Indian as a friend only when the Indian humiliates himself and
places himself under his order.[233]

2) Never trust white lawyers. Indians should instead get ready to take
up their own defense in court.[234]

3) Never to plead guilty to charges even when coerced or threatened.[235]

4) Not to pay attention to the old political parties, liberal or conservative, because "politics is the element that each day buries us in the
cemetery of sadness and pain."[236]

5) Never to give up the struggle. Lame recommended above all perseverance (which sometimes he called "patriotism"[237] — i.e., unswerving
allegiance to the cause of justice). For Lame "the cause" was simultaneously social and political, as well as religious:

God has clearly rewarded perseverance, but perseverance to the
end, that is, the patriotism of him who knew how to engage in great
battles against the three powerful enemies: the devil, the world, and
the flesh.[238]

6) Finally, Lame believed in the importance of standing up and con-
fronting the *legal* system of injustice. One of his priorities was to educate
the Indian "to speak at the right time,"[239] with courage, as Lame himself
had done:

I have always looked for danger as my companion, and with civil
courage I have spoken out to the most frightful judge, to the most
intelligent lawyer, courage that I bequeath as an example to all
Indian children.[240]

Becoming enlightened about the judicial system would allow the Indians,
Lame believed, to take up their own defense successfully, before courts
and tribunals.

However, the native religious prophet failed to integrate all these
exhortations and challenges within a clear strategy for action towards
the liberating goals implicit in his messianic ideology, a failure that is
not unrelated to the ambiguity already observed in the definition of his
messianic role. As a result, one finds in "Los Pensamientos" two dis-
crepant lines of action proposed to Indian followers: on the one hand, he
incited militant mobilization to resist injustice and to reclaim their right,
thus doing justice for themselves against a social order that hated the
Indians bitterly; and on the other hand, he insisted on the need to resort
to legal and judicial procedures within the framework provided by the
national society.

The first line of action is more in consonance with his analysis of the Indian condition in terms of a radical social dualism between "Indians" and "non-Indians"; the second reveals his "double consciousness" which identified him with the Indian tradition as well as with "the national conscience," a moral entity to which presumably both Indians and non-Indians could belong.[241] The latter idea explains Lame's belief that, although regional authorities were venal and totally corrupt, the national authorities in Bogotá were impartial and fair.[242]

Insofar as Lame came to define his role in terms of equipping his followers for survival in the midst of an inimical society (as an educator rather than an eschatological prophet), his ideology and strategy became basically adaptive and followed the route that had traditionally led Indian communities to cultural and physical extinction.

This latter route has been known as the *via juridica* (the legal way), which consisted in the pleading of the Indian case through the only means that the system of domination left open to them (legalistic and judicial procedures) and through which their defeat was certain.[243] As a matter of fact, Lame's juridical struggles (*via juridica*), for which he felt legitimate pride because of what they represented in terms of his own intellectual development, were easily absorbed or effectively counteracted by the dominant society, to the point of neutralizing them entirely.

CHAPTER IV

Critical Interpretation of Lame's Religious Thought

Lame's reflection on the meaning of faith takes place in the context of the historical situation of Andean Indian communities. As has been shown in chapter 2, such a situation, in its basic structural elements, is the continuation of the conditions of exploitation, domination, oppression, and repression imposed by the conqueror over the indigenous people since the early time of the European conquest of America. In its totality, it signifies a condition of "dehumanization" in which Indians are seen by the dominant society not as persons but as "nonpersons," and are therefore maintained on the margins of all decision-making processes relative to their own future.

It has also been shown that at the time of Lame's emergence as a leader, the traditional forms of Indian life which had developed over a period of centuries were under strong attack from important sectors of the national society. These sectors were pressing for the "development" of Indian regions which meant, in fact, the disintegration of Indian communities and the transformation of the Indian population into a floating labor force which was badly needed in haciendas, ranches, plantations, and public works.

As part of these developments, the traditional *resguardos* were being declared officially "extinct" and their communal lands partitioned and distributed to individual Indian families, a process that almost always led to the eventual appropriation of Indian lands by white and mestizo members of the dominant society through indebtedness, eviction, or other forms of violence. Many Indians were being forced to migrate for entire seasons to faraway areas and to become part-time or full-time wage earners on haciendas or plantations. Thus, as the corporate Indian community was threatened with extinction, the Indians found themselves every day in greater contact with the national society and caught up in the net of social and political processes based on literacy, legalism, and the monetary economy, all of which were alien to the traditional Indian culture. Under pressure for rapid acculturation, the psychological and cultural identity of the indigenous population was deeply shaken, its self-reliance profoundly weakened, and its condition of dependence and powerlessness sharply increased.[1]

All these conditions are clearly reflected in Lame's religious thought which can best be understood as the voice of the voiceless, the protest of the victims of "progress," whose very survival was being decided by powerful forces that seemed totally out of their control. Lame's theology is thus a reflection on the meaning of God and of the Christian faith, arising from the depths of oppression and insecurity as experienced by the indigenous population of southwestern Colombia. As shall be shown presently, it is a theology that reflects such conditions by denying them any moral and theological legitimacy. It is therefore by definition a prophetic theology.

INDIAN REBEL AND RELIGIOUS PROPHET

Essential to the understanding of his religious thought is the characterization of Lame himself as a religious figure. However, the fact must be underlined from the very start that the Indian leader does not appear on the scene in the first place as a religious personality but as a rebel, as a fighter, as a man struggling against injustice. He was, as his fellow Indians say, "a warrior" (*un guerreante*).[2] According to his own account, Lame's initial act of rebellion was provoked by his patron's cruelty towards his father which reached its explosive point on one specific occasion, setting afire Lame's immense reservoir of anger and indignation.[3] From that moment on, Lame's life was plunged into a protracted war with the dominant society. In his own words:

I started on a road full of thorns and thistles, and along that road I had to cross two rivers, one of tears and the other of blood.... This Indian ... has been hated, slandered, chained, jailed, and insulted by word and deed by the descendants of the Spanish.... Because I have been put in jail 108 times in Tolima by non-Indians.[4]

It is in the context of this embattled life that Lame's religious experience in the jail of Popayán as well as his later reflection on the meaning of the faith are to be understood. The question is not, therefore, whether his faith motivated his rebellion, but rather whether it can be understood at all apart from his struggle against injustice.

The answer to this question is clearly negative because the manuscript "Los Pensamientos" makes it abundantly clear that Lame's religious thought was radically affected by the permanent struggles of his life, at least in three decisive respects. In the first place, his militant involvement opened new vistas onto the history of the Indian people, which he came to regard as "the history of suffering" that began on October 12, 1492. In the second place, his experience as a rebel allowed him to perceive aspects of the Christian faith that remained hidden to other Indians and which he develops in his manuscript. In the third place, Lame's example as a "warrior" as well as his insights as an indigenous intellectual prompted his followers to recognize him as a special kind of religious leader, best understood as a prophet.[5]

In a broad social and ideological sense, the concept of prophet applies to strong religious personalities who may arise in a variety of historical and cultural situations, bringing to them definite religious messages. Another fundamental characteristic of prophets has to do with a special source of inspiration which transcends ordinary human ingenuity, with the correlative capacity to articulate and express profound religious knowledge, aspirations, and emotions immanent to the society which recognizes them as prophets. Both of these characteristics convey to prophets a special authority that elevates their personality above the general level of the community and lifts up their message to the status of divine revelation. A third characteristic has to do with the intimate relationship between prophets and their message. Prophets incorporate and bear witness to truth that the community recognizes as divine.

In all these respects Manuel Quintín Lame can be said to be prophet, as has already been made clear in the exposition of his religious thought. However, were these spiritual characteristics the only factors which turned his rebellious personality into a prophetic figure able to elicit recognition and to command moral authority over a group of followers? The biographical information available suggests that besides his religious characteristics Lame could also impress his followers with one major virtue which he, and very few other Indians, possessed: he could claim a relatively wide experience of the white world. He had acquired this "knowledge" through his enrollment in the army, his participation in various combats, his travels to remote places, his acquaintance with "learned men," and above all, his capacity to read.[6]

Lame, therefore, was able to claim for himself the role of an "interpreter" of the white world to the Indians of the mountains who lived "in the darkness of ignorance."[7] And he could show evidence that he was able to deal critically with that surrounding society which exerted its power and domination over Indian peoples.[8]

Beyond this broad characterization, the Judeo-Christian tradition lays a special emphasis on two major dimensions of the prophet that are also present in Quintín Lame: a strong sense of commitment to radical moral reform, and an eschatological awareness and perspective of his message.[9] The first dimension dominated Lame's entire career as an Indian rebel, a cause for which he found legitimation in his experience with "the numinous", and which became the best summary of his life according to the epitaph on his tomb: "Here lies the Indian Manuel Quintín Lame who . . . [refused] to abandon the defense of his race which has been left dead, expropriated, weak, ignorant, illiterate, pitifully and sadly abandoned by civilization."[10] The second dimension (the eschatological emphasis) is the leitmotif of his manuscript "Los Pensamientos," whose message hinges on the momentous affirmation that "the day shall come when a handful of Indians shall reclaim their rights, as God reclaimed humanity . . . from the tyranny of the devil."[11]

There is, however, a major contrast between the biblical prophets and Quintín Lame: it has to do with the heightened sense of self-reliance and self-worth which according to Lame's testimony issued from his numinous experience. On one occasion he made reference to the prophet Isaiah's vision in the temple, thus showing awareness of biblical prophecy and setting his own experience in line with similar encounters with the numinous in the Judeo-Christian tradition.[12] But when one examines the biblical theophanies, such as Isaiah's, and compares them with Lame's, the contrast becomes evident. Biblical theophanies invariably elicit in the human subject a deep sense of unworthiness, as when Abraham ventured to plead with God for the men of Sodom, and says: "Behold, I have taken upon myself to speak to the Lord, I who am but dust and ashes."[13] This spontaneous recognition of unworthiness in the presence of the Holy is accompanied with a concomitant feeling of submergence and prostration, "a diminution of the self into nothingness."[14] Isaiah said: "I am a man of unclean lips and dwell among people of unclean lips" — not only the self, but the tribe or "the people" to whom the self belongs is depreciated or devalued in the presence of the absolute value of the numinous reality. In the New Testament also, the Apostle Peter cried in the presence of Jesus, "Depart from me for I am a sinful man, O Lord."

These spontaneous outbursts in the presence of the numinous have no parallel in Quintín Lame's experience. In his case, the religious experience did not evoke a confession of unworthiness or sinfulness either of himself or of the Indians, but rather a feeling of self-reliance and self-worth, a fascination with the potentialities of his mind, pride in being an Indian, and the highest expectations for the Indian future. In other words, rather than evoking a sense of inner defilement and unworthiness, the numinous experience elicited in Lame a keen awareness of the spark of light shining in his own mind amidst the darkness of ignorance and repression in which the Indians were forced to live under the conditions created by white civilization.[15]

Thus, Lame's prophetic message is marked by the strongest affirmation of Indian self-worth and of the greatness of the Indian "destiny": it expresses the Indian aspiration to survive the Western thrust that was sweeping with renewed force the Indian communities, not as marginal remnants or as dead instruments of white self-enrichment, but with the dignity worthy of a human being. The major contribution which Lame made towards this goal is represented in his "doctrine" and "discipline" (i.e., his prophetic theology) which — as shall presently be shown — is marked by the intellectual attempt to integrate Christianity within the history, categories, and traditional values of the indigenous communities of the Andes.

CULTURAL *MESTIZAJE*

Manuel Quintín Lame defined himself as a Catholic. The religious picture that he portrays of himself in "Los Pensamientos" is that of a devout believer in God, "the Supreme Judge of every human conscience."[16] However, it would be a mistake to assume that these familiar concepts carry with them in Lame's mind the same noetic content as traditional Christian doctrine. "Los Pensamientos" reveals, for example, that the Supreme Reality in which Lame believes is neither the transcendental "Wholly Other" nor the purely personal God of certain Western traditions. His understanding of God does not quite fit these Western formulations because Lame's faith was more in line with the prophetic tradition of Israel, in its relation to history, even though it was also enriched with the naturalistic worldview characteristic of the Indian communities of the Andes.

It has been shown that Lame took pride in the fact that he was "a legitimate Indian," not a mestizo. In his veins ran "pure Indian blood with not even a sprinkle of Spanish blood stained with envy, selfishness, and contempt."[17] But if this was true of his body, it is not true of his mind: the major characteristic of Lame's religious thought is its *mestizaje* (miscegenation, commixture). His mind brings in a mixture of worlds, a mixture of histories, a mixture of cosmologies and theologies, a mixture of philosophies of life, and a mixture of eschatological and historical hopes. This combination of cultures and spiritualities is expressed throughout his manuscript "Los Pensamientos."

It is clear that in the course of centuries the forced cultural contact introduced by the Spanish conquest produced in the indigenous population a variety of mixtures, adaptations, and syncretisms.[18] However, cultural contact never took place, as it were, in "neutral conditions" but in very specific ones characterized by conquest and colonial domination. The uniqueness of Lame's religious *mestizaje* resides in the fact that it came into being in the context of his rebellion. Struggle becomes the crucible for the peculiar blend that takes place in Lame's thought, as shall be shown presently with regard to the major themes of his theology. For the sake of convenience, these major themes shall be analyzed around the three larger areas of concentration of his religious thought: first, Lame's conception of God as related to nature; secondly, his perspective on history and eschatology; and thirdly, his understanding of the nature and role of Jesus Christ, "the liberator of humanity."

The Nature of God or "Divine Nature"

The vitality of both cultural traditions is forcefully expressed in Lame's concept of God. He believed in a God revealed in nature to the extent of becoming indistinguishable from it. Although in some passages Lame seems to be repeating the Catholic formula "God, the Creator," most of the time he refers rather to "God, Divine Nature," or to "Divine Nature," or simply to "Nature" as the only source of knowledge and wisdom in a way that closely identifies the divine reality with its medium of revelation. One passage of "Los Pensamientos" refers to "the immense fields which Divine Nature has."[19] In another passage Lame uses the formula "God Divine Nature, formed by three powerful kingdoms: vegetable, mineral, and animal."[20] And elsewhere, when he refers to the processes of nature as the source of wisdom, he adds: "Nature is God's Book and God's Science: it is infinite while man's science is finite."[21] In none of these instances can it be assumed that in Lame's mind there is a sharp distinction between a created nature and an uncreated God. This understanding is reinforced by the fact that Lame squarely rejected the biblical doctrine of creation "in six days," which he called "a fallacious interpretation."[22] He asked: "Why is it that nothing has been said of the birth of that Omnipotent Artisan or Architect who supposedly worked six days and then rested the seventh?"[23] — implying that to fix the duration of creation is tantamount to fixing the origin of God.[24]

In one passage Lame mentions casually "the Nature of the Muschca, that is, the Sun God,"[25] and a few pages later he explains that "Muschca [is] the God of Divinity, who created everything that is seen and is not seen," but adds that "through faith all we Catholics believe this is true."[26] Thus it is clear that for Lame his Indian ancestors also believed in the true God — "Muschca," the Sun God. In Lame's mind the synthesis of the two religious traditions has been achieved to the point where to believe in "Muschca" as Creator is the same as to believe in God the Creator, according to the Catholic faith.

Still another expression of Lame's naturalistic worldview is provided by his belief that "the man of faith and good works" is able to hear God's voice in the phenomena of nature:

In the whisper from afar, through living faith coupled with good works...it [God's voice] crosses suddenly in the interior of the poor little Indian and makes him hear the words of the Majesty which made man out of nothing, after its own image and semblance, and tells him: "Hear the words of God in the mountains, all over the desert, as they cross in the soft winds, with a mild perfume of wild flowers; watch his shadow in the waters that move so magnificently; watch his shadow in the midst of the immensity above us."[27]

And again:

> The Palace of Wisdom lies before man's eyes.... Behold its divine
> shadow that dwells in the waters that flow and their movement
> never ceases; behold its shadow in the midst of the immensity above
> us; behold the star that rises in the East called "the Sun"...behold
> therein the shadows of the Palace of Wisdom.[28]

For Lame, nature is God's theophany to such an extent and in such a
fullness that it becomes the supreme and ultimate source of knowledge
and wisdom, and thus indistinguishable from God.
    In many passages the concept of God stands in the place of "Natural
Law," or "the Divine Order of Things," categories that come easily to
Lame's mind. In most instances, this conception of the divinity lies implicit, but towards the end of his work Lame thanks God for having
spared his life despite the hate of his deadly enemies, and then goes on to
explain: "that Supreme God to whom I am grateful is Divine Nature,
upon which human nature depends."[29]
    A similar religious blend is present in Lame's belief in what he calls
"the mystery of the Trinity"[30] or "the mystery of the most holy trinity."[31]
Lame takes for granted that this concept of the deity is in accord with
orthodox Catholic doctrine, but in fact it expresses a more indigenous
interpretation as suggested by the following key paragraph:

> Because the gift of inspiration makes him ["the man of high faith"]
> know the grove of the three virtues, the first of which goes down
> into the depths, the second stretches out, and the third rises and
> places itself in the small cells of the infinite. *It is as though they
> were three gods, like the gods of Nature, the first of which shakes its
> long white mane, and the second and third shoot out (*crispan*) their
> mane of lightning bolts and write their legends on the immense
> shores of the Harem, displaying their impetus.*[32]

Here Lame seems to draw the outline of a theology that is reminiscent of
certain pre-Columbian traditions of the Andes and Mesoamerica.[33]
    The trinitarian form of the divinity seems to explode in Lame's thought
with the status accorded by him to the Virgin Mary, "the Empress of the
Heavenly Court."[34] In many passages of "Los Pensamientos" the Virgin,
after whose name Lame always adds, "conceived without sin," tends to
displace Jesus Christ, assuming the place of God. This happens, for
example, when Lame refers interchangeably to Nature and the Virgin as
"the Queen of my thought,"[35] or else as "the Maker and designer of my
mind,"[36] or when Lame calls the Virgin Mary "Noah's Ark of Salvation."[37]
    Here again it is not difficult to see the synthesis that has taken place
between Catholic thought and indigenous mythology. In effect, several

times in "Los Pensamientos" Lame substitutes "the old woman Ocllo"[38] for the Virgin Mary and for nature, and calls her also "the Queen of my mind" or "the image of my thought,"[39] thus integrating the Virgin Mary within the Andean mythology in which there had always existed a feminine deity, associated in some regions with the moon and in others with a messenger from God who would have acted as intermediary to bring wisdom and practical knowledge to the Indians.[40] In certain traditions of pre-Columbian mythology as well as in popular religious practice, the pluriformity of the divinity admits of a fourth member, Pachamama or Mother Earth.[41] It is not surprising, therefore, that to christianized Indians like Quintin Lame the Virgin Mary is naturally incorporated into the divinity, and often associated with the earth and the fertility forces of nature.[42]

Nowhere is there a clearer indication of the nature and significance of Lame's religious *mestizaje* than in his own description of his numinous experience. This momentous experience of God ("the mysterious image"[43] or "the Image of my thought"[44] or "the mysterious shadow of Jehovah"[45]) is described sometimes as an experience with nature: "as when lightning tears the majestic mantle that the gods wear in the late hours of the night. Suddenly the wayfarer sees through lightning the blue garment that nature wears. In the same way I also met the image mentioned before."[46] As has been shown before,[47] for Lame the significance of the experience resided in the fact that it confirmed and legitimized his rebellion and his struggle, turning it into a "vocation." In his own words: "It was then that my thought was awakened socially and morally to combat injustice."[48] Thus, Lame's religious thought involves not the denial, but the affirmation of Indian tradition and Indian thought, one of whose basic tenets is the awareness of God's presense in nature, with corresponding demands on human behavior vis-à-vis ecological stewardship.

Eschatological and Historical Hope

The reality and depth of Lame's religious and cultural *mestizaje* is clearly revealed in his interpretation of history. It represents a remarkable effort to integrate within the vision and experience of the Andean world the eschatological thrust of the Judeo-Christian tradition.[49] It also attempts to achieve the transformation of both cultural traditions into an indigenous Christian vision: a prophetic theology of struggle and hope for the Indian people.

Lame is concerned with "the passing of time and of humankind along with it" (*el correr de los tiempos, y con ellos el hombre*),[50] and conceives "time" philosophically as a moral agent that judges human beings. But he also thinks of time historically, in terms of ages and periods, and above all in terms of the Indian "destiny." This historical vision consists of four aspects.

(1)   In the first place, Lame refers to "the prehistory of the Indian race,"[51] to which he relates all the traditions known to him about origins: the beginnings of Indian arts and skills, together with the legendary figures and heroes both masculine and feminine associated with those early stages of Indian life. In connection with this prehistoric time Lame mentions legends about an early age of conflict and internecine wars between Indian kings and chiefs.[52]

(2)   Secondly, Lame refers with pride to his ancestors and their great accomplishments, such as monuments and works of art "of extraordinary beauty" which have withstood the test of time ("which the wrath of centuries has not been able to destroy").[53] However, despite Lame's emphasis on his ancestors he never mentions specific names or dates except in the case of Juan Tama, the cultural hero of the Páez Indians, whom Lame claims as his forebear. But besides this, it is very little in fact that Lame knows about Indian civilization as it actually developed before the conquest.

(3)   In the third place, Lame concentrates on the history of sufferings which started "on October 12 of 1492," a date that he often repeats as the point in time when the Indians became "proscribed, persecuted, hated, and abandoned"[54] — a condition that is illustrated paradigmatically in the life of Lame himself.

(4)   Lastly, Lame refers to "the future of Indian race" which he conceives in millennial terms as "the prairie of our great destiny" — that is, the time when "the white man shall become the tenant of the Indians."[55]

How does Lame see the Western world and Christianity in relation to his vision of history? This is for Lame an important question which he solves by incorporating one within the other. In Lame's mind Indian history is intertwined with biblical history: heroes of the Bible — Moses, Noah, David, Daniel, Jesus — appear in Lame's book as part of Indian history, and very often Lame himself interprets his own experience in terms of the experiences of those biblical figures. Jesus Christ himself, "the Liberator of humanity," is described and referred to in terms so close to the Indian experience that he appears to be completely absorbed within Indian history: an Indian attends his birth, bringing him presents; he is raised and develops as a child in the same way that Indian children are raised; and Lame himself in his messianic role compares his experiences with those of the Christian messiah.[56]

Whites and Western civilization appear in Lame's manuscript only as a negative force: the sinister side of history. European civilization is not even credited with bringing the gospel to the Indians; according to Lame evangelists had already come to the New World before the conquest.[57] Western civilization, "consumed by hate, envy, and pride," does not realize that it shall come to an end under the ineluctable punishment of "the law of compensation." This final retribution will be inflicted individually at the moment of the white man's death, when time, the fiercest and staunchest enemy of humankind, catches up with the evildoer. It shall also have a collective application at the end of history when the white man shall become "the tenant of the Indian."

It is clear that a synthesis has taken place in Lame's mind, in which the Western understanding of history has been enriched with indigenous traditions of the Andes. The resulting interpretation shares with the Western philosophy of history its linear and eschatological orientation: it is future-bound heading towards a moral transformation. But it differs radically in its view that Indians (proscribed, dispossessed, and weak) are in fact at the center of the historical process, whose culmination shall consist in the full vindication of the Indians by means of a symmetrical reversal of historical conditions. Thus, what one sees taking place in Lame is in fact the appropriation and transformation by the Indian mind of the eschatological ideology of the Judeo-Christian tradition, an intellectual and cultural attempt that is not new among the indigenous populations of the Andes, but one which has seldom been articulated in writing by Indians themselves. Hence the importance of Lame's version.

Lame's intellectual attempt is reminiscent of the monumental *Chronicle* of Guaman Poma, the Indian intellectual of the seventeenth century.[58] Poma, like Lame, perceived the biblical world and the Western world from the perspective of Indian history and experience.[59] In his famous *Corónica* he sets a parallelism between the epochs of Indian history and the ages of biblical history, but the parallelism is not absolute: there is an effort of integration and synthesis.

Separated in time by three hundred years, these two Indian intellectuals of the Andean world share a vision of history strikingly similar. Both are concerned fundamentally with Indian history; both see the European conquest as the source of the present Indian condition; both perceive the biblical world and the Western world through the Indian vision of history; and both expect a decisive intervention that would restore the original condition of the Indians. This last feature is the most striking element common to both. It is a vision that focuses on the Indian *destiny*, and sees present conditions under the conquest and colonial domination as a historical (in Poma also "cosmic") cataclysm whose disastrous effects shall come to an end by a "restoration" — that is, the return to the original and right order of things.

Eschatological hope does not exclude historical hope in Lame's theology:

> *There is an Indian race that sleeps down there in those cemeteries in the bowels of the earth, where great men of my race suffocated, passed to eternity;* because they built their camps in the center of the earth to defend themselves from the knife of the Spanish, *and they remain there up to this day,* etc., etc.[60]

A few pages later Lame reiterates the same myth, adding a more explicit eschatological note:

> Many Indian families dug their gloomy settlements in the bowels of the earth to escape the knife of the wicked who charged like wolves against the Indian people of Colombia in 1502, 1503, and 1509.... *but justice shall arrive and the Colombian Indian shall regain his throne, etc., etc.*[61]

Later on in "Los Pensamientos" Lame adds that the Indian ancestors took along with them their treasures "into the bowels of the earth," where they have been kept to this day.[62] Still another reference suggests that true wisdom is hidden with the ancestors in the underworld.[63]

Set in the context of Lame's eschatological vision which hinges on the announcement that "the time shall come when the Indian shall regain his throne," and "the white man shall become the tenant of the Indian," it becomes quite clear that Lame has made room within his conception of history for the basic elements of certain popular traditions of the Andes, which carry with them implicit interpretations of history.[64] Those basic elements are: (1) the calamity of the Spanish conquest caused segments of the Indian race to escape into the underworld; (2) they remain there to this day; and (3) the time shall come when restoration will take place by means of a symmetrical reversal of historical conditions.

However, there are also indications of the transforming process which these autocthonous myths experienced in Lame's mind, a process not always explicit but certainly implied in certain references to the generations of Indians "who are still asleep in the mind of God," or who are asleep "in those immense fields of Divine Nature."[65] Thus, Lame seems to have believed in a latent humanity, a people not yet risen as such but destined to become the protagonists of history. Such a people is the Indian tribes.

Sometimes Lame seems to hope in the decisive intervention of the ancestors who had built their settlements "in the bowels of the earth" at the time of the conquest. In one crucial passage, however, he provides an allegorical interpretation of this myth which has the effect of bringing its eschatological message from the indeterminate future into the historical present:

> Humanity, wrapped up in pride, ... thirsty for the riches of my ancestors who are today in large settlements *in the bowels of the Guananí earth* ... Today, after 447 years ... in the forests of southern Colombia called Tierradentro ... it is born, as it had to be born *in the bowels of ignorance, of ineptitude, and illiteracy of the Guananí race,* the idea of the Indian man who studied in the mother forest.[66]

It is not difficult to perceive the transformation that the chthonic myth of the Andes has undergone in Lame's mind: in the first place, he suggests that the underground world is not physical but *sociological* in nature: "the bowels of ignorance, of ineptitude and illiteracy"; and in the second place, that the eschatological time has already begun: "the idea of the Indian man" has been born, and the time of restoration has started. The original order of the world, which was radically upset by the cataclysm of the conquest in 1492, begins to be restored 447 years later, in 1939, the year when Lame finished his manuscript. A new epoch has been opened in the history of the Indian people.

This being the case, What is it that has happened to the millenarian thrust of Lame's ideology? This question points to the decisive transformation of Lame's religious thought as a believer in Christ.

The Indian Appropriation of Christ, "The Liberator of Humanity"

With this title Lame refers consistently to Jesus Christ,[67] sometimes addressing him as "the Liberator of the wretched poor,"[68] and in one passage as "the Divine Liberator."[69] In spite of its probable origin in political and military rhetoric,[70] Lame's use of the concept "liberator of humanity" is not primarily political, but theological. It refers to "humanity" not as a quantity, but as a value that stands in need of being rescued: a human worth that has been repressed and needs to be liberated. Thus, in Lame's religious thought the title "Liberator of humanity" refers specifically to three human realities that in Lame's mind stand in need of liberation: first, the individual human soul; secondly, the Indian people or "the wretched poor"; and thirdly, the human potential of the Indian intellect which is "asleep" in ignorance and unconsciousness.

The first interpretation conceives Jesus as the liberator of individual human souls from the tyranny of the devil.[71] This individualized interpretation, however, is restricted almost entirely to the last chapter of Lame's manuscript where he indulges in speculation about "the road to heaven."[72] In that chapter he repeats the popular belief of Christ's redemption originally preached by the Spanish missionaries and widely held today by the Latin American masses. Their belief is that Christ's liberation consists in: (1) "chasing away the devil from our hearts";[73] and (2) releasing the soul from "jail" where it is kept prisoner by the devil, a freedom obtained through the payment of a "debt" which has been incurred "by the error of the old Adam."[74] According to these popular beliefs, the final liberation would be consummated by the flight of the individual soul from its terrestrial "jail" into immortality, thus receiving its reward for a life of suffering and struggle.[75]

It has not been possible to determine whether this spiritualized interpretation of the concept of liberation corresponds to a certain stage or period of Lame's religious development, or whether it was always a part of his spiritual world as the basic line of popular religiosity common to the Indian peasantry of the Colombian countryside. What is certain is that these beliefs tend to recede to the background of Lame's prophetic theology which runs across his entire work. In the context of this theology the idea of Jesus' redemption is closely associated, not so much with the soul's flight into immortality, as with the historical hope of Indian liberation, as a people, from the white man and his civilization.

This second concept of Jesus, as the liberator "of the wretched poor,"[76] does have strong political and social overtones, particularly because of Lame's interpretation of the historical condition of the Indian people as one of captivity under Guagaz (the white man) ever since October 12, 1492. In Lame's thought this condition of captivity involves social and political oppression and repression because the white man has kept the Indian "under his boot and under his contempt";[77] and "he who defends his right is persecuted as a fugitive robber."[78] This keen socio-political awareness makes the belief in Jesus as the "liberator" of the Indians ("the wretched poor") a potentially subversive doctrine because it is associated with Lame's emphatic announcements that "justice shall arrive and the Colombian Indian shall regain his throne"[79] and that "the day shall come when the Indians shall rescue their rights in Colombia, and the white man shall become the tenant of the Indian."[80]

However, there is still a third interpretation of the role of Christ in Indian liberation implicit in Lame's religious thought, one that reveals an entirely new dimension to Lame's theology. It is the tendency to historicize eschatological hope by bringing it into the present span of Indian existence. This perspective focuses attention on *the human potential* latent in the Indian people, a potential that needs to be liberated and brought into fruition through Indian awareness, self-reliance, and education. The humanity of the Indians is "asleep" and needs to be awakened.[81] At present, the Indian is a crippled giant bitten by "the snake of ignorance and illiteracy,"[82] and "left to die of hunger, like a rat trapped in a hole."[83]

Thus, in this version the picture of the Indian condition is not less but more dramatic and even desperate in relation to the other interpretations. It still has to do with a condition of "captivity." But attention is not directed now towards the oppressor (neither "the tyranny of the devil" nor "the white man's boot and contempt" are the immediate villains) but towards "the snake of ignorance and illiteracy," an enemy that presumably the Indians would be able to overcome themselves by following Lame's example.

The liberating power of Jesus derives from the fact of his identification with the Indian: he who is "the divine man, the immortal man, who has his empire in that immortality unknown to us,"[84] has in fact become an Indian.[85] This understanding of Jesus Christ is decisively determined by Lame's perception that there is a very special relationship between "the liberator of humanity" and "the wretched poor,"[86] a belief that he based on four complementary observations.

First, Jesus and the Indians have in common a condition of insecurity and poverty.[87]

Secondly, Jesus belongs in the natural world of the Indian, not in the artificial world of "civilization." Jesus' knowledge was not acquired "in famous academic halls" but in reading the books of poetry and philosophy "of Nature."[88]

Thirdly, Jesus, like the Indian, suffered social discrimination and persecution from the powerful of society.[89]

Finally, the beneficiaries of Christ's liberation are "the wretched poor," because the liberator of humanity did not come to favor the rich but to console the poor.[90]

This appropriation of Jesus is in consonance with a similar idea that pervades Lame's theology: that the Indians are in fact the biblical "people of God," and that salvation history as told in the Bible is constantly reenacted in the life and suffering of the "wretched poor." Jesus' promises are addressed to the Indian, not to the non-Indian, because "God taught to his apostles, 'blessed are the poor in spirit because theirs is the Kingdom of heaven'":

He [Jesus] did not say, "blessed are the rich, the white, the lawyers, the intelligent, etc." What he taught was peace and concord among men, *but among those of good will!*[91]

Thus, an important aspect of Lame's theology is the appropriation of the Christian God in behalf of the Indians, thus rescuing "the Liberator of humanity" from his own captivity in the bonds of white-mestizo society.

This "indigenization" of Christ dominates Lame's religious thought and provides the ideological support for two major implications of his prophetic message. In the first place, Christ "the Liberator" is in some sense incarnate in the Indian people so that the Indians themselves shall be the agents of their own liberation. According to Lame the day shall come when "a handful of Indians shall form a column to reclaim their rights,"[92] and in the same way that God has rescued humanity from the tyranny of the devil, "the Indian race shall rescue its rights in Colombia."[93] This idea appears a third time in "Los Pensamientos" where Lame insists that the moment shall arrive "when the Indians shall rise to confront the Colombian colossus and to reconquer their domains."[94]

Accordingly, Lame does not expect liberation to come by God's fiat, by a sudden miraculous intervention from above, or by the rising of the ancestors from their settlements in the underworld, but rather through the historical involvement of Indians in their own liberation.

The second implication of the Indian appropriation of Christ is that Lame himself becomes the messianic prophet of the Indians, whose moral and intellectual leadership is indispensable for Indian liberation because he is the one Indian whose being has been transformed from an animal-like creature into a full human being.[95] Jesus is the one who discovered "the Giant of his mind"[96] and "the eagle of his thought,"[97] and, above all, the one who has been called, like Moses, to lead the Indians out of slavery.[98]

Thus, what Lame has done in the articulation of his prophetic theology is to appropriate Christianity for the Indians without surrendering either their identity or their history. In his version of the messianic hope, both Christian eschatology as well as the elements of Andean traditions come together and become transformed not only in terms of Lame's own vision and prophetic call, but also in terms of the present struggle for Indian survival. In this "historicization" of eschatological hope, the focus of responsibility has shifted from heaven to earth, from the ancestors to current Indian generations, from Christ to Lame. The burden of responsibility for the historical outcome of the Indian struggle is now placed on Lame's own ability as agitator, organizer, and political strategist. This major ideological development is best understood in the context of the crisis of survival through which the Indian communities were passing during the time of Lame's activity, both in Cauca Indígena and in the southern Tolima area, and which was intimately related to the capitalist development of the Colombian countryside.

THE CRISIS OF SURVIVAL:
"FROM THE MOUNTAIN TO THE VALLEY"

Early in "Los Pensamientos" Lame makes the somewhat cryptic statement that he has "come down from the Mountain to the Valley" to write his work and to defend his proscribed people.[99] Throughout the entire manuscript the opposition between the "Mountain" and the "Valley" comes naturally to his mind.[100]

Indian communities of Cauca Indígena have made their habitat in the rugged and inaccessible geography of the Colombian Andes with its high plateaus, its rocky peaks, and its steep slopes. In former times there were Indian communities in the lowlands, where the climate is gentler and the earth more fertile. But the conquest and colonization process forced the Indians to seek refuge in higher places, leaving behind the rich lands of the valleys to the white and mestizo conquistadores and colonizers, who have now established there haciendas, plantations, cities, and towns. Thus, every communication that takes place between the Indians and the whites or mestizos involves a literal "descent" from the mountain to the valley.

It is clear, however, that the expression "from the Mountain to the Valley" has, for Lame, a deeper, metaphorical meaning, one that comes across quite clearly in a number of passages where Lame contrasts the Indian way of life with "civilization."[101] In Lame's mind the "Mountain" stands for natural knowledge and natural wisdom; it represents the natural way of things, which is also the Indian way and Indian culture. The "Valley," on the contrary, stands for non-Indian civilization: the urban way of life, the seat of artificiality, materialism, and the moral corruption of white and mestizo society.[102]

Lame insists very strongly that he is the product of the "Mountain" and strives to take distance from the "Valley." He wants to make it absolutely clear to his readers that even though he has descended to the "Valley," he has done so without the intention of accommodating himself in it: assimilation is not his ultimate goal.[103]

Lame insists that his preparation to fulfill his messianic task did not take place in the "Valley" but on the "Mountain." It did not consist in any kind of schooling or "education" of the type that whites receive in schools and universities. "I don't rely," he says, "on the learning or idea of any civic men — I have not studied their feats, their origins and ends."[104] Rather he claims to have come down from the "Mountain" already equipped with the true knowledge and wisdom that can be acquired only in prolonged contact with nature.

Lame refers to St. Augustine and other white intellectuals who had had "the privilege" of education and contrasts himself with them because it was "nature that educated me under its shade... and taught me to think how to think."[105] For Lame "natural education" is not so much an accumulation of wisdom, or even knowledge of the right interpretation of events, but an orientation of the mind: "I rather rely on the compass that is in the sanctuary of my heart."[106] Lame believed that he himself and his manuscript were the product of this "natural education." To the readers of "Los Pensamientos" he explained:

Herein is found the thinking of the child of the forests, where he was born and reared, and educated in the same way that the birds are educated to sing, and their chicks are trained to fly, by clapping their wings until the day when they shall challenge space.[107]

Educated by nature and experience, Lame has come down "from the Mountain to the Valley" with a purpose: to take up the defense of his proscribed and persecuted people, the victim of white civilization.

It is in the context of this struggle that Lame's cultural *mestizaje* is best understood. He learned to read and write Spanish; he acquainted himself with the exchange value of products and labor; he learned the legislation and the judicial procedures of the dominant society; he adopted the Christian religion; he made friends and allies with prominent members of the national society. That is to say, in Lame ("the poor little Indian") the "Mountain" and the "Valley" have come together in the context of the Indian struggle for survival and eventual liberation. Thus, Lame's insistence in contrasting the "Mountain" with the "Valley" reveals his awareness of the tension between two radically opposed perspectives on life and the world, two worldviews, two styles of life that have come into contact creating a crisis that threatened Indian survival.[108]

Furthermore, Lame's insistence on identifying the source of his messianic motivation, as well as of his knowledge and of his loyalty, in the world represented by the "Mountain" points towards one of the most fundamental clues for the understanding of his religious thought: Lame enters into contact with civilization and with Christianity as a member of an Indian society that shares specific values and attitudes that are part of Indian humanity and cannot be discarded or surrendered without at the same time disappearing as human society. It is from the perspective of those values and attitudes, as they have developed historically in the Indian communities of the Andes, marking them with a distinctive kind of spirituality, that Lame reflects on the meaning of Western civilization, and of the Christian faith.

At the heart of this Indian spirituality there is a certain quality of relationship to the natural environment. This quality could best be characterized as an intersubjective relationship with nature,[109] which Lame elevates to the level of a sacred or religious relationship, so much so that alienation from nature is equated in "Los Pensamientos" with alienation from God. The specific kinds of knowledge and wisdom that are inherent in nature are only partially revealed by Lame. However, he claims to have found in nature all the secrets of reality and the consummation of his theodicy.[110] Lame cites towards the end of "Los Pensamientos" his "bibliography" — that is to say, his sources:

The first book: to watch the blowing of the four winds of the earth.

The second: to gaze at the Mansion of the four winds of Heaven.

The third: to observe the rise of the solar star in the East, and to watch when it dies in the twilight, and to realize that man, born of a woman, dies also in the same way.

The fourth book: to contemplate the smile of all gardens, sowed and tended by that Young Lady who dresses in blue and who crowns herself with flowers, and perfumes herself at her interminable dresser, etc., etc.

The fifth book: the unending choir of songs.

The sixth book: the beautiful garden of forest zoology.

The seventh book: to listen carefully to the conversation of the streams in the forest, which seemed to me like a concert of children passing from ecstacy to ecstacy.

The eighth book: the Idyll.

The ninth book: the book of true love, because it is not the lovers' secretary.

The tenth book: to study the harmonious rules of that lady by the name of Nature, in the Palace of her three kingdoms.

The eleventh book: on agriculture and on who are its owners, that is to say, the users.

The twelfth: the book of wild husbandry.

The thirteenth: the book of hygiene.

The fourteenth: the Metaphysics of the supreme reasons of this world which are found in this book.

The fifteenth: ontology, which points out and looks after being in general and its immediate attributes, etc.[111]

Lame's point is that through careful observation and intimacy with nature it was possible for him to acquire true wisdom and to become the kind of intellectual who was able to challenge the dominant society.

One aspect of this special relationship with nature is the Indian's attachment to the land. Lame was concerned with the Indians' alienation from the land imposed upon them by the partition, distribution, and eventual sale of Indian reservations (*resguardos*). This concern was at the very center of his militant activity as an Indian prophet, not only for economic reasons, but mainly because of the cultural and spiritual values that were at stake. He was keenly aware of the fact that for the Indians to survive with dignity depended on the possibility to survive with land, because "land is not only the fruit of our work, the source of our food, but also the core of our social organization."[112] Thus, for Lame as well as for the Indian peoples of the Andes, the very idea of "selling land" in the total and definitive sense, implicit in the white man's formula of "real sale and perpetual alienation," signified not only a practice contrary to the laws of nature, a form of treason to the spiritual power upon which life itself depended, but also the loss of the physical base of social survival.[113]

Related to the same kind of spirituality is the Indian capacity of adaptation to the physical conditions of life determined by the natural resources and other conditions of the natural environment. It is in this context that Lame's denunciation of white greed and of the illusory happiness provided by money acquires all its force as another recurrent theme of his prophetic religious thought. He charged that the white man's acquisitive obsession could lead only to frustration and bitterness ("the poverty of the white man is sad . . . shameful"). He contrasted the white man's plight with that of the Indian who in the midst of his poverty was "satisfied" with his meager possessions and his simple life.[114]

In the context of these imponderable spiritual values one is able to understand Lame's reactions to various aspects of the encroaching civilization, particularly his attitude towards "money." The spiritual crisis that a monetary economy was producing in Indian communities transpires throughout "Los Pensamientos."[115] In book II, chapter 6, Lame makes the point that money is "man's best friend" because even in moments of personal disgrace, such as when one has fallen prisoner, and relatives and friends are unable to help, lawyers are able to offer release "for a handful of money." And he confesses that he has learned about this "liberating" power of money from "civil knowledge" (as opposed to "natural knowledge").[116]

However, the ambiguous and illusory nature of the "friendship" offered by money is present all the time in Lame's thought. Gold, for example, which had a symbolic and artistic value in Indian culture ("gold was a live phenomenon . . . able to speak") has been turned into the source of "ruin, misery and death" because of the white man's envy and greed.[117] For Lame, money conveys a false sense of prosperity and happiness which causes the white man to fall into a trap because "he does not think of his enemy, which is time."[118] Thus, the white man who piles up money does not at the same time cultivate virtue ("wisdom"); in Lame's experience the enemies of the Indians are "the experts of usury and sophisms."[119]

Thus, the human impoverishment that Lame sees taking place because of alienation from nature and from the land, and because of obsession with material possessions, particularly with money, are among Lame's most persistent concerns throughout his manuscript. He was aware of the social developments taking place that were destructive of the quality of life and of the human being, and he expressed his protest against such developments.[120] This is the background of Lame's vehement plea to his fellow Indians, "not to rush like women in love, abandoning their parent's love, etc., etc., in search of the great society of civilization."[121] It is also the basis for his insistence on the superior quality of Indian culture. His "Indian consciousness," so offensive to his antagonists, is in fact a major feature of his ideology and fills implicitly or explicitly the pages of "Los Pensamientos." In Lame's theology of struggle and hope, of promise and activism, of faith and self-reliance, "Indian consciousness" plays a major role as hermeneutical key for interpretation of the Christian faith.

Conclusions

The study of Manuel Quintín Lame's experience and religious thought has made two things patently clear: first, that the author of "Los Pensamientos" was at the same time an Indian rebel and a man of faith, who carried on a lifelong struggle against the oppression suffered by Indians at the hands of the dominant national society in the Colombian Andes; and secondly, that in the course of his struggle Lame was able to achieve in his own mind and to articulate in his manuscript an understanding of the Christian faith that is distinctly prophetic in nature and which provided moral legitimation to and motivation for his cause. These findings make an important contribution to the understanding of the nature and potentialities of popular theology, and raise major issues and questions for the theological activity and pastoral work of the Christian church in Latin America.

Those who have investigated specific forms of popular religiosity in Latin America, including local and regional versions of folk Catholicism, Afro-American religious cults, and Protestant Pentecostalism, to mention only the most widespread, have concluded most often that these forms of religiosity tend to function as a substitute satisfaction, easily turned into an ideology of domination by ruling groups and to engender conformist and passive attitudes, irresponsive to the challenges of qualitative social development.[1] In the specific case of Indian peasant populations of the Colombian Andes, most students of religion have considered that the Christian missions have allowed Christianity to be incorporated within the naturalistic worldview of the Indian culture which identified God with the cosmos and with the forces of nature, resulting in a "naturalistic religiosity" that is blamed for a wide spectrum of regrettable social and religious attitudes. Examples would be the absence of a kind of faith that issues from a personal encounter with God, for God is not conceived as a person but as a "force"; concentration on ritual without understanding the religious content of the faith; and the feeling of indigence and powerlessness whereby the believer feels almost crushed by the forces of nature and society.[2] As a consequence, it has been concluded, the Indian-peasant populations of the Colombian countryside have developed passive and defeatist attitudes, the tendency to conformism that regards the status quo as "the will of God," and a pervasive fatalism that stands in the way of "progress" and development.[3]

Is this, however, the last word about the popular religiosity of the Andes? The study of Manuel Quintín Lame has shown that certain forms of popular Christianity are capable of evolution and even of transformation from a passive and fatalistic religion of social resignation into a militant faith of struggle and hope.[4]

TOWARD A THEOLOGY "FROM BELOW"

Regarding the specific nature of Lame's theological thought, my analysis of "Los Pensamientos" has made it clear that Lame's "theology" is not the product of a Western, evolutionary, and academically reified approach to theological thinking, but a reflection on the meaning of faith from the perspective of the experience of oppression and domination, of conflict and rebellion, that characterized Lame's life and also the entire history of the Indian regions of the country. It is clear also that Lame did not attempt to reformulate Christian doctrines by applying or adapting them to specific conditions, but to reinterpret them *from within* the Indian world. His manuscript provides, therefore, a unique contribution towards the development of a nonacademic "popular" theology, articulated by an indigenous Christian prophet, through the appropriation and reinterpretation of selected Christian symbols and themes, the reclamation of ancestral traditions of the Andes which Lame fills with new meaning and fresh emotion, as well as through the affirmation of the traditional values of Indian communities developed in the course of centuries.[5]

As to doctrinal content, my study of "Los Pensamientos" has revealed a way of thinking about God that is in line with the ancient prophetic tradition of Israel[6] whose two distinctive features are also characteristic of Lame's faith: on the one hand, a paramount concern with justice as the dominant criterion of genuine faith and acceptable worship; and on the other, a definite eschatological orientation that sees historical events in terms of their final destiny and consummation. Thus, Lame's theology, in its core, does not introduce new doctrinal material. However, the characteristic way in which Lame appropriates the biblical faith for himself and for the Indian world, in terms of the specific history and human condition of the Colombian Andes, and the fact that the activation of his religious faith takes place as part of his experience as a rebel and fighter for Indian liberation, raise serious issues and challenges to the theology and pastoral practice of the church in Latin America.

For purposes of identification and analysis, these issues and challenges can be summarized in three major points. The first one is a critique of the church's conception of God as expressed not only in the church's teaching, but mainly in its practice and way of relating to various social groups. The second has to do with Lame's interpretation of eschatology, as a central dimension of the Christian faith. The third is a challenge to develop a socio-political ethic in terms of the historical experience of Indian peoples. All these points are intimately related to each other, and together they constitute a prophetic critique that anticipates the major lines of contemporary "liberation theology," for which it opens new perspectives and poses new questions.

Regarding the first point, it is important to remember that Lame's interpretation of the Christian faith establishes the strongest possible connection between the mystical and the political dimensions of faith. For the Indian rebel this connection consisted quite explicitly in the fact that the divinity has taken the side of "the wretched poor" (the Indians) in the historic conflict characteristic of the Indian peasant areas of the Andes. In this regard Lame's theological contribution resides in the "indigenization" of the Christian God, which he did by affirming on the one hand the continuity between the Christian God and the God of his Indian ancestors, and on the other hand, by associating the Virgin Mary with the indigenous beliefs in mother nature, and by elevating her to the same level of the Christian God.

It was not Lame's intention to challenge any doctrinal formulations about the trinity, or to question the radical monotheism of the Judeo-Christian tradition. Rather, his concern was social and political: to affirm the common humanity and equal dignity of the Indian people by establishing the universality of God, which included the history and cultural traditions of the Indian world. Thus, in Lame's theology, religious faith and cultic activity stop being the alienating practice characteristic of rural Catholicism, and become for oppressed peoples and despised cultures a way of affirming their own worth and their own humanity.

In worship believers do not empty themselves for the sake of an alienated God, but rather enrich and elevate their material and ordinary existence by filling it with the divinity. This is the "infrastructural" meaning of the cult of the Virgin which in Lame occupies such an important place, and which with different names (*Virgen de Guadalupe, Virgen Morena, Virgen de las Lajas,* etc.) is practiced throughout Latin America.[7] This "indigenized" conception of God expresses the need to bring God closer to the poor, so that the faith may be able to activate their daily struggle and to give divine meaning to their justified protest. If this indigenization fails to take place, the God of the church will prove to be not the biblical God, whose nature is justice and liberation, but just the idol or fetish of the dominant society — that is, a god of oppression.

This prophetic faith raises a major challenge to the traditional practice of the church, for Catholic preaching and education has been deeply embedded in the mentality of the conquest and in the Constantinian experience of colonial times. Its Thomistic theology, which posits a certain order of creation as the will of God, has in practice served to justify the conquest and the colonial domination of the Indian, and to justify as well the class structure of the society created or decisively determined by those historical facts. In the realm of ethics, "the angry God theology" taught by missionaries implied the submission to a code of behavior whose principal virtues are obedience to established authority, humility, conformity with one's station in life and, above all, renunciation of every form of rebellion, which was assumed to be rooted in arrogance and pride typified by the devil. Inasmuch as the anxiety and fear produced in

believers by the failure to live up to expectations (fear of eternal punishment, fear of untimely death, fear of physical suffering) could be assuaged
only through the sacramental system of the church, one end result of
Christian missionary activity among Indians was in practice further dependence and subordination to the religious institution and, through it,
to the national society and the state.

Lame's challenge to the church to break this alliance with dominators
and to trust only in the inherent truth and power of the gospel — for "the
church is defended by God" — demanded major changes in theology,
ecclesiology, and ethics for which the church was not ready at the time.
But the same challenge will reappear thirty years later, before the Second
Vatican Council. The same demand is currently being made by growing
segments of the church, particularly from the poor and from base level
Christian communities, on theological and pastoral grounds similar to
those suggested by Lame.[8] It is a challenge that becomes more relevant
every day, particularly in view of the emergence of new ideologies of
domination and political oppression, such as the "doctrine of national
security," that attempt to manipulate the institutional church and its
traditional symbols in the service of a certain system of domination that
is unjust and oppressive towards the most vulnerable segments of the
population. It attempts to establish itself as the "totalized reality," the
idol or fetish, outside which no rights are recognized and no human
dignity respected.[9]

The second major issue raised by Lame's interpretation of the faith has
to do with his emphasis on eschatology. It is here that the fundamental
rupture and innovation was introduced by Christian theology with respect
to the pre-Columbian systems of religiosity that prevailed throughout the
Andean region — that is, the belief that all of creation, including human
history, is future-bound, moving towards its definitive completion and
fulfillment in accordance with its original intention and potentiality. This
is a doctrine that can give meaning and theological illumination to the
perennial quest and dream of humanity, as well as release a special teleo-
logical energy that may be channeled in a variety of ways in various
cultures and conditions. Although central to the religion of the Bible,[10]
the eschatological dimension has not occupied its proper place in the
theological reflection and pastoral work of the church in Latin America.
Even though at the time of the original European conquest of the Andes
in the sixteenth century there were important millennial currents and
eschatological expectations within the Catholic Church which interpreted the very discovery of "the New World" in eschatological terms,[11]
with time Christianity became firmly established in the colonial system,
and the church lost its eschatological edge. In its preaching and catechetical task, as has been shown in the case of the Cauca Indígena region, the
missionary enterprise of the church presented a spiritualized and individualized version of eschatology (concerned with individual sins and
with the personal punishment that these were bound to bring upon the

individual believer both at the moment of physical death and at the "final judgment" of each individual), but without a collective vision of a radical transformation of human society. This vision is the central doctrinal element of Lame's theology.

For the church to be able to understand itself and its message in terms of the eschatological vision intrinsic to the Christian faith in a way that makes sense to the masses of the poor of Latin America, it must be ready to make a major realignment of its own historical commitment, this time to the cause of the poor and oppressed, the despised racial groups, the rejected cultures, the marginalized and excluded peoples of Latin America. Because it is not possible to do theology true to the eschatological vision of Christianity from a position of power, in association with oppressors and rendering homage to the idols and fetishes of various systems of domination, a truly prophetic theology can be done only from the perspective of those who struggle and hope for liberation.

This is why Lame's theology has a distinctly prophetic quality: it is a reflection on the meaning of faith that arises from conditions in which faith is genuine and possible. And when this happens, one of the characteristics of such theology is that it does not follow the same lines of interpretation, and does not lay the same emphases, as the theologies done from the perspective of any system of domination. As has been shown, for example, Lame's eschatological vision has two major features: the first lays the emphasis on retribution ("the law of compensation"), according to which "God's wrath" is addressed against oppressors on this side of the grave as well as after death; the second stresses the promise of conditions of justice in a radically new human society in which "the wretched poor" (*los pobres infelices*) will be vindicated and rewarded.

These are the major classic themes of the religions of the oppressed everywhere, and also characteristic emphases of biblical eschatology.[12] These are also the themes that every system of domination finds the most heretical and dangerous because of their clearly "subversive" nature. It is no surprise, therefore, that these eschatological themes have been absent or conveniently spiritualized in all versions of Constantinian Christianity. Lame's theology is a reminder to the church that it is precisely this radical edge of Christian theology that the masses of the poor understand the most and cherish the most, the dimension of the faith that foments their hope and gives meaning to their struggle.

The third, and certainly the most serious, question raised by Lame's prophetic faith has to do with socio-political ethics. Will the church in Latin America be able to develop a socio-political ethic of struggle and hope that is true to the eschatological vision of the Christian faith? What Lame himself attempted to do in this regard is an important dimension of his contribution to the development of a truly popular theology. It concentrates on the historical struggles of Indian peoples to their final victory and liberation. His main points may be summarized as follows. Indian history, which became a "history of suffering" ever since October 12, 1492, and the sacred history in which God accomplishes mighty deeds of liberation, are one and the same history. Consequently, there is no other arena for Christian believers to express their faith in than the one characterized by the Indian struggle to assert their human rights in the face of white-mestizo dominators "who hate the Indian to death." In this conflict God is definitely on the side of the oppressed, as manifested in the biblical record, in Jesus Christ "the liberator of humanity," and in the way in which historical events finally unfold, even those in which evil seems to prevail temporarily.

It is clear, therefore, that Lame's religious thought involves a historical (not simply personal) concept of sin, as well as a historical concept of salvation or liberation. To be sure, for Lame sin is also psychological and personal, a "stain" on the soul, "a Satanic hate" that is irrational and absurd. The liberation of the soul is certainly his preoccupation. However, Lame's major ethical concern has to do with the historical (social and political) forms of domination, and with the cultural ethos that accompanies them, as expressed, for example, in white-mestizo discrimination and "hate" of everything Indian. The final victory over these historical manifestations of sin will be achieved "one day." This is eschatological hope. Meantime, however, what is the Christian believer supposed to do? Lame's answer is that the Christian believer (the person of "faith and works") shows the integrity and authenticity of the faith by resisting oppression and by struggling for liberation. Prophetic faith is, therefore, inherently subversive, demanding activism towards the transformation of existing conditions.

The "historization" of eschatology that one observes in Lame's religious development does not mean the reduction of the eschatological vision to the limited dimensions of Lame's own programs and activities. The liberation of Christ is not equated with either political or social liberation. But historization does take place, and in a double sense. On the one hand, looking at human history in the way that Lame viewed it — as the arena where divine liberation is at work — widened his perspective and gave what was at stake in the political and social battleground all its depth and true meaning. In this way eschatological hope becomes historical to the extent that persons of faith and good will get involved in struggles for justice, bringing about victories that will have an exemplary and motivating effect on present and future generations, which are "still asleep in the mind of God." Lame viewed in this light, for example, his own "victory" that made possible the reconstitution of the _resguardo_ of southern Tolima. He was aware of the ultimate significance of his own temporal strivings and struggles. On the other hand, Lame's eschatological vision invested the historical activity of the Indians with a new dignity, transforming their self-image from that of a despised and depressed group (the stereotype projected by the dominant society) into that of the protagonists of liberation history, the human agents through whom Christian hope will become a reality.

It is quite clear that the traditional social doctrine of the Catholic church, to the extent that it was known to Lame, as expressed in the church's own practice, was not prepared to deal with the issues raised by Lame's experience and vision.[13] Only the momentous changes that have taken place within the church since the Second Vatican Council, the Cuban revolution, and the emergence and development of radically new perspectives in Latin American theology are bringing into focus the background issues that were present in Lame's own struggle with the church and with society, as well as the repercussions and implications of the major themes of his manuscript "Los Pensamientos." Thus, Lame's theology enters on its own right into the current debate between the traditional church patronized by the ruling establishments, and the protesting and struggling theology that is emerging among the poor as interpreted by those who have decided to adopt their position and perspective as their own, by making an "option for the poor." This vein of Christian theology is better known as liberation theology.[14]

LAME AND LIBERATION THEOLOGY

With regard to the fundamental theological task of developing a sociopolitical ethic, the contribution of liberation theology centers on the question of reclaiming history from the perspective of theology. Samuel Silva Gotay has aptly summarized this contribution:

> Salvation is a process that takes place in history, the one and only history that exists. History is the struggle for salvation, for the establishment of the kingdom of God. Human beings make history by their participation in social forces. History is not predetermined; its future is open and humankind is free to build in it the utopia that has been accumulating in its historical memory. In other words, human struggles are not in vain. History follows a dialectical process of the development of social forces in an autonomous way, one in which humankind participates to shape its own destiny, a process in which God is present as a force that pulls the process towards the future, which is already present in the historical memory of Christians committed to the promise of a reign of justice.[15]

It is quite clear that Lame's major insights regarding God's liberating activity in history, and the interrelations among history, eschatology, and human responsibility, find in the thought of liberation theologians repercussions they could not find in the traditional "social doctrine" of the church. The implications of this kind of thinking vis-à-vis the nature and significance of Christian activity in the world, and of theological reflection itself, as they are being articulated today by liberation theologians in Latin America are no less important. Some of these implications are the following:

(1) The practice of the Christian faith is inherently political by its very nature. By accepting the responsibility of building in history the real world, whose nature is essentially political, the Christian faith rediscovers itself as political practice.

(2) The "idealist" philosophy that dominated Christian eschatology in the past gives way now to the historical character of the reign of God. In this way, ethics becomes relativized in order to respond concretely to the realities of a history that is being forged in struggle after struggle;

(3) Theology, therefore, becomes the reflection on the participation of Christians in the historical process of liberation. It applies to their political practice criteria derived from a prophetic faith in terms of hope and commitment to justice.[16]

These are implications that apply also to Lame's thought and practice. They are either explicit or implicit throughout "Los Pensamientos," as well as in his public activity as an Indian rebel and prophetic figure. However, regarding the challenge to develop a socio-political ethic of struggle and hope in the light of the eschatological vision of the Christian faith, contemporary liberation theology has carried the task much further than Lame did, and along new and unexpected paths. This development can be summarized in two points that also provide the ground for a serious critique of Lame's thought and practice.

In the first place, theological reflection has changed its point of departure: it does not start any longer with metaphysical doctrines and then deduce conclusions to be applied to concrete historical realities. Rather, the process begins with social reality itself. This change of approach applies also to Lame. However, as liberation theologians point out, this is an approach that requires the incorporation of the social sciences with adequate analytical tools in order to know reality with the intention of transforming it. Liberation theologians believe that accurate social analysis is required to discern "the signs of the times" on the basis of which appropriate and effective practice can take place.

In this respect Lame's theological reflection is found seriously wanting. It is not only that the Indian prophet was unaware of the Marxist categories of analysis and such Marxist notions as economic dependency, praxis, class struggle, and revolution, which most liberation theologians have consciously adopted as the most appropriate and "scientific" for the social analysis of societies like that of Colombia. Rather, it is the fact that Lame lacked adequate analytical tools to understand the situation of Indian peasant areas of Colombia in their relation to the economy and politics of the national and the international orders. His rudimentary sociology was simplistic in assuming that the dichotomy Indian/non-Indian was the only explanatory key to understand the condition and problematic of Colombian society. Besides, his "psychologistic" analysis (based on attitudes — virtues and vices) of the groups in conflict did not provide adequate knowledge of the root causes and complexity of the social problems. As a consequence Lame was not able to avoid ambivalence and contradiction in his own practice, as reflected, for instance, in his misplaced trust in some intellectual members of the ruling white-mestizo elites on the one hand and, on the other, in his frustration with an important segment of the Indian population, both in Tolima and in Cauca — enemies of his campaigns.

In the second place, liberation theology realizes the need of the Christian faith to adopt a concrete and explicit ideology (i.e., a conception of history and society) that gives expression and articulation to the self-projection forward in history and the political strategy of the poor and oppressed. It is clear in this perspective that without an accurate analysis of the historical situation, it is also impossible to identify and define the "historical project"[17] capable of realization and likely to elicit commitment and meaningful activism on the part of the segments of society that share the vision of a new social order.

Here again, Lame's political ethics reveals its inadequacy. Without a scientific analysis of the concrete historical configuration of Colombian society, Lame's model or "project" to be achieved through Indian activism was far from clear. Sometimes it expressed the nostalgia of the Indian past, and the ideal of reconstituting Indian communities in conditions of semi-isolation, with their own organizations and cultural values. At other times, the project involved a definite integration within the national society that would require of the Indian peasants literacy, command of the legal and political systems of the dominant society, as well as economic education and capacity of adaptation to the changes taking place in the countryside. The contradiction of these two "projects," as well as their practical impossibility, made Lame's activism to a large extent meaningless.

The serious shortcomings of Lame's ethics do not undermine the validity of his prophetic stance, or make his challenges less pressing for the church at large, and also for liberation theology. Even though the liberation perspective has provided fundamental insights to appreciate and evaluate Lame's contribution, it is still true that one major issue that Lame's thought and activity raised in his own time, both for the church and for society at large, is still standing. It has to do with "the Indian question." Can the ideological perspective adopted by liberation theology take full account of the uniqueness and the specific historical potential of the "Indian consciousness" that permeates Lame's thought, as a reality distinct, for example, from "class consciousness"? What would this recognition of the ethnic factor mean for the formulation of a "historical project" in which an Indian people may participate, one that would not simply pronounce the death sentence on Indian communities and culture? In other words, will liberation theologians be able to avoid falling victims themselves of totalizing ideologies that make no room for the "otherness" of indigenous populations, for their distinctiveness, and thus assure that their theological reflection will be free from the engulfing tendencies of the European mentality?

Thus, the insights, reflections, and perspectives contributed by Manuel Quintín Lame still pose a major challenge even to those who are trying today to comprehend and formulate a truly popular theology, one that emerges "from below," because this goal cannot be achieved without the direct participation of the oppressed themselves. In this regard there are positive signs in the quest and awareness of "roots" that is expressed, for example, by one of the major voices in the contemporary theological discussion in Latin America, Gustavo Gutiérrez:

> We shall not have our great leap forward, into a whole new theological perspective, until the marginalized and exploited have begun to become the artisans of their own liberation — *until their voice makes itself heard directly, without mediations, without interpreters* — until they themselves take account, in the light of their own values, of their own experience of the Lord in their efforts to liberate themselves....
>
> Our theology will have no proper, distinct focus of its own until it takes its point of departure in the social practice of the Latin American peoples — the lowly, repressed, and, today as yet, silent peoples of Latin America.[18]

APPENDIX

English Translation of Quintín Lame's Manuscript, "Los Pensamientos del Indio que se Educó dentro de las Selvas Colombianas," The Thoughts of the Indian Educated in the Colombian Forests[1]

PROLOGUE

1. A small idea has taken shape, just a few days ago, to the right side of a concert of thoughts which were being engendered and born (for quite some time) but which could not blossom due to the insects that day and night plagued the garden of the Indian. Hearts soaked in bile and bitterness whose lips sprayed poison: the lips of non-Indians, because their intelligence is stained with the poison of envy and selfishness, not understanding that I was a man, born of a woman, and that the world, the human soul, and God are the three beings whose existence natural reason was able to discover. The first is called Theodicy, or science of God, the second is Psychology, or science of the human soul, and the third is Cosmology, or science of the world.

2. But in the forest I knew the cloud of deceit of non-Indians: in the forests that witnessed my birth the 31st of October of 1883. The cloud of deceit [which wanted] to destroy the garden of Quintín Lame was like pyramids of ice, which were destroying the farmer's garden. But the shade of faith, hope, and charity worked in favor of my race, proscribed

and persecuted since the 12th day of October of 1492 to the very day
when this book be finished. But the captain conquistador who discovered
our possession and our Guananí race, to which I belong, died in the city
of Valladolid in the arms of misery and hunger, etc., etc.

3. And everyone who has committed ruinous actions against the Indian
race has been attacked by misery, together with natural death, which
assails man with the scythe in its hand. Because it was for the sake of the
wretched poor that the Liberator of Humanity came into the world.

4. It is called "The Colombian Thinker before the Ruins,"[2] because I
refused to obey that which was unjust, iniquitous, and absurd. Because I
regarded it a heroic and sacred thing not to submit to injustice and
inequity, even when it carried the signature of the most frightful Colombian
judge. History shall lift up my name in the face of the voluminous charges
that have been made before Courts, Town Halls, and Governorships in
the Departments of Cauca, capital Popayán; Huila, capital Neiva; Caldas,
capital Manizales; Tolima, capital Ibagué; Nariño, capital Pasto.

5. Justice shall call upon the historian to point out where to find the
deposit of my actions, and in which jails I wrestled with men of the
highest Colombian civilization, who called me brother wolf, and who
charged and accused me. But those men had to bow their heads when the
empire of justice thundered, punishing injustice born in the hearts of
non-Indian men against me, ordering that the strong locks of jails and
penitentiaries be opened so that I could enjoy the broadest freedom,
thanks to God. Those men, together with the investigating judges, ordered
a search after me to put me in jail as if I were a robber, because I held
gatherings with my people in the Departments of Nariño, capital Pasto;
Cauca, capital Popayán; Huila, capital Neiva; Tolima, capital Ibagué.
And Dr. Guillermo Valencia, as representative of the Lower Chamber,
requested that I be expatriated from Colombia, but the President of
the house argued that such expatriation required consultation with the
Minister of Government, Dr. Abadía Méndez — actions that are recorded
in the Annals of the House of Representatives. Besides, in one of the
chapters of this work I shall cite the events, the ruins and the severe and
unjust punishments against myself and against my Indian race of Colombia.

6. This book will serve as a horizon in the midst of darkness for the
Indian generations who are asleep in those immense fields of Divine
Nature. Because the white man is the sworn enemy of the Indian who
does not knock at the door of deceit, who does not want promises, who
does not sell cheap; and the public functionary joins the capitalist landholder and the lawyer to cause the Indian to lose his plot of land, his
cattle, etc.

7. It is not true that only those who have studied fifteen or twenty
years, who have learned to think about thinking, are the ones who have a
vocation, etc., having ascended from the Valley to the Mountain. Because

I was born and reared in the mountain and from the mountain I have come down to the valley to write the present work.

8. There was an oak tree, old and robust, cultivated by nature. I say "cultivated by nature" because a garden of flowers had grown on it, of the kind that civilized people call parasite flowers and which we Indians call *chitemas*, in the dialect of my Páez ancestors. Climbing on that tree at the age of six I was able to contemplate another treetop, even taller, proud and haughty, that crowned over the virgin forests which had witnessed my birth and that of my ancestors before and after October 12 of 1492. That tree was known as "the Oak of Lebanon" and it seemed to hail the two almighty natures, one human and the other divine, when the four winds of the earth passed by.

9. A thought came to me that as high as that tree would be placed my ideas in the Colombian nation, when I should come down from the Mountain to the Valley to take up the defense of my Indian race, proscribed, persecuted, despised, plundered, and murdered by non-Indians. Because this is what is shown by the deposit of actions, and confirmed by the witness of the past, witness that came together with today's announcement, that I should prepare myself for the defense of future generations of the Indian race of Colombia.

10. I started on a road full of thorns and thistles, and along that road I had to cross two rivers, one of tears and the other of blood, rivers that ran like the crystal-clear waters of Nature, the same rivers that bathe the five parts of the world, dragging along sand, because the waters never cease to run carrying the sand; and thus has been humanity passing along before the infinite intelligence which created humanity, a humanity that has been passing and has passed, without being able to understand what is written in the beautiful book called "The Book of God." Such humanity, wrapped up in pride, thirsty for riches, for the riches of my ancestors who are today in large settlements, in the bowels of the Guananí earth, in order to protect their riches and their lives from the persecution of those who arrived the 12th of October of 1492 calling themselves Spanish conquistadores.

11. Today, after 447 years ("The Ruins") in the forests of southern Colombia called *Tierradentro,* the Ruins of the Colombian Colossus, it is born, as it had to be born, in the bowels of ignorance, of ineptitude, and illiteracy of the Guananí race, the idea of the Indian who studied in the Mother Forest, using for pencil a piece of wooden coal, for slateboard a flat piece of the same wood, and for a pen a small iron needle which the Indian carried stuck in his straw hat, made with the kind of straw that is found in the same forest.

12. I cannot take pride in sophisms saying that I spent a long time studying in a school or a college. My college was faith coupled with an untiring enthusiasm, because when I asked my father, Sr. Don Mariano Lame, to give me education, that is, to send me to school, he gave me instead a shovel, an ax, a machete, and a sickle, and sent me with my seven brothers to clear the forest. However, with that overpowering enthusiasm which I felt inside me, I thought that I should instead learn to write using a piece of wood, and a piece of coal, and with a needle on the leaf of a tree. The result was that knowingly I took a number of papers that belonged to my aged uncle, Leonardo Chantre.

13. The non-Indian men of Cauca banded together and requested that I be condemned and sent to the penitentiary of Tunja, charging me with eighteen crimes which had not even crossed my mind but which had been created by the intelligence of a poet, the same one who wrote *Anarcos*.[3] He, together with other non-Indian capitalists, called upon the attorney Avelino Córdoba Bravo from the city of El Bordo, to accuse me, and to bury my complaints. But Doctor Bravo was frightened when he went to the Court and requested the lawsuit against the Indian Quintín Lame, because he saw the bulk of the material and said to the secretary Alonso Delgado that he was not asking for all lawsuits and judicial cases that were being held against all the prisoners detained in the jail of Popayán, to which the secretary answered: "Doctor, wait a moment and you will have still more fun." And he brought two extraordinary bundles of documents and placing them on the table said: "This is the lawsuit against the Indian Quintín Lame," to which my accuser Bravo asked whether the Government had spent all that paper and still had not been able to condemn the Indian Quintín Lame. And the secretary answered: "No."

14. In a separate chapter of this work I shall develop every one of these episodes without fear of telling the truth, without fear that the narrow straights or the sad things disturb me, nor letting the happy ones engross me. Because inside the Indian's mind, his thoughts disciplined by Nature, every event is unerasable, and every day leaves in his heart a memory in the same way that the clock marks the hours. Such is my memory, thanks to the omnipotence of the one who created me and gave me life down to this day; because neither the things that happened pass away, nor the future things shall take place. In the same way that after four hundred forty-seven years I am making my work known to the Colombian public. However, it is not with proper or learned language, but with the experience of some years of suffering that I have been putting together little by little the present book. Because human nature has educated me in the same way that it educated the birds of the remote forests, who sing their melodious tunes and build their small houses, without a teacher; who also sang to the little Indian when Nature surrounded and fondled me, and scattered over me flowers, leaves, and morning dew, in the days when I also enjoyed the tender kiss of my mother. May she rest in peace.

MANUEL QUINTÍN LAME CH.

BOOK I

Chapter 1
The Indigene who Learns Lessons from Nature

15. The indigene receives his lessons from nature out there in the forest, not from the collection of studies made by the most recent and renowned thinkers, men who have received magisterial classical education in all the sciences, pagan as well as Christian, about all humanity.

16. Herein is found the thinking of the child of the forests, where he was born and reared, and educated in the same way that the birds are educated to sing, and their chicks are trained to fly, by clapping their wings until the day when they shall challenge space and cross it with extraordinary intelligence; and as they take off for the sky they regard each other with loving care, the male and the female, as they make use of the wisdom which Nature has taught us. Because out there in the lonely forest is found the Book of Love Relations, the Book of Philosophy. Out there one finds the true poetry, the true philosophy, the true literature. Because out there Nature has an interminable concert of songs, a choir of philosophers who exchange thoughts every day, but who never are able to climb the walls where the mystery of the divine laws of human nature is located, which is subordinated to Divine Nature; and this takes place every day and every night. But the choir of non-Indian men who have rushed to the great classrooms in Colleges and Universities, beginning with the primary school, etc., they have not and will not be able to have a conference with that book of poetry, nor with that book of Philosophy, which has three powerful kingdoms. But the children of antiquity, and the children of the Middle Ages, and the children of the present age, those who were cuddled in cradles of gold and cradles of crystal, were not able to know those three kingdoms. But the child who was born in an inn, on a cradle of straw, did go through all the pages of the book of poetry, of the book of philosophy, of the book of literature, books which he had studied from eternity; he knew where to find the garden that God had created at the beginning of the world for the first man and the first woman; a garden that is hidden from the sight and from the mind of those great men who have burned their eyelashes studying, and who are today amazed, lying down in eternity: the warrior with his sword, the ruler with his scepter, and the learned man with his pen, and tomorrow I myself with my interpretation.

17. The eagle of the little Indian's interpretation is escorted by a choir of pigeons: not the doves that hum in the garden, but the wild pigeons that sigh in the deep forest, on the grayish top of the laurel tree, forming a concert that surrounds the Giant in his Palace, the palace of my thought. This idyll is such that it itself sings, it itself blossoms, it perfumes itself, it renews itself, it cultivates itself, it warms itself up with the heat waves and the icy winds of the same season of passing times.

18. The concert of philosophers which the three powerful kingdoms have, form a book, a logic, where all the fundamental theorems are to be found, both of the science of the material world and also the science of the spiritual world. Where is the cradle of wisdom to be found? The cradle of wisdom lies hidden under cruel mountains, according to the dreams of the Indian who went up to visit the newly born baby who was lying in a cradle of straw, in one of the corridors of the "House of Bethlehem," the one who left the Stone of philosophy, etc., the Indian who brought him a present of gold as a man and as a King of kings.

19. Science has a very large garden and few are the men who have seen it, even from afar. But the poor little Indian has seen it from very near, together with those disciples which Nature has created and still creates in the forest during those moments of interminable conversation between the brooks and the fountains; those moments when the tiger snoars, the lion roars, the snake whistles, the cricket sings, and the wild pigeon sighs flying across the forest. It is the moment of recess which Wisdom, the teacher, has ordained harmoniously to her disciples; afterwards the four winds of the earth which are the sowers of nature, cross over. What is Nature?

20. Nature is God's Book and God's Science: it is infinite, but man's science is finite; because even when the white man studies he knows nothing, because his heart is filled with pride and envy against the poor ignorant, etc. The white man hates the Indian unto death: outwardly his lips are full of smiles, but his intention is to humiliate him. I mean "to humiliate him" by making him say certain words and thus be able to strike deals. These actions and intentions I will later develop with frankness.

21. But the Indian Quintín Lame was able to interpret the thinking of the ant and of other insects that human nature breeds. The thought of the tiniest ant is the same as that of the condor when he is getting dressed in his cave, and it is the same thought of the tiger cubs, and it is the same thought of the children of men: because when the ant snaps open the buckle of her wings to get out of her hole, she does not follow the path of the others, but rather climbs a heap of sand and stretching her wings, pretends to challenge the sky and feels powerful. But just as she begins her walk the enemy falls upon her, in the same way that error assails man. As the cub of the tiger gets ready to jump on his prey, so has the white man done to the Indian and this has been happening since October 12 of 1492 up to this day of 1939. But there is an Indian race that sleeps down there in those cemeteries in the bowels of the earth, where great men of my race suffocated, passed to eternity; because they built their camps in the center of the earth to defend themselves of the Spanish knife, and they remain there to this day, etc., etc.

Chapter 2
The Image of my Thought

22. Twice I met the image of thought, and I met it in rapture in spite of having passed swiftly, as when lightning tears the majestic mantle that the gods wear in the late hours of the night. Suddenly the wayfarer sees through lightning the blue garment that nature wears. In the same way I also met the image mentioned before after eleven months of having been held incommunicado in one of the dungeons of Popayán charged with eighteen crimes, fabricated by famous minds headed by one poet and one lawyer who were the classic nymphs of Popayán; those "nymphs" had decided to place the author of this book in shackles with an iron bar of twenty-eight pounds between my feet, to force me to abandon and despise the image of my thought, the image which I had regarded in rapture with a faith higher than that of Moses, the leader of the people of Israel, which gave me the assurance that I was destined to overcome those men who had studied fifteen or twenty years, and make them bow their heads, those aged men seventy or eighty years old, those poets who had written *Anarcos,* who had published a telegram saying that I was a person of horrible character, a rogue, a crook and so forth, but who did not have the civil courage to stand up as my accusers the day of the trial when I myself took up my defense in the Superior Court of Popayán. But my faith of being saved began in God and ended in God, the Supreme Judge of the human conscience. That image carried me from ecstasy to ecstasy, and from image to image, becoming my true friends who visited me and still visit me in the dungeons when hunger, pain, and sadness used to attack me. When the year ended, my detention as incommunicado ended, too, and I entered into communication.

23. I had been held incommunicado since the day I was captured on the Bridge El Cofre because of a treason on May 9 of 1915. And on May 9 of 1916 the blacksmith came in hastily, armed with hammer and chisel and said: "Señor Lame, I have come to take off the bar between your feet. Congratulations!"

24. Reply to the telegram published in the newspaper, *El Domingo:* "I don't accept the insults which Dr. Guillermo Valencia hurls at me in his telegram. But if Dr. Guillermo Valencia's pen is good for writing *Anarcos,* Manuel Quintín Lame's pen will be good for the defense of Colombia. Sincerely yours, Manuel Quintín Lame."

25. It was in the image of my mind where I studied all the phenomena and longings which were dancing around in the enemy camp against the poor little Indian.

26. Dr. Laurentino Quintana said, "Quintín Lame is not the one called to defend himself against countless charges which are recorded in the lawsuit of over 8,000 pages long."

27. My accuser, requested by Dr. Guillermo Valencia, Ignacio Muñoz, and countless other aristocrats, enemies of the image which the Indian Quintín Lame has had and still has until this day, the image which had accompanied me out there in the forest, mentioned before in chapter 1 and which still accompanies me today; thereupon the thought of the Indian is purified to become an idea, ideas which have been like indestructible walls when stormed by man's enemy which is Time and its elements: the rain poured down, the winds blew, the rivers flooded and stormed the edifice; the one that had been laid out by the infinite intelligence which had made the armor of this first man and the beauty of the first woman. Today the poor little Indian finds himself within those walls which I myself built with my tears and blood caused by the envy and contempt of the Spaniards who first arrived in our land on October 12 of 1492 to make themselves rich and who treated us like beasts of burden, and still continue to do so.

28. There was also the son of Don Francisco Casas [born] in 1474, who in the year 1510 arrived with the expedition of Dominican Friars headed by Friar Pedro de Córdoba and in the year 1512 headed towards Cuba with Pánfilo de Narvaez and protested against the abuses which the white man inflicted upon the indigenous people: because Friar Bartolomé de Las Casas had observed the misery and injustice which the Indians suffered and this Protector was thereby hated by the most powerful people in the Court, which sometimes placed his life in danger.

29. The same thing has happened to me. I have always looked for danger as my companion, and with civil courage I have spoken out to the most frightful judge, to the most intelligent lawyer, courage which I bequeath as an example to all the Indian children of good will of the entire Colombian country. Because to be a lawyer one does not need a degree; the diploma is Truth in its sharpness and the unmasking of the false lawyer because he does not rely on the law but in the spirit of a business. The true lawyer is the study of universal law, abstract, concrete, natural and positive, because man has a body in common with the minerals, life in common with the plants, sensibility in common with the beasts, and reason in common with pure spirits, for which reason he was called microcosm.

Chapter 3
The Virtue of the Indian Reared by the Loving Care of Nature in the Mother Forest

30. This chapter is dedicated solely to demonstrate the value of virtue when accompanied by faith, because faith without good works is dead. He who fears God does right, and he who seeks justice will possess it, coming out to meet him as a venerable mother. She feeds him with bread of life and intelligence and she gives the poor little Indian to drink the healthy water of wisdom, and she settled herself in the immense valley which has three prairies where there are three gardens of *Abana* tended by Nature, where |in| the pure air is born that which gave new youth to the spirit of several of my philosophical understandings. In the same way shall be born tomorrow a communion of Indigenous people: legitimate descendants of our Guananí land, children of those hated tribes persecuted by non-Indians; but the Law of Compensation does exist, gentlemen, and in itself it is avenging justice, because the act committed by the old Adam and by old Eve's whim was paid after four thousand years.

31. The Indigenous race here in Colombia has been hated by all capitalism, and very few priests and religious have spoken out for it, because their thoughts have been far removed from the ideas of Father Friar Bartolomé de Las Casas, because there have not been priests from our own race to point out the true right that the Indians of Colombia have: we the legitimate Indians, not those in whose veins already runs Spanish blood stained with envy, selfishness, and pride, and whose conscience from generation to generation comes down stained with sprinkles of Indian bloodshed.

32. The prairie of science is where human law and meditation are found, the Law of Unity. When in man reigns peace and harmony between the inferior and the superior parts, between the image or imagination and the intelligence, between the passions and the reason, then the understanding or the light of reason, which is participation in the divine light, shows in secret to the man of high faith what he was created for. Because such a gift of inspiration makes him know the grove of the three virtues, the first of which goes down into the depths, the second stretches out, and the third rises and places itself in the small cells of the infinite. It is as though they were three gods, like the gods of Nature, the first of which shakes its long white mane, and the second and third shoot out their mane of lightning bolts and write their legends on the immense shores of the Harem, displaying their impetus in the midst of the prayer which the god of inspiration released out there in the prairies, above which crosses the eagle of psychology, as it contemplates the palace where human thought is engendered and takes the name of Giant of the ignorant person's thought. However, I am wise for the good and ignorant for evil, not having looked even from afar to a school or a college, or learned from anybody even the letter "o," to which Francisco José de Caldas referred when he was climbing with a serene forehead the steps leading to the gallows.

33. Likewise, many Indian families dug their gloomy settlements in the bowels of the earth to escape the knife of the wicked who charged like wolves against the Indian people of Colombia in 1502, 1503 and 1509. That crime is hidden, gentlemen, but justice shall arrive and the Colombian Indian shall regain his throne, etc., etc. I am not a prophet, but I have been and I am the apostle of my race, and none of the men of the white race who have waged war against me in the departments of Nariño, Cauca, Valle de

Cauca, Huila, and Tolima have been able to laugh, as was said by Señor José María Barona, "the day when the Indian Quintín Lame will be carried to the dungeons of Tunja, I shall throw three parties. . . ."

34. Doctor José Hilario Cuéllar said on the occasion of a fiscal visit that it would be easier to separate the waters of the Cauca and Magdalena rivers after they have become one river for a long distance than it would be for the Indian Quintín Lame (yours truly) to separate the Indian and the white races, especially in politics. But such magistrate or district attorney was wrong because such a thought fell down, as when the tree shakes off its flowers and the leaves, the leaves become a toy of the wind, because in the same way logic has become a toy until this day, the logic born in fact in the image of my thought which has been given birth this day in the cradle of Colombian civilization.

Chapter 4
The Prehistory of the Indian Race before October 12 [1492]

35. One hundred years before October 12 the Indian Güelpa, in a meeting of wise men in the temple of Cacharpa, the palace where holocausts were burned to the sun, as to a merciful god, having sung three times the hymn to the sun, a quarrel developed, after which Cacharpa called the attention of all and announced to the entire Sanhedrin in slow words, in the Indian dialect, that very soon the wise men and the Indian sovereigns would fall into the hands of Guagaz. Time passed and with time wars developed between the Indian sovereigns who disputed among themselves river banks, prairies, and fields, and tore each other to pieces with wooden spears, arrows, and poisoned darts, with poison extracted from plants. . . .

36. And what shall I say [about the time] when the Nature of Muschca, that is, the Sun God, made appear two sages, woman and man, the woman to teach how to weave gold and to cross it, that is, to knit it; and the man to carve stone and make hieroglyphs on it, to make faces of men, and animals, and of fowl; also to make fetishes, crocodiles, and golden birds with their chicks, crickets, frogs, lizards, snakes, and so on. The wrath of centuries has not been able to destroy such writings, nor have the ages been able to do away with the fetishes made of clay, which my ancestors glued together with resins from trees. What shall I say of the historian of Bochica, who split the cliffs to form the Tequendama water falls, but who has not been able to explain how and why the figure of this sage appears on the face of the rocks, because many historians lack civil courage, and others lack honesty.

37. But 447 years having passed, one of the descendants of the Indian race [came forward], the grandson of the Indian Juan Tama de Estrella (and what is the meaning of "de Estrella"? . . . in another publication it shall be made known!).

38. I wished to speak of those icy altitudes of my race, proscribed and abandoned by the Colombian civilization, which arrived October 12 of 1492. Because today I resemble the wayfarer who found the titanic creations of men, lost in the primitive sands out there in the desert, where they had challenged the centuries with powerful buildings, built with mortar and granite; but time stands against man's fantastic pride. A sage says that time flees and never comes back, but that is not the case. Time wears a glove wherein man's evil actions are kept, and slowly punishes him, bending his body like the bow of an arrow, and takes away his riches in those moments when man sinks in a material or civil calamity: the ruler dethroned, the warrior defeated, and the wise man comes near the shadow of the Tower of Babel. But he who believes that God loves him and who has hope in God, the creator and regulator of time, is never defeated and if he is, the defeats of yesterday help him to achieve the victories of tomorrow. Because the patriot has always achieved victory thanks to his patriotism, for patriotism has been the immortal crown of the great patriots, such as Simón Bolívar, San Martín, and Ricaurte who set his arsenal on fire and blew himself up into the air to write his immortality against the King of Spain.

39. In the same way I set myself today to write the present work which shall become the basis for the children of the indigenous race, who are still asleep in the mind of God, our Lord.

40. Smoke is the natural sign of fire and footprints [are signs] that someone crossed the valley; the man who on the top of high cliffs did his writing accompanied by that mirror that never loses its luster, because he was carried in the arms of that mysterious image, the same that accompanied me in the dungeon, and helped me carry the iron bar between by ankles, and which was an agent that talked to me in the interior of my spirit, pointing to me the present and announcing the future. And it said to me, "Blessed the man who thinks on the things of tomorrow, and who foresees them, interpreting their spirit; and cursed be the man that cares only about the present."

41. On those cliffs where I was writing my defense like a hermit in the mountains of Orep, my persecutors never reached [me], those whose hearts were full of bile and bitterness and their lips full of poison. But I had entrusted my campaign, my actions, and my goals to the Immaculate Mother of the Creator, source of Wisdom, and through faith I am able today to stand before the tribunal of those men who refined the purity of their language in the colleges of Colombia and Europe, [whereas] I am the Indian who carved my language through constancy, and came to know the Palace of the Giant of my thought, which was pointed out to me by the unequivocal finger of the Queen of Nature, out there under the old oak tree which had witnessed my birth.

42. He has been, is, and will always be great, who first through faith rises to God Divine Nature, to which human nature is subordinated, and which is constituted by three powerful kingdoms — vegetable, mineral, and animal.

43. How could I best develop the internal and external cores of these three kingdoms? Very well: man in a state of foolishness is a wild jackass. If he cuts his finger, he is frightened; if he doesn't bathe, smells of copper, etc. That wild jackass has the same desires as a man has; that mineral kingdom flees, hiding away from man, etc., etc. When that logic appeared to me it was from afar when I was contemplating the valley and could also glance at the garden of that logic which was colored with flowers and each flower produced a canteen where the children of ignorance could quench their thirst in the future, those children who are still asleep in the unknown.

44. The garden of man's universal logic is very large and in its midst three great palaces are built in whose center wisdom is found rocking in a cradle, contemplating the mystery of the Trinity. For this reason Wisdom has never been, is not, and shall never be destroyed. Christian philosophers have not yet interpreted that garden and even less the pagan philosophers. The earth said: "The garden of science is not inside me." And the sea answered: "It is not inside me either." And what shall I say of the soul of my thought? And what could be the soul of man's soul? Well I can answer: it is good works. And what are the good works? They are faith and charity, which rise like incense to the throne of our celestial Father to placate the wrath of this Justice, as was said at the beginning of chapter 3.

Chapter 5
The Experience

45. Experience has two powerful walls, one visible, the other invisible, walls which have served as powerful trenches to protect me from the fire of my enemy, in the field where fierce combats are waged, material, civil, and moral. For this one needs a good and unique memory. In the first wall are stored all the actions that swirled around man since the moment when he first used his reason: like the Indian who never forgets the white man who struck a physical blow at his father and insulted him with words, or his brother or his wife. The Indian does not say a word but in his interior he nurtures the thought of the fighting cock and takes revenge by causing an ulcer to grow in the white man's stomach, which in their language some persons call "a spell." The white man steals the farm from the Indian by making him drunk, having him sign documents of debt without owing anything, dragging him to the courts to legalize the despoil, and the judge cooperates by saying to the Indian: "It is better for you to pay." One protests, "What should I pay if I don't owe anything?" The Indian is told then to appoint a lawyer; the Indian names a lawyer but the liar, thief, or swindler who dragged him to court meets with the lawyer of the Indian who wants to protect his right or his property or his cattle, etc., and offers to split the money that he is getting if the lawyer agrees to lose the case, because "We the white and mestizo need to protect each other, while those Indians are nothing...."

46. The second wall of experience is to say what one knows, and to say it at the right time and season, because it is safer to be silent than to talk, because the wound that is covered is never touched by the fly and soon heals. The Indian caudillo, advocate, or leader consults inwardly or externally by means of the sacred heart of Mary, conceived without sin, in whose heart dwells and rules the mystery of the Trinity, because she is the cradle of wisdom, which I mentioned in chapter 4.

47. In the whisper from afar, through living faith coupled with good works, out in the distant sea, in the murmur of the wind as it shakes the foliage of the old oak trees, out in the desert where the solitude is silent, it [God's voice] crosses suddenly in the interior of the poor little Indian and makes him hear the words of the Majesty which made man out of nothing, after its own image and semblance, and tells him: "Hear the words of God in the mountains, all over the desert, as they cross in the soft winds, with a mild perfume of wild flowers; watch his shadow in the waters that move so magnificently; watch his shadow in the midst of the immensity above us. He told me, "Your name is written in the book of the predestined of the Lord. Through your faith God has given you your life; in the midst of your affliction and your struggle, God has consoled you in ecstasies, ecstasies which the celestial bodies have not been able to describe to this day, because a mysterious cipher is marked in your heart, a cipher that the learned never found in their forty or so years of study, etc., etc."

48. I studied ontology in the forests, and its immediate attributes when I investigated the supreme reasons of God, of man, and of the world, and it taught me that the world, the human soul, and God are the three beings whose existence I wanted to discover, supported by a very high faith. For this reason my conduct has not been reproached to this day by the most famous minds that wrote pagan philosophy and Christian philosophy, neither by any of the historians or jurists of the present age.

Chapter 6
The Passing of Time and of Humanity

49. Time is the most powerful and the fiercest enemy of the proud and the envious. Time with truth looks down upon the miserable career of man, born of a woman. His state is like the grass and its flower: if a wind blows, the flower falls and the earth which sustained it before does not recognize it any longer, and the name of a man, good or bad, passes along in the lips of living humanity, as does the lint when it is blown away by the wind like the leaf of a tree that is the toy of the wind and of the running waters. The waters have a spirit which my ancestors called the god of the rivers, who made himself known before the majesty of an Indian empress under the name of Múschcate, who is the false god (*el dios supuesto*), and Múschca, the God of Divinity, who created out of nothing everything that is seen and is not seen, and through faith all we Catholics believe this is true.

50. And why? Because none of the most famous artisans born of human nature has been able to stop the clock built by the eternal hand of him who made nature and man. This clock which works above man's head and which is never slow or fast is what is called natural law, established by the eternal wisdom which ordered the tireless running of the waters and the places where they stop running, deposits that remain still according to the command of natural law. In the same way it established the time when the dawn displays its beauty; and likewise at the precise time commanded by natural law the star that illumines humanity appears; and everything happens harmoniously along with man and above man; as I said before that lint and leaf are the toys of the wind, because if a man is good he will undergo a good death, because as is a man's life so is his death, and according to his death so is eternity.

51. Liars and vulgar skeptics speak of human reincarnation; but this is a sophism that attempts to answer the question: "For what purpose did God create man?" This question should be answered |honestly| by the free thinkers, the deceitful nonbelievers who have deceived the illiterate and weak Indigenous peoples in the departments of Colombian territory, telling them that the wisdom of God is not true. I wish to refer in this chapter to a number of non-Indian men who have asked me to walk in their paths, to follow their teachings, to develop their doctrines, in favor and in defense of my people. But I offered them all the flower of contempt and went on with a very high faith searching the road of the good, and on that road I found righteousness, which has accompanied me to this day when all the intellectuals have said that "what the Indian Quintín Lame hides under his hair is a mystery," and this for not having studied in any of their schools or colleges. But I had known the Garden of Science protected by a beehive of golden bees which buzz around the flowers of science and around the imagination of the poor little Indian, out there in the forests accompanied by solitude; out there in the dungeon accompanied by the imagination; in the penitentiary accompanied by faith and charity towards my fellow prisoners who cried, but whom I consoled. Because I have been in jail 108 times in Tolima by non-Indians, and on none of those 108 occasions have I needed a lawyer or a defense attorney to make my defense before 4,000 and more liars, bribers, who had committed perjury, belonging to the white and mestizo race, who have joined the investigators and the judges, and the mayors, and the town councils, and the clerks, who also had joined the director of the Ibagué Penitentiary, Señor Jesús Elias Quijano, so that he would not allow any message about my defense to come through to me in my defense. But I chased out the pressure and slander piled up by my enemies who were men of knowledge and experience; who were entrenched inside the walls of doubt on the frontiers of insanity and pride, non-Indians who made up accusations against me but which they could not prove before the law or before reason. And for this reason justice came out to meet me in the same way and with the same affection with which my mother used to receive me after three months of absence. And the same thing happened successively with all the other accusations. It is true that there were Indians who accused me also, but they were bribed by the white and the mestizo, and for that reason I exposed all the bribers before the public because I had been inspired by God, the supreme judge of the human conscience.

52. The life of the proud and envious man is like the flower which the tree rejects and falls down upon mother earth and while lying there cries out saying, "I rejected the tree"; the tree which is Nature's clothing as it gets ready to blossom again, and to produce new leaves and to become greater than yesterday.

53. The same thing has happened to me, who educated myself in the forests and formed myself there, and in the forests I became acquainted with the Book of Philosophy and also came to know the palace where the giant of my thought was placed to which I referred in chapters 3 and 4. And it was there also where I met the three kingdoms which human nature has in the form of three flower gardens; where some flowers are superior and others are inferior, and where I came to know that the inferior flower is the support and decoration of that which is superior, because inferior sciences serve as the basis for the superior sciences, and the superior for the inferior.

54. Nature showed me also the idyll of poetry in the midst of that white layer where the queen dresses herself like a bride who brings forth the bridal gown of her innocence in the moment of climbing the steps towards the altar where the poets of the Eucharist chant and to swear her marriage carrying a lighted candle in her hand. However, in all of this there is no material reality, because many times there has been deceit, etc., etc.

55. But in the Queen about whom I have been speaking there is reality, because from the very beginning of the world she gathered the seeds yielded by the garden, sown by Divine Nature in the garden of Paradise, where the first man was sentenced and the first woman was condemned, farmers who were exiled by that sentence given by the supreme judge of human conscience of whom I have been speaking before.

56. That Queen called Nature which ontology had referred me to, out there in the forest where I caught a glimpse of the garden of science called Theodicy which taught me how to interpret human thought and how to defend myself; because by night it was a sanctuary of light, and by day the sanctuary was surrounded by the whitest cloud when I used to climb the steps to receive God's bread in the Eucharist every Sunday when Mass was said in the jail chapel. The day when I was getting ready for that Monday when I had to face the judge who was plotting to turn the unjust trial against me; for this reason I say in truth and good faith that God is above everything and more powerful than anything.

Chapter 7
The Judicial Lesson

57. In the judicial section of this chapter I intend to demonstrate with frankness to the Indian population of Colombia that their duties and their rights, as well as their domains, are today bitten, and the bite infected (*la mordedura engangrenada*) by the snake of ignorance, ineptitude, or illiteracy. But Indians who can interpret the first six chapers of this book shall be able to rise with the greatest aplomb to confront the Colombian Colossus, and to reconquer their territories, in the same way that I also took back the Indian *resguardos* of Ortega and parts of Chaparral in Tolima. My campaign began in April 1922 and ended on December 31, 1938. And in the year 1939 I began officially as Governor to defend the domains which had been reclaimed, together with the Indian Council which was formed by twelve Indian men, a victory achieved with my pen and my example; and thinking everything over, considering that there was danger in delay, I ordered those twelve men to rule rightly so that their government would become an example for the future.

58. Likewise the parents of an Indian family who bear a child endowed with intelligence must get this book [i.e., child] to be like a mirror that never loses its shine, in the midst of icy pyramids, or in the heat waves produced by the birds of prey of our enemies. But they will not prevail, provided that such a young man or young men rest their ideologies on God, through faith, because science accompanied by faith rests on God, the designer (*ordenador*) of the Universe and of Natural Law.

59. I have been and I am the man who sits with pride in the midst of my race, and in the midst of my enemies, who mocked me, who slandered me, who called me names; [in the midst] of the authorities who tortured me, tying me by the neck and the arms, as if I were a runaway murderer. This is what Dr. Alvarez Guzmán did, as mayor of Ortega, to make himself famous among his own kind. He set a post at the door of the dungeon of the Ortega jail, and had me tied to it by the neck, and arms, and around the waist, without movement for three days and three nights; and did not allow food to be handed out to me; he also opened the doors of the jail building and asked the people of Ortega, men and women, to visit and stare at me from the balcony, to show that he knew how to punish the Indian Quintín Lame: thus he displayed his greatness and demonstrated his courage, immortalized in the pages of history assigned to Nero.

60. We Indians ought to abandon and refuse the gifts of the whites, the bluffing mouthful (*pedantezco palabrerío*) that says: "I care for you as one of my family, as a true friend, and it is because of this love that I ask you to sell me your produce at a lower price, etc., etc.

61. The white lawyer says to the Indian (who has a legitimate complaint against a white man): "Your lawsuit does not look good at all, it is very difficult, but if you pay me 800 pesos, putting down half of it in advance, in a week your case shall be won." The Indian answers: I have only 200 pesos with me." The white man says: "No, no, only if you give me 400!" The Indian answers: "In two weeks I'll bring them." Says the white man: "No! Bring them in a week" (and he promises and swears that the lawsuit will be won in favor of the Indian). The Indian brings the 400 pesos, and two months later comes back to ask: "How is my case going, Mr. Lawyer?" But the lawyer who is a loafer and a liar says: "I have done everything possible! The outcome lies almost entirely in my hands, but today I am broke. Give me 100 pesos, which I will appreciate as if it were a present." The Indian says: "Today I have nothing, but in a week I'll bring the 100 pesos, or at least fifty." Five months later, failing to hear from the lawyer again, the Indian asks the secretary of the Court about it, and she says: "It is already two months since your lawyer presented a brief, but he never came back again!" "But he told me that the case was practically won!" says the Indian. The secretary answers: "That man is really swindling you. Find yourself a good, honest lawyer, who at least shows up at the office!" But by this time the Indian's money has run out, he sinks in misery, and the lawsuit is won by the other side. The lawyer of the poor Indian is now happy because secretly he was in cahoots with the defendant!

62. That is why in the lawyer's house there is hunger, there is misery, there is ruin; that is, in the house of the lawyer who has no conscience, and will die in ruin as did Christopher Columbus who died in the city of Valladolid.

63. These were the powerful reasons which made me learn to interpret the science of criminology and civil law, supported by faith in the Supreme Judge, the owner of all human consciences, because of having been the first magistrate who penetrated the mind of the chief of the eternal armies, who was thinking of rebelling against the Infinite Mercy.

64. The same Supreme Judge pronounced sentence for the second time, on the earth, in the garden which he had planted and where he had placed a guardian or steward together with a woman, whose dresser was a lake that was in the garden, and the steward or farmer had joy in contemplating the beauty of the flowers and the fruits. The place where the second sin was committed, which many historians say was the serpent which offered an apple, etc., which is not true, because it was the laws of human nature which ordered the strict fulfillment of its laws; because the animal kingdom reveals to us such fulfillment with understandable precision that philosophers call logic and psychology, because they claim to have studied; but I say it because I have interpreted it by observing diverse living creatures.

65. The first man and the first woman were personally notified by the Supreme Judge of their sentence of banishment, because he himself had so determined, because he created humanity after his own image and endowed it also with knowledge, and for that reason made appear his divinity in one of the daughters of Israel by the name of Mary conceived without sin, who pleads before that Supreme Judge on behalf of us who come to her with a very high faith.

66. It is here where the Christian philosopher develops his ideology to demonstrate to humanity that he is in fact a philosopher, and that to be able to soar had first to stand on the stone of philosophy; because my book shall be criticized by many short-sighted people who are deprived of man's imagination which I came to know out there in the desert, in the jail, and in the dungeon when I was tied to the post, to quench the wisdom of the mayor of Ortega, Alvarez Guzmán, in 1931. And what shall I say of the episodes which Dr. Miguel Arroyo Diez carried out in Cauca, together with Dr. Guillermo Valencia and many other intellectuals against the Indian Quintín Lame, myself, in order to humiliate him, and have him condemned without defense and against the law and the national constitution. But that Supreme Judge to whom I have been referring throughout this chapter is the stream that never stops running, never stops shedding its light on humanity, because the law that has regulated nature [was made] by God, who made the Universe out of nothing; likewise the clock that is fixed in the infinite, and which no silversmith or liar in the entire world has been able to cut or twist even one of its parts, was built by the artisan who lives out there in the Palace of Immortality, wherein reality exists, the reality that is known by the soul of the person who has lived uprightly.

67. The jurisprudence that I learned was taught to me in those fields of struggle where I was accompanied by that image that was just beginning to fly from image to image, which I kept looking at, being today more beautiful than it was yesterday; and I figured that tomorrow it would be more beautiful than today, and that man's wisdom would be more exact, [to be able] to gather the flowers of science in the garden cultivated by the first man and the first woman; a garden sown by the Supreme Judge who reigns in the Palace of Immortality, as mentioned before, because in the future man shall be wiser than yesterday, and tomorrow wiser than today.

68. Hear, you Indians! The elements of proof are three: the first is confession; the second is the testimony of witnesses, and the third is written documents. But be careful not to make the confession of anything, because oral confession is retribution in action; the defense is in your own lips, and so is your conviction; one should never confess his deeds before any civil authority or criminal investigation; [because] there are around many prosecutors who threaten the ignorant with torture, with the dungeon, and with exile, with sentences of twenty years, etc., etc. But the man who allows a prosecutor or a judge to intimidate him should not reside in Colombia. There are many judges and prosecutors who say "Don't deny it, don't deny it! Because there are testimonies that say that it was you who did it." But what they want is to become famous by means that lie ouside the law, outside reason and justice.

69. Justice is the right that every person has, and that is why it is called distributive, commutative, and legal. It is like the man who has the intention of committing a crime and discloses that intention. Such action is a material element [of proof] so that the defense attorney will not be able in the future to defend the accused, and the accused himself will not be able to deny unless he shows proof of insanity.

70. Man establishes the criterion [for his life] which [if chosen wisely] will allow him to see realities with the clarity of truth, and his will [will be] the perfect example of uprightness and honesty when he determines to direct all his actions towards justice, and to enter the chamber of the highest ministry of life, and lead human destinies.

71. The Indian is hated by the white man, is abhorred unto death when he attempts to criticize his actions. The Indian cannot go with a white man to a coffeehouse, to a hotel, or sit at the table as his guest, no matter how dressed up he might be, because the white man degrades himself before his own, looks down on him with arrogance, etc., etc. This is even more so when the Indian has penetrated the garden of science and the white man remains outside unable to enter, things which I realized when I came down from the mountains where I had seen the Prairies of Science, and understood how high, profound, and broad is the science of philosophy. I do not wish to mention the powerful bark which covers the principal tree of the science mentioned above, because philosophers say that there is a key to philosophy, but I do not know it, even though I could interpret it in case of need.

72. The Colombian Indian must have his representation, first, in the Senate of the Republic and in the lower house, in the assemblies of the departments, and in the city councils for the following reasons: (a) because the legislature gives orders and passes laws against the communal properties of Indians because of our ignorance; (b) because the legislature would have us distribute our *resguardo* lands, but it does not likewise order the large white landholders (*latifundistas*) to do the same; because in the same way that a weak race is asked by law to distribute what belongs to it, so it should be asked of a race which is strong on account of its intelligence and cunning; (c) because it is the most appropriate means for our race, which is proscribed and abandoned by Colombian civilization.

Chapter 8
The Prosecution, Humbug, and Deceit against the Indian on Trial

73. Three frightful and vindictive judges of the Superior Courts of Popayán, Neiva, and Ibagué, together with governors, busy themselves extraordinarily (in my prosecution), together with the judges of the lower circuits, the municipal judges, the town mayors, etc.

74. In Popayán it was Doctor Miguel Arroyo Diez and Doctor Guillermo Valencia who infected the conscience of the judges against the accused Manuel Quintín Lame for having learned to think how to think. In Neiva it was Sr. Ricardo Perdomo C., and Doctor Luis Ignacio Andrade, and in Ibagué the director of the jail, Jesús Elias Quijano, and Doctor Marco A. Vidales, judge of the Superior Court.

75. It is said that Popayán is the cradle of sages, the cradle of poets, the cradle of philosophers, the cradle of the most famous jurists; but I did not consult with any one of them about my own defense in the years 1918 and 1919 when I was preparing it, like the chicks of the fowl when they flap their wings to challenge the infinite space on their own for the first time and to cross it; [likewise] I presented my bravest defense in the midst of all those learned men of the present age.

76. One of the prosecutors, together with the alternate prosecutor, came to the jail and called me apart to inquire how and in what way I was to begin my defense, so as to help me, saying that they owned no lands to protect, etc. But I immediately saw their ploy and answered them with a question about how were they going to begin their accusation against me. And they said: "We are not going to accuse you, but to defend you, etc., etc."

77. But when I looked at these young men with their lips bathed with smiles, suddenly the Queen appeared to me, the same who had consoled me out there in the forests, and in the dungeon, and in the jail when I was held incommunicado for one entire year, dragging around the dungeon of Popayán iron shackles weighing twenty-eight pounds by order of the aristocrats of Popayán mentioned before.

78. And who was this Queen? It was the very image of my thought which had been engendered in the deep and extensive Prairie of my body and my spiritual soul, within the sanctuary of my heart, which is the compass in a man's life, which compass oriented me when I had to cross two swollen rivers, one of tears, the other of blood; which compass pointed to me two paths, one of thistle, the other of thorns; but both of them to the right side, because on the left side was lying my non-Indian enemy, crouched like a tiger, ready to devour the Giant who was building the Palace of my thought, that is to say, the thought of the Indian who educated himself in the midst of the mother forest, so as to be able to confront and to fool those poets with ellipsis, when (one of them) who was running for president of the country asked me in several letters to tell the Indians that they should vote for him; to confront those minds which had been carved in the schools of Europe; to confront the pricking thorns of the rose gardens which had blossomed and were crowned with white flowers, or rather, what the poor little Indian today calls flowers, which covered the cemetery of illusions of those aged men, seventy or eighty years old, who ended their lives buried with their capes on. And today the eagle of my thought flies across those fields, transformed into logic and psychology according to the promise of that image that has not left me to this day, thanks to God's mercy, because God is above all things, and the man who rests on God's omnipotence is powerful, and is able to pass through files of two hundred thousand cannons and guns fired by slanderers, bribers, and perjurers against the Indian who attempts to assert his right before them. Such were the kinds of men who attempted to place me on the bench of the accused, because they tried to defend the bloody, cowardly, and villainous crime committed in the late hours of the night, on March 12, 1922, by Sr. Ricardo Perdomo C., and Sr. Luis Solano, the latter being the chief of police of Neiva. Ricardo Perdomo C. yelled at the top of his voice, "Don't mind killing Indians; I have money to pay for them to the government." Thus he ordered officer Solano and his policemen. This fact is documented in the official records of the trial, part 3, where the slander against me is formulated, and also in parts 1, 2, and 4, where are recorded the machinations which those non-Indians mounted against the Indian race of San Andrés de los Dujos, San Roque del Caguán, and San Antonio de Hortalesillas, in the Neiva district. This crime was directed and paid by the millionaire Ricardo Perdomo C., who was the boss of the governor of the department and of the judges of the so-called Court of Justice, but which in fact it was not.

79. And why [did these things happen]? The Law of Compensation answers this question. Because this law ordained that the Conservative Party should be buried under its own ruins, and be placed under the orders of the Liberal Party, etc., etc., and to die, like the man who first came to these lands with the title of conquistador, on October 12, 1492, also died. Because there is nothing stable for us humans in this world, because time is the enemy, tenacious, invisible, and powerful, against the man who is puffed up with pride. This happened to the Colossus of Rhodes, of whom we were told by the traveler, the same who discovered in the course of time man's titanic creations, in the primeval sands where the first man set foot, and which the first woman contemplated.

80. What shall I say of the great attempts against me, made by non-Indian men of Tolima, men of little minds, whose intelligence was clogged by cynicism, hate, envy, and deceit, to answer the Indian Manuel Quintín Lame, myself. But as God has said, "the gates of hell shall not prevail against the gates of heaven," because truth is a Queen whose throne is in heaven, and whose habitat is the bosom of God.

81. The jury was formed by five members who began considering whether I was guilty or not of the seven charges made against me by the evil minds of the mayor Angel María Salcedo, of Ortega, and the mayor of Coyaima, Gavino Tovar, etc., etc., whose evil minds were endorsed by certifications of the municipal councils of Chaparral, Ortega, and Coyaima.

82. But then the luminous fountain of my imagination began to roar against the lie, the infamy, the robbery, the patricidal and criminal deceit

of all the non-Indian men of Tolima; and I realized that I was a sand storm raised by the hurricane produced by evil minds, first, of those who had sworn before God to administer commutative, distributive, and legal justice; and secondly, by commercial firms of Chaparral and Ortega which, by means of sophisms, tied up to them the authority of the Reverend Father Rafael A. Parejas, as stated in the record of my defense, with documents that I collected in a personal inspection of the district of Ortega.

83. This Sanhedrin of liars had made it a habit to hang Indians by their feet to make them say what they were told to say, that is, declarations against me; they did this to the Indians Joaquín Ducuara, Felix Moreno, and Eufrasio Ducuara, and their declarations are recorded in the record of the defense against the indictment and the tribunal.

84. The fountain that I mentioned before is, as I said, luminous, because it was destined to destroy the edifice of the insane man built by the evil mind that I have been referring to; but the fountain had overflowed and its currents were going to destroy the edifice, and to smash the thought of the non-Indian, thanks to the thought of him who had been hated, not because he was a sinner, but because of shaping the good in the heart of the Indian of Tolima, my brother.

85. How nervous was the judge of the Superior Court when the jury was ready to pronounce its verdict on the seven charges made against me, which Judge Vidales had requested to be [a verdict of] guilty. His face was then rose-colored, but when the jury declared: "The Indian Quintín Lame is innocent of all the seven charges of which he was accused before this court," because four members had voted in favor and one against, the face of Judge Doctor Marco A. Vidales turned pale like a white flower; and the Superior Court said: "The tribunal has decided wisely."

86. Thus, justice emanates from God: that image, which always is by my side, kept saying to me: "You are free! You are free!"

87. Therefore, I knew that Justice had already taken away the keys from the jailer to set free the little Indian, Manuel Quintín Lame, myself; and all the learned men with their heads down left the room, where they had been watching for several days.

88. I was the accused, and I myself was the defense attorney, against the charges of several judges, of several mayors, of several prosecutors, of several municipal councils, and of several commercial firms! When I had started my defense the second judge, Marco A. Vidales, tried to deny me the right to my own defense, but I immediately appealed to Article 1620 of the Judicial Code, and the president of the Court indicated with a nod of the head what was the right thing to do against the wrong that was going to be committed against me. I was going to defend myself before men against the unjust charges imputed against me in Tolima, because I was an Indian and the advocate of the Indian, who has been and continues to be deceived, and who finds himself like the child who cries out in the cradle for the presence and loving care of his mother, when he feels hungry, and thirsty, and cold.

Chapter 9
The Condition of the Indigene in Darkness

89. Ignorance exceeds everything and everywhere, because it pretends to know all, whereas wisdom claims to know nothing; because ignorance says everything that comes to mind, but wisdom says only what is just and appropriate.

90. Why? Because ignorance sails in darkness as in a polar night. But I was able to know the white gardens of the sea, and to discover therein the bird that was asleep, which was the image of my mind, which was to make me know the immense bridge across which I should pass to visit the garden of the sciences, and in the future to know the song of that bird which was awakened in the midst of nature, when it shakes its long head of hair, white like foam. But through faith it is possible to hear the song of that bird, which is the bird of man's immortality, when the human soul turns into immortal soul; which bird in the future, when man exhales his last sigh, shall fly away to know and to sing in the mansion that was given to Abel the innocent, to Noah the just, to Abraham the generous, etc., where to the son of God was to ascend — body and soul, four thousand years later, to the mansion which is waiting for all of us who have defended the ten commandments of God's law, and have obeyed them. Everything else has been easy (*obra de carpintería*) because it has been changed by men. Because man is good until the day he so wishes, and the same thing when he is bad. That is why God has clearly rewarded perseverance, but perseverance to the end, that is, the patriotism of him who knew how to engage in great battles against the three powerful enemies: the devil, the world, and the flesh.

91. I said, "until the day he so wishes," thinking of the change of ideas of men like Calvin and Luther, the case of the swindler Vicente Arenas with whom I was detained in the jail of Ibagué, chatting on many subjects.

92. Consider the patriotism of Saint Rita de Cacia, for whose faith she received the name of Saint Rita of the Impossible; consider the name of Saint Rosalia de Palermo, as well as the name and charity of Saint Isidro the Farmer; of Saint Roque the medicine man (*médico yerbatero*); and so on and so forth. I could cite a whole list of saints, but time does not allow, because I have much work to do, material and intellectual, in defense of my race and obligation.

93. What I have said I said because the white man's race, which is my enemy, fierce but not all-powerful, has said, and keeps saying, publicly, that the Indian Quintín Lame, myself, is asinine, a swindler, a crook, a thief; they want to ignore all my deeds in the same way that the Jews requested the Roman governor to remove the *INRI* from the cross, etc., and the Caesars wished to hide the mystery of Easter, that is, of the resurrection of him who had died on the cross, and been buried in the garden, on whose tomb a heavy rock had been laid, and a guard, etc. Likewise, Dr. Guillermo Valencia, together with a handful of aristocrats from Cauca who supported him, non-Indians, wished to divorce or destroy my thought by means of cynicism and violence, and had me sent to the dungeon, carrying iron shackles weighing twenty-eight pounds, for an entire year incommunicado, as is stated in the records of the indictment. And they ordered to let it be known that the Indian Quintín Lame had been exiled, or had died; this notwithstanding he is still alive, for which reason they said: "the Indian has to be treated roughly, because it is the only way to fill him with terror," etc.

94. However, on one occasion I bumped into the famous poet on Florian Street in Bogotá, and when he stepped down from the sidewalk, I called his attention, and he responded courteously, and I said: "Doctor, give me those five flowers," and we shook hands, thus proving to him that I was not anymore the Indian wolf but the little brother wolf, that I was not anymore the wild beast, or the wild ghost that shrieks in the forests, but only a wild pigeon, who had flown over the mountains and the forests, in order to know where to find the gardens of science, so as to be able to whisper to the poet who had caught a glimpse of human love in his poems. In that moment came to my mind the order of expatriation from Colombia which he had proposed as House Representative; and also the letter in which he asked me to order all the Indian councils of Cauca |to vote for him| when he was running for president of Colombia; because it is not that Dr. Guillermo Valencia expelled me from Cauca, as some lackeys from Tolima say, but that he wanted me exiled from Colombia, and Dr. Abadía Méndez, the Minister of State, spoke in my favor, as has been said before.

95. I don't rely on the learning or idea of any civic men — I have not studied their feats, their origins and ends; I rely rather on the compass that is in the sanctuary of my heart, which is not an enigma, as some intellectuals and journalists have said, but rather the fountain where the Queen of my imagination swims, as in the ponds to which reference is made in the Old Testament, and also in the New, because the old scriptures were reformed by the New Adam, who came to pay for the crime of the old one, for which crime the door to the mansion of bliss was closed, and Abel, the innocent, could not enter, neither the holy fathers of old times, who remained waiting in a mansion.

96. Because the earth was populated twice, the first time by the descendants of Adam and Eve, and the second by those of Noah, who escaped God's punishment, thanks to the same God, in a mansion called the Ark. In that Ark I myself have found protection against slander, bribery, and perjury, and also defense against the assault of the Colombian judicial system. It was while sailing in the Ark that I, the poor little Indian, came to know the sleeping bird to which I have referred before; and when it woke up, my thought too was awakened, socially and morally, to be able to combat injustice, which is born in the white man's heart, my enemy. It is there also that the flood had its origin, and also the icy waterfalls, which intended to destroy the eagle of my thought. But I was sailing in the Ark, taking care of that bird with which Nature had endowed me; and today is the day when I set loose the wild pigeon [of my mind] to carry the olive branch of my thought transformed into idea, which will be known by all who have hated, and still hate me, wishing my death; and that wild pigeon, born and raised in the forest, flies close to the most famous minds [of Colombia] to whisper in their ears; those men who walked on the road built by Christopher Colombus on October 12, 1492, when it was inaugurated and known by the peoples of Europe, to come here to persecute and murder us like rapacious wolves, without realizing that we, like wolves, are children of nature, but the foreigners are not children of nature but children of rocks, because the rock is an inherent being, which has been turned into flames, because rocks are the house of fire. For this reason the white man's heart is the house of envy and persecution against the poor, ignorant Indian, taking advantage of his ignorance and weakness. But the weak and asinine Indian brings forth today a work called "Los Pensamientos" which marks the collapse of the Colombian Colossus, because what has been said is the truth and nothing but the truth. Because the Law of Compensation is drawing near, and many intellectuals don't realize it.

Chapter 10
The Harem of Justice

97. You are honorable, if you are just! I must acknowledge in this chapter raising the torch that is the messenger of truth, and not of error, the good will of certain non-Indian men, among those who form the national government of Colombia, because since 1910 to this day I have been received with all my petitions on behalf of all Indian *resguardos* of the departments of Nariño, Cauca, Valle del Cauca, Huila, and Tolima.

98. I keep in my possession a letter from Dr. Marco Fidel Suarez, let him rest in peace, dated August 11, 1912, when he was the Minister of Foreign Relations of Colombia. It was his answer to my letter which I had addressed to him, because his name and his good intelligence filled the entire country. And he wrote: "Señor Quintín Lame, Popayán Jail, etc. You are on the way towards greatness, like other famous indigenous men have been in other lands. Keep the same personal faith in all your doings, etc., etc."

99. And what should I say of the Supreme Court of Justice to which I have appealed since 1907? When I first addressed to it an ill-conceived petition, because the bird mentioned in chapter 9 had not yet awakened, but was still asleep amidst the gardens and lakes which Divine nature possesses. However, the Court realized my ineptitude and also the intention which prompted my petition in behalf of my people. Because, in spite of being in jail, I have been like the hunter's dog which barks louder the closer it is to the hiding wolf.

100. I am also grateful for the Supreme Court decision in 1930 against the unjust prosecution which the aristocrats of Neiva initiated against me, using the District Court as their agent to execute the will of the tyrant Ricardo Perdomo C., who washed his feet in Indian blood in the locality of Los Limpios, district of Neiva, on March 12, as mentioned before. And the District Court declared them innocent, both the physical actors and their aristocrats and accomplices, thus washing its hands and insulting justice, reason, and morality, as the Roman governor had done against the second person of the trinity, known as Jesus Christ, King of the Jews.

101. A warrant was issued for my arrest and I took refuge in the mountains of Tolima for six months during which time I was able to collect evidence against the evil administration of justice of the District Court of Neiva and the Governorship. It was then that I received the telegram from the Minister of State, Carlos E. Restrepo, saying: "Señor Manuel Quintín Lame — Ortega. The Supreme Court of Justice rendered a verdict in your favor on the indictment against you over the crime of Los Limpios, district of Neiva, etc."

102. How grateful I was to our God, the Supreme Judge of every human conscience, to whom I had entrusted my struggle, as the Omnipotent General to defeat the potent generals, as in effect I defeated them, thanks be to God.

103. In the same way it was announced through the mouth of the prophets the arrival of the liberator of humanity; but he did not come to favor the very rich, but for the sake of the wretched poor, hated by the white man, persecuted by the white man, slandered by the white man, and deceitfully indicted by the white man. And in spite of all that, I have not needed, or asked for, any intellectual lesson or class [from the white man], but rather I have developed my own thinking in this work, which the white man will label in many ways, because the whites of the departments of Nariño, Cauca, Valle del Cauca, Huila, and Tolima are my most tenacious and deadly enemies.

104. But how could I say the same of the whites of Bogotá who, since 1907, have not even said to me: Indian, are your eyes black? The same of the other departments of Colombia. But through my faith, which I state in writing in this book, there shall rise tomorrow a handful of indigenous men, who shall take over the desks, the rostrums, the platforms, the tribunals, because the intelligence of the Indian race surpasses, and shall surpass extraordinarily, the white man's intelligence, through a very high faith, as stated and demonstrated in this book.

105. What shall I say to the Indians who lived before October 12 of 1492? The wrath of centuries has not been able to destroy the inscriptions on hard rocks on the crest of steep mountains. And why has the white race not been able to interpret the Spirit contained or embodied in Indian lakes? The Indian naively has given everything to the white man without realizing the superiority of Indian intelligence. Consider the history of the Veda Indians, of the Egyptian Indians, of the Japanese Indians; the pagodas of India reveal a knowledge that the white doctor does not and will not possess, because the latter relies on the mineral kingdom, while the Indian [relies] on the vegetable and animal [kingdoms] to prepare the decisive medicine, and so on.

106. The members of the jury who expected [my conviction] with sophisms and false arguments, in the Superior Court of Neiva, were sweating, raving to hear my conviction, but their nervousness miscarried, vomiting pieces of poisoned barbed wire, when they heard the thunder of justice, thanks to my shrewdness and faith. Because I had known that the jury had said that, whether I was guilty or not, I would have to be punished, because the Caesar, Ricardo Perdomo C., had spent so much money on it.

107. In book number two of the judicial records is found the confession of Señor Luis Solano who requested that justice be done to him as the perpetrator of the crime of Los Limpios. But the jury, in spite of that, did not condemn him!

108. This is justice as practiced by the Conservative Party of Neiva in 1923, 1924, and until 1930. I don't know the justice practiced by the Liberal Party of Neiva, but soon I will and then I will write a second work. Because I take distance from what I don't know, because this is the first book produced by the Indian wolf, that is to say, the first thought turned into an idea.

109. *Atallo Cundulcunca* (the condor's nest). The condor of my thought and the eagle of my psyche [is] the indigenous psychology, which was formed when those condors soared like singing swallows and established their nest in the highest peaks, or else under the shade of ancient oak trees, and shouted in the midst of that immense solitude which surrounded me, as recorded in chapter 1 of this book.

110. I came to know that the aristocracy of Neiva was not satisfied; because all the functionaries, the Mayor, the Judges, the Chief of Police, busy themselves by certifying against me before the Mayor of Ortega. Then I realized that those functionaries did not think of tomorrow but only of today, because as the saying goes, "Let him who has a tail of straw not come close to the fire."

Chapter 11
The Mist in the Thought of the Indian
Educated in the Mother Forest

111. There are times when mist takes possession of the domains of the forest in all their extension; when mist pays a visit to the forest and takes possession of its shade; in like manner I have taken possession of nature's garden: during brief moments, hours, nights, days, weeks, when the mist lives under the mother forest, I have been there too, plucking the flowers. And the hunter of game sometimes loses his trail and his skill, but I have not lost my compass in the darkness, etc. And the musical concert of nature never misses the opportune hour to sing its stanzas with spiritual accent, and it is spiritual because it strikes man's spiritual attention when he exclaims: "What beauty! What greatness!"

112. One finds the condor's nest so neatly prepared, the little houses of sundry birds so well built, the beehive with its guardian at the door, and likewise everything so harmoniously arranged. Because nature has taught her harmonious sons to those whom she has educated for generations, not like the white man, the enemy of the Indian, who has learned to read and write through teachers; and the same nature possesses her own reserves which predators squeeze with their lips, stealing her perfumes and fruits, while the wind which owns them passes by.

113. While my enemy paces around, thinks, and builds his idyll of lies, I have captured the vapors emanating from his evil mind, which distills poisonous fumes against the ignorant Indian. But such fumes have not been able to poison the compass which brought down to the prairies the [Indian] who educated himself in the forests, as has been said in chapter 1.

114. In the mother forest is found the beautiful book entitled The Idyll; the beautiful book called The Key of Sciences, or the Knowledge of Man; and there is also found the book called Philosophy, where the three kingdoms — the vegetable, the animal, and the mineral — live visibly and harmoniously together: the mineral serving the animal, and the animal serving the vegetable. And why? This question has already been answered in chapters 1 and 2 of this work.

115. I am like the guardian bee standing at the door of the beehive keeping out the lazy drones which want to eat without working: drones who are like those others who arrived on October 12 of 1492 and seized our wealth, our laws and customs, as well as our religion. And being Catholic, apostolic, and Roman, the veterans of Mother Spain did not behave towards us like priests, but rather as poisonous snakes to kill us with the poison of envy; and such envy persists to this day. After 447 years it has not disappeared, because the Indian is always under the white man's boot like a slave; and the Indian who defends his right is persecuted like a fugitive robber by the non-Indian. This enemy seeks a thousand ways to smash materially, morally, and socially the indigene when he has come close to the garden of science. But I have, thanks to God, known not only the garden of science, but the Garden of Sciences, and because of that am ready to answer any subject that the reader finds obscure or doubtful.

116. But I have to defend at all costs the national conscience, which is a glorious party where indigenes have found refuge to this day from our enemies and persecutors. Consider the intelligence of Don José María Mallarino and Don José Manuel Pontón in the year 1606; and also the intelligence of Pope Saint Pius V in favor of the Indian *resguardos* of the Poenza Valley, today's Popayán, in the locality of "Los Cerrillos," according to his ruling which is found in Volume VI of Tierras del Cauca, in the history that is kept in the colonial archives of this city; and also the defense of the Indians of Fray Bartolomé de Las Casas before the Spanish Courts; and also the thought of the liberator Simón Bolívar on behalf of Indians of Pasto, when he wrote a beautiful letter to the candidate for governor stressing the courage of the Indians from Calibío, who fought under Captain Cabal, in the locality of Piendamó, against the enraged Sámano. In spite of this there is not in Colombia a statue of Atahualpa, or Bochica, as there are in some sister republics; because Colombia is the house of envy and hate against the Indian; even some priests are the enemies of my campaigns and my struggles, like Father Gonzalo Vidal who wrote a leaflet entitled "Camisa de Once Varas," in Popayán, department of Cauca, which I answered, with due regard to the spiritual authority of a priest. This happened in 1914, for which reason the same priest refused to be my witness in 1918 and I had to report him to his superior.

117. Consider also Dr. Miguel Abadía Mendez's defense on my behalf, when Dr. Guillermo Valencia requested Congress to exile me from Colombia. Consider also the time when I offered president Dr. Olaya Herrera, in [Bogotá], to go spontaneously with 5,000 Indians to punish General Sánchez Cerro who had invaded the Amazonian border, because I wished to go personally with those 5,000 youth to cross swords with the invader, with the Colombian flag waving above our heads; something which I had done before, in 1903 and 1904, at the time of the invasion of our border with Ecuador by General Avelino Rosas. I belonged to the Calibío battalion, and after the combat I received the decoration of lieutenant, under Colonel Bernal. But history says nothing of this, because of the cowardice and envy of historians. I wished to cite the combat in which I took part, but I don't, in order not to sow suspicion in the hearts of my own people, so that tomorrow, without regard for party colors, they may join together like noble giants to punish any insolent invader who dares to insult our motherland.

118. We should pay no attention, O Indians of Colombia, to the politics of self-enrichment which the old parties, liberal and conservative, have practiced towards us. And why? Because two days before elections, and the evening before elections, they seem to be courting a beautiful woman, offering a thousand things, that is to say, a thousand promises, and then the deceived woman finds herself pregnant, cornered by sadness and pain, etc. The same has happened to the remnants of my race, which live today in this Colombian land since October 12 of 1492, hated, deceived, persecuted, trampled underfoot, and robbed by non-Indians of Colombia, from all the thirteen departments of Colombia, except the district of Santa Fé de Bogotá, department of Cundinamarca, where our complaints have always been heard, because the Indian never forgets the one who did him good, or the one who struck him a blow!

119. White gentlemen: Hear the word of the Indian wolf, transformed today in thoughts, to mark the transfiguration of the wild wolf, as I have been called by poets, historians, journalists, writers, and lawyers.

120. The wild jackass has been transfigured, but not in an extraordinary manner, around that sublime lake, when the mystery of light transformed the head of the wild wolf into that of a man. Why? Because that wild wolf is the son of nature, and the men who have deprived him [of character], who have embalmed his reason through a thousand slanders, are not [sons of nature], even though they considered themselves not stupid. But in this book they can take a glance into the mind of that ass which came down from the forests to visit the valleys of civilization; but this became a torture to the poor ass, because it placed him under the boot, under contempt, because he was an Indian of yellow race, the descendant of the original inhabitants of this Guananí land, hated by the white man to this day. However, my appearance is spiritual in the midst of my enemies, who placed me in shackles, and held me incommunicado for a year in the dungeon, to place a gag on my rare virtues, which I met in the mountain. It is not the picture as interpreted by Rafael: the picture of hate and envy against the Colombian Indian. But the Law of Compensation, gentlemen, is drawing near!

BOOK II

Chapter 1
The Pollen of Humanity

121. Pollen is a germ created by God since the beginning of the world: hear that, you philosophers, intellectuals, poets, etc., etc.

122. There is a legend in the Bible, about which wrote Dr. Friar Luis de León; but that legend is written in unlikely language, and is not founded on firm ground, or purpose; because the waters that bathe the territory of humanity have a destination; and the four winds of the earth have their home (towards which they go); and likewise, the four winds of Heaven, as well as the sands that are washed away by the waters.

123. It is said that the world was created in six days; but there is no satisfactory proof that this is so (hear this, you Christian and pagan philosophers!); because everthing that is said about the creation of the world has been passed by word of mouth without any proof to guarantee that the world was in fact created in six days.

124. To my way of thinking, the creation of the world has taken place in great epochs, because the eternal intelligence is incomprehensible to human intelligence. Why? Because [God's] mercy is infinite!

125. The earth is round like an orange, and it turns around on its axis every twenty-four hours, and in that time the sun lights it and warms it; and when we see the sun, it is daytime, and when we do not, we find ourselves in darkness of night. And why is it that in this movement of the earth the waters do not spill over and run all over? Because the natural law is eternal, and rests in God, etc. Man has not and will not be able to know the spirit that forms that law, because it begins in God, and ends in God, who is the supreme legislator of the law.

126. Christian as well as pagan philosophers say that the first woman was deceived in paradise by the snake which presented her with an apple; but this supposition is a sophism, etc., etc. Because, let me ask them, who deceived the vegetable kingdom into producing flowers and fruits? Why is it not said of a second snake which deceived that kingdom? As has been said in chapter 1 of this work, man has his body in common with the minerals; his life with the plants; his sensibility with the beasts; and his reason with the spirit; etc.

127. God, that is to say, Jehovah, [is] the true Muschca, in the language taught by Ollo, the woman who appeared to educate my race three hundred years before October 12 [1492]; but she was not born of a woman; she was sent by Nature to educate my race; because she appeared, or was found, in the mountains that form the northern coasts of Mexico, etc. She taught some Indian peoples one language, and others another and so forth.

128. Why is it that the fly, the spider, the cricket, the ant, the butterfly, the bee, the beasts of the forests, the fish of the waters, the fowl, the cattle, horses, donkeys, goats, sheep and swine, etc., etc., etc., all of them, when the time comes the female seeks the male? Because herein lies the logic, which is a true microscope that allows me to see the sheepfold of deceit, and to interpret it, because man was created by God after his own image and semblance.

129. And what shall I say of the woman of the story? Today in her bosom lies the mystery of the most holy trinity; the woman who was the wife of a carpenter, is today the Empress of the heavenly court, more beautiful than the sunrise, brighter than the sun, prettier than all the gardens of nature.

130. I have a question for all the geniuses who have carved ["sculptured"] their intelligence for twenty years in a college, or in several of them, whereas mine is the thought of one who educated himself in the forests, thanks to that little old woman, Ollo, who is and has been the image of my mind, and who pointed out to me the right way to confront all my accusers of very fluffy brains, who were all of them from the city of Popayán, the seat of the old empire of Queen Poenza (hear that, non-Indian people!). I now ask them why the wrath of centuries and ages has not been able to destroy or to erase up to this day the legends that mark the tombs of our prehistory; cemeteries which are found, some of them in the bowels of the earth, others in a large number of lakes, and still others the deposit of the great riches of my sovereign ancestors who commanded hosts and who in some cases had not been born of a woman, such as Sinviora, the founder of temples to the divinity of the Sun, who also taught the Indians the right way to worship the sun, and how to fast, and the right way to live together as men and women, and how to get married, and by whom; and the rules for Indian women to follow, the single woman, and the widow, and what penalty to impose on the Indian woman who had a child, being single; and to the widow who had children without first getting married once again. He also provided fathers and mothers with the medicine to abate or diminish their urge or strength, when nature imposes its law on the young male or the young female.

131. It was Nature who commanded the first woman to begin fulfilling its law, for she was the predestined mother of humanity, of whom the Empress of the heavenly wonders was to be born; who ascended body and soul [into heaven], and to whom all her devotees pray saying: "Oh, Mary, conceived without sin, intercede on behalf of us sinners who come to thee!"

132. How could it be said and sustained that the first woman was deceived when she was going to be the mother of the Empress and the Empress was to be the mother of the Divine Liberator?

Chapter 2
The Palace of Wisdom

133. The Palace of Wisdom is the place where peace, reason, and justice reign! Where is the Palace of Wisdom? Well, one needs to consider what palace, where, how, and in what form.

134. I leave aside the titanic palaces of humanity, because some of them have been destroyed and others humiliated; because the man who calls himself wise, is not wise, and the thinker has not come down deep enough, or climbed high enough, or reached far enough to be able to interpret where the Palace of Wisdom is to be found. And, when was it built, and by whom? It has been interpreted and made known to humanity that the world had been created in six days, a fallacious interpretation of what God supposedly said: on the first day, let there be light, etc.; on the second day he supposedly divided the waters; on the third day he supposedly ordered the inferior waters to gather in one place, etc.; on the fourth day he supposedly created the sun, the moon, etc.; on the fifth day supposedly he created the fowl, etc.; on the sixth day he supposedly ordered the earth to produce animals, etc.; and on the seventh day he supposedly rested and blessed the creation, etc., etc. But where is the proof of all this, "sophers" or "philo-sophers"?

135. Why is it that nothing has been said of the birth of that Omnipotent Artisan or Architect who supposedly worked six days and then rested the seventh?

136. I said before, in chapter 4, book I, of this work, that the earth and the sea were said not to know the Palace of Wisdom. And why? Because to this day nobody has been able to know, nor will ever know, the tribunal of God's higher designs. However, by a divine miracle, the poor little Indian is able to say "maybe," by considering Noah's defense in the ark; considering the defense of the people of Israel; considering the defense of the prophet cast into the lake [*sic*] of lions; considering the defense of those three young men who were thrown, with their hands tied, into the fire by order of King Nebuchadnezzar of Babylon; it seems to me that these extraordinary events had their origin in the man of integrity, that is to say, in the man of good faith, because through faith accompanied with good works the human being is very great, both on earth and also before the tribunal of God's justice.

137. Now, why is it that the above events appear in the Gospels, and why is it that the early Christians were ready to defend the Gospel with their swords? Why the mystery of the Annunciation and the Incarnation of the Son of God and his birth in the inn of Bethlehem? Why was it that Herod did not capture the three monarchs who asked him permission to pass to Bethlehem? And why is there the Gospel in the heights and peace on earth, but only to the man of good will? And why is it that there is evidence in the Gospel about all these mysteries whereas the mystery of the creation of the world does not appear in the Gospel?

138. The eviction of Adam and Eve was the sentence of that Supreme Judge, that is, the truth; it is reason and it is justice; because in one word it is the reality of the good, and the material reality of man, because man's legitimate reality is his death, and according to a man's life so is his death, and according to his death so is eternity. Now, any Christian philosopher could try to deny my reasoning, but it has to be with reasons and proved facts about the creation of the world in six days.

139. The Palace of Wisdom lies before man's eyes, and man has not been able to interpret it, but its interpretation is given in chapter 4, book II, of this work.

140. The waters flow whispering, but man does not interpret their smile and their talk as they pass by or when man passes across their route; the gentle winds blow, but man does not know where they go; some of them carry the perfume of flowers because they have crossed through the gardens of Nature; others carry the smell of the dust of the earth.

These winds go by playing with the fur of the animal kingdom and with the leaves of the vegetable kingdom.

141. Behold its divine shadow that dwells in the waters that flow and their movement never ceases; behold its shadow in the midst of the immensity that hovers over us; behold the star that rises in the East called "the Sun"; behold the concert of the major stars which form the clock that is fixed above our heads; behold the harmonious and sweet singing of those choirs that inhabit the forests; behold the inner law of the forest when it is the wild pigeon's turn or the lark's turn to sing, or the play and singing of a concert of locusts, or a concert of crickets, whose strident songs hit the ear of that man who was being educated in the mountains under the forests with the oak trees as witnesses, which had also witnessed my birth; behold therein the shadows of the Palace of Wisdom!

142. I wish to develop my thinking about the laws of the monarch of the seas, the monarch of the woods, the monarch of the fowl which cross the sky, the monarch of humanity.

143. Let's think first of minerals, because gold was once a phenomenon that was able to speak like man does today, but it was filled with pride; however, before October 12 of 1492, gold was the intimate friend of my ancestors, who kept large quantities of it in storehouses and deposits, in the mansions of our sovereign Zipas, Zaques, etc., etc. But five days after October 12 a number of gold deposits turned into stone and others into water, because the metal understood the poison of the envy of *Guagaz,* which in Castillian means "white-rational man." Pride, envy, and selfishness cause *Guagaz,* the white man, to fall in ruin, in misery, as was the case with the famous conquistador Christopher Columbus, who died in the city of Valladolid.

144. The poverty of the white man is sad, painful, shameful, because of his envy and bad faith towards the poor Indian, due to our ignorance, simplicity, and illiteracy.

145. Today the white man is full of bread, full of praise and visits, because he has money; but he is unaware of his enemy, which is tenacious, powerful, and invisible. And what is it? It is time, because time never turns back, but it gathers in its glove all of man's remains, and counts one by one the steps remaining to reach the point when it will execute the Law of Compensation.

146. The poverty of the Indian is not seen, because the Indian dresses badly, eats badly, works under the rays of the sun all day long, with the help of the cocoa vice or tobacco; if he gets a crop, he is satisfied; if not, he is also satisfied; if he has money, he is satisfied; if not, he is also satisfied; if he has salt, he eats his food with salt; if not, he eats without it; whereas the white man, if he does not have all of this, detests and curses his lot, and becomes like the rotten trunk of a tree thrown out in the garden, eaten by worms; but the Indian, even in his old age, sits down to pluck grass in his garden. The Indian lives up to one hundred years, and the white man reaches only forty or sixty at the most; after sixty, he becomes bent because his blood is degenerated, etc. Indians did not reveal various secrets to the white man, secrets that nature has planted in the vegetable kingdom, which Ollo taught them, and which I should explain in what follows, but I don't do it because of the bad faith of the white man against my race.

147. I have spoken of the Palace of Wisdom which is among us, but we do not know how to interpret it because the foliage of the trees reveals its meaning, some saying yes, and others saying no. Who is the Queen who owns that Palace? It is nature who causes man to be born, and makes perfect the beauty of the woman. This Queen wears a blue mantle that never fades, she crowns herself with flowers, and with white lemon blossoms, like a bride bringing her innocence to the altar. She keeps a book on her dresser which no wise man of antiquity, of the Middle Ages, or of the present age has been able to know; a book that contains unknown phenomena. Nature puts an end to man's life in an instant, and also to his goods, that is, to his wealth, because Nature has very powerful forces against all humanity. That is why the suicide blows off his skull, and the high mountain ridges are witnesses of men who have frozen their hearts because of a futile whim: cowards! It is true that man after birth cries because of realizing that his sentence is confirmed, etc. But God said, "Help yourself and I shall be your help"! This is why the man who commits suicide is cursed, because he takes God's right, and when he comes to the tribunal of God's justice, God disowns him saying: "Who has called you? I do not know you."

148. Many men commit suicide because a woman betrayed them or refused them or because they failed in business; others because of pride. The woman who commits suicide should be left alone because she is like a snake, because each one of the proud hairs of her head turns into a snake when she combs or does her hair at the fountain. But we should develop the mystery of the Immaculate Conception when [the woman] caught the snake and "placed it under her foot." Here is required good judgment and thinking because the woman who is consecrated should not wear long hair. For her there is the monastery for nuns, for sisters and for mothers; for her there is the thought of Saint Rosalia of Palermo, and the interpretation of the image of my thought, because one of the daughters of Israel was crowned Universal Queen of all creation, and in her lies the mystery of the most Holy Trinity.

149. Women today do not wait for a man's declaration of love, that is, the word demonstrating to humanity that it was not true that originally the snake deceived the first woman; she had in her hair, and still has today, thousands of snakes, and therefore, it was she who deceived the first man when the appointed time had come, because the laws of nature had to be fulfilled, as is the case today in all the animal and vegetable kingdoms.

Chapter 3
Marriage and Passion

150. Marriage was sacred because in it the saints were born, and from a marriage was born the liberator of humanity, although he was not born like the rest of us. He is the son of an old carpenter named Joseph; and his parents did not busy themselves searching for jewelers to make a cradle of gold or crystal, like the ones in which Adrian, Trajan, and Theodosious, the sons of the Caesars, were rocked. Because Joseph's son was rocked in a humble cradle made of straw, as the chicks of the fowl which are rocked by the four winds of the earth, in the same way that the children of the Indian marriage are born, on a pile of wild straw, as was the case with the one who writes this book, who is the legitimate son of Mariano Lame and Dolores Chantre; Mariano Lame the legitimate son of Angel Mariano Lame; Angel Mariano Lame the legitimate son of Jacobo Lame; and Jacobo was the one who fled from the hamlet of Lame on the highest crest of Tierradentro, because of the sentence of the governor of that *parcialidad* due to disobedience. And when Jacobo Lame arrived in Silvia and appeared before the chief of that region, he could not remember his name, which was Estrella y Cayapu, on his mother's side; and for this reason the Indian chief named him Jacobo Lame. For this reason my name is Manuel Quintín Lame, and until this day non-Indians have regarded me and still regard me with the greatest contempt so that if their looks were machine guns firing in secret, the Indian Quintín Lame would have already lost his material life.

151. In the white man's marriage I have seen extraordinary happenings which have served me for information. But in the house of the Indian marriage one finds humility, peace, tranquility; the children of the Indian marriage live naked, sleep naked, move around naked, and work naked outdoors until they themselves earn their clothes, but their clothes are very different from the white man's clothes.

152. When the first child is born to the marriage of an Indian girl and an Indian chief, a fiesta is celebrated. If the newly born is a girl, all the women of the area come, if it is a boy, all the men come to the fiesta, bringing music and offering different kinds of music to the child and also all kinds of working tools for the garden. For ten minutes the child is placed on the tools on the floor and on the musical instruments; and also on several jewels that are given as presents. The same is done by the women to the girl, according to the work that awaits the newly born.

153. When I asked my father, Mariano Lame, to send me to school, he yelled at me twice: "Do you want school?" "Do you want school?" I answered, "Yes, *señor.*" Then he handed over to me a machete, an ax, a sickle, a shovel, and a bar, saying: "This is the real school of the Indian! Get going with your brothers to cut wheat and to clear the forest!" For a moment my heart was pierced with sadness, but then came gladness, together with the thought that I should fight against my father's command, as is described in chapters 2 and 3 of this book.

154. Because I am an Indian, a legitimate Indian, for which I am proud, because through my veins does not as yet run Spanish blood, thanks be to God! As an Indian, I have not known the sheepfolds which are the gardens of the old zoology produced by the ancient and current civilization. But on my own I have been able to know fully this zoological garden, which is referred to in chapters 1-4 of this book.

155. In the Indian marriage the matron, or the woman of the house, is the legislator inside the home, and the man is the legislator outside the home, and together they are the household's gods of the home. When children are born, the parents become the second gods of the earth to struggle with the rearing of the newly born, and so on and so forth. Because all of us Indians should educate our children, teaching them how to know God, through the Most Holy Virgin, who is the spouse of Joseph, the carpenter, mentioned before, and through the Most Holy Virgin we rise towards God; but it needs to be with a unique and living faith, and with such a perfect charity that the left hand does not feel the movement when the right hand is about to do a charity; and knowing who is truly in need of charity, which is what is called alms, because there are many healthy persons going around begging as a business; because I have visited some towns and cities in the Colombian territory, many times as a prisoner, other times free.

156. Charity is meant to be given — hear this well, you Indians — to an ailing person, to a prisoner, to one traveling on foot, who is exhausted with thirst and hunger. This is the true charity; this is the incense that appeases the divine wrath! And what is this incense? It is through the Virgin Mary that it reaches up to God, because she is the charitable mother towards all her children who say the rosary with faith and constancy. And she was the maker and designer of the image of my mind, and she took me by the hand to point out to me, one by one, all the flowers of the garden (of my thought) of wisdom, when I came to know what is human intelligence, that is, good understanding or science. And up to this day non-Indian men have been unable to divorce me from it, nowhere in Colombia, thanks be to God!

157. Passion has a place within the marriage that is truly marriage, that is to say, where the household gods struggle to establish an internal legislation. And sometimes they cry and other times whisper in each other's ear, like a couple of pigeons, the woman with a prudent love towards the male or husband, because the Holy Spirit has said that in true marriage the woman is the devout sex, because she gives shape to two kinds of persons for the service of humanity and heaven. And when her son makes a mistake, she calls upon God to punish him, not upon the devil. Why do I say this? Because there are some mothers who insult the child with crude words, forgetting that he is the child of her innocence, the child of her love, the child of her will to control, not realizing that it was these three elements which combined in shaping the child in her womb; forgetting that tomorrow she will have to render accounts before that frightful Supreme Judge who condemned the first man and the first woman to abandon the garden which they were cultivating; forgetting that tomorrow will arrive, the "tomorrow" of which I have been talking all the time, when the irreversible hour comes to know reality; the "tomorrow" that surprised the powerful ruler who had to depart wearing his scepter with no time to say goodbye to his people; which also surprised the wise man still holding the steel pen in his hand, but without yet knowing the Palace of Wisdom, which human nature holds, where the bird of immortality sings, at the precise minute when one could not hear any longer the tick-tock of the machine that moves the human armature, which then becomes food of the birds of prey. However, what is that bird that sings? That bird is the human soul which left flying over the garden which the man cultivated with his good works on this earth, such as charity, prayer, fasting, confession rightly made, and the practice of penance, before the arrival of that "tomorrow" which was not tomorrow any longer, but today!

158. Man, therefore, should work as if he were going to live one hundred years and should live as if death would arrive at this very moment, because the righteous man thinks about life, but even much more about death. And who prepared this man? My mother. Oh, my dear mother. May she rest in peace!

159. Let's remember Joseph the Carpenter who intended to accuse his wife before the judges when he knew that she was pregnant, etc. Let's remember also when Jesus got lost and was found by his parents. In the same manner shall be found the children who were abandoned by their parents because of a whim, because through her faith that mother found her son again; for this reason the child needs to be brought up holding bread in one hand and the flog in the other, and calling upon God to punish him, not upon the devil. This is the beginning and the end of a mother who educates her children when they start to know material things.

160. Let's remember the warrior who died with the sword in his sheath, who had abandoned his troops, and the guards did not have the courage to report him to the general, or to the commanding officer, etc. And death jumped on him, giving him no time to sound the alarm. Let's remember the greedy rich man who became one of the martyrs of the devil, and how was death for this rich man? He pleads before the Sanhedrin of doctors saying, "Don't let me die, because I have money." But they look at each other and give no answer because they also will have to die despite being doctors.

161. I wished to tell the story of greedy rich men whose deaths I had to witness, and describe how terrible their deaths were, but I stop for now in this chapter and in another book I shall explain it in detail.

Chapter 4
The Unjust Trial of the Indian who Came down from the Mountain to the Valley of Civilization

162. I have to share a thought which has been struggling to be born in the interior of the son of the forests, so that men may know it and also the children and the youth who stroll around reading books where science is written, but they learn to say what they read, and to know what they are supposed to say; whereas the son of the forests says only what he has seen and witnessed, because the witness that is able to say "I saw it" is the basis of right and justice, commutative, distributive, and legal, before God and men.

163. Non-Indian youth, with their personal interests in mind, learn what is written in those books, be it the truth or not, because many writers write what they want, some out of passion, others with a lack of civil courage. Because many historians, lacking integrity, rely on a kind of science that is the enemy of history, and which to this day wages war against it. Because in the same way that the hawk wages war against the wild pigeon of the forests, and the fox against the hen, and the big fish against the little one, the spider against the fly, and the woman against the woman, so has the Colombian white man waged war against me, because he has considered himself the only one who possesses science and knowledge, over against me, the Indian Quintín Lame. But he has mistaken my thought, which now appears without beauty, like the philosopher who drew the laws of thought and the astronomer who figured the movement of the stars; like the poet who sings his stanzas interpreting the love of the human heart; like the smith who pierces and shapes the finest metals with his chisel and who is able to set a machine in motion, a machine that needs to have life, which produces motion thanks to three elements: gasoline, fire, and oil.

164. What shall I say of the heroic life lived in the midst of the sublime darkness of ignorance? But I with a reverent thought have created or renewed day by day a sacrifice, in silence, so as to fulfill the goal dedicated to the gratitude of my Indian brethren who lie in ignorance, who need to know my simplicity and lowliness, sprinkled with blood and bathed in tears every moment, and every day of my life. Because I receive slander coming from non-Indians with a smile, like the mother who looks out for her children who have gone astray with her countenance full of love, a countenance and smile that spread over the wickedness and contempt of her children.

165. Thus, slowly, I have come to see in the midst of such darkness what the Indian is called to become in the future, because he has the right to lead the destiny of humanity because the Indian has his head in the same place as the white man and so is with the rest of his body; because man bows his head before the motive, not before a white face.

166. The judicial records show the ways in which the judges dealt with me in the district of Popayán and how they held me incommunicado for an entire year in the dungeons of Popayán and how they forbade that even a piece of paper wrapping a candy bar reach me, much less a book. But that "image" of which I have been writing since the beginning of the book shall best interpret my experience to the Indians who still lie asleep in the nest of ignorance like a rat left starving to death trapped in a hole; but once they study with attention the present book, they shall hear the ring of the bell in the same way that the prisoner hears the sound of the bell at eight o'clock in the evening when a friend comes to pay him a visit. The aristocrats of Popayán who plunged me in the dungeon intended to isolate my knowledge from the Indians, but they were not as smart as the prisoner, because once I was left alone with a guard, a man called "the good" used to visit me bringing in and taking out communications every week to different places and in different forms.

167. The law of fatalism, the law of pride, the law of envy, the law of lies, the law of hate, the law of slander, the law of contempt, the law of threats, the law of bribes and deceit, like birds of prey, fell upon me, as if they were to eat a rotten dog but could not do any harm because instead of a dead dog, they found a lion locked behind steel bars! Even though the seven vices raged against the seven virtues of the Indian Quintín Lame, they could not prevail, because their blow could not penetrate the steel cage; the black birds of prey looked like black rats who lacked the courage to confront the Indian wolf who had been transformed into a polar bird who was sailing and resting on the white foam of the sea, as he continues to do still today, knowing as he does the spirits or gods of the seas, and all their powerful elements. They have not been able and shall not be able to prevail against the men of very high faith, because God is infinite and his mercy is more profound than the seas, deeper than hell, more vast than the heavens, more beautiful than the paradise of the heavenly courts. Its equal is only the Palace inhabited by the Lamb which was destined to be sacrificed on the cross in defense of humanity; the Lamb that was tempted by the devil; the Lamb that came to take away the sins of the old Adam, that is to say, error; likewise the daughter of Joachim and Ana, who was destined to pay for old Eve's whim, taking off the crown of thorns of the Lamb from the cross; for these reasons the gates of hell have not prevailed, and shall never prevail, over God's mercy. That is why the sea of slander could not drown the poor little Indian who writes these thoughts when he had to carry a thick iron bar of twenty-eight pounds and iron shackles, with my hands tied with handcuffs, on my back, thrown on the ground like a pig for the slaughter. This happened at the police barracks in Popayán at the hands of the "brave" Leonardo Ramírez who received the orders from the governor before I was put in the dungeon for one entire year incommunicado. These events took place on May 12 of 1915, because I was captured on the 9th, on the bridge of the

El Cofre River, because of treason, which the conservative government paid in the amount of 400 pesos. With this money Judas Iscariot bought a mint to make gold coins, and as he had sold me, he was also sold, and was caught red-handed by the police: because he who kills with a knife shall die by the knife, and man shall be judged according to the way he has judged others, and with the rod that measures others shall he himself also be measured (words of the Holy Spirit).

168. Of the civilians who took the name of judicial persons, and of the men who were consecrated to defend with their authority God's house, only a very few follow the commandments of that Lamb which was sacrificed on the cross; because there are many priests who hate the Indian and obey the white man, not realizing that the priest is the one who should gather the sheep in the fold, with that love, that goodness which God taught the apostles when he took them to the mountain to educate them, saying: "Blessed are the poor in spirit because theirs is the kingdom of heaven"; but he did not say "blessed are the rich, the white, the lawyers, the intelligent, etc." What he taught was peace and concord among men, but among those of good will.

169. Let's remember the voice that was heard from on high when the Lamb that was to be sacrificed for the redemption of the world was born: "blessed he who comes in the name of the Lord, who brings peace to the earth"; but it refers to men of good will, and this good will is not found in every priest, Illustrious Bishop of Tolima, Most Illustrious Archbishop of Colombia, and Your Holiness Pius XII. Do you ask why? Well, this is the thought of the wild jackass, who lives in the wilds, who climbed the cedar of Lebanon, to the proud treetop, to catch a glimpse of the majestic genius of the forest, to which I referred in chapters 1-4 of book I. That cedar tree crowns the majesty of the Colombian forests, which are shaken by the four winds of the earth; and that proud treetop, swung by the four winds of heaven, greets the powerful artesan who built the clock that is placed above our heads, and which regulates and fulfills the laws of nature; but these laws are incomprehensible to many, because nature holds phenomena that are unknown to men.

170. Consider, for example, the temple to the god of the rivers; and the temple of the gods and the miracles of my ancestors; consider the gospels that were preached to Indian multitudes by the priests of my ancestors, three hundred years before October 12 [1492], etc., etc.

171. That man named Jesus, who is the second person of the Most Holy Trinity, is the man who instituted the good, because he was the spiritual teacher who called to himself the children, healed the sick, gave life to the dead, gave food to the hungry, and drink to the thirsty, and who ordered Christians to fulfill his commandments. But many priests baptize first the child of the white man, and a long time afterwards the child of the Indian. I wished to mention the places, and the names of the priests, but I reserve them for later. Many priests say, "I belong to the Company of Jesus," but it is only words. I do not accuse all the priests of Colombia, only some who are weak, because we are all born of a woman, and this human weakness derives from the fact that God placed error in man's brain, and there it will remain until the day when we all shall appear in Tofafar Valley, before the tribunal in which the sheep shall be separated from the goats.

Chapter 5
Spiritual Manna

172. The good Christian's manna is Christ; because "Christian" means the one that is Christ's, the one who is given to his holy service; like the sacrifices of major and minor cattle that were offered by the ancient Christians to placate God's wrath, etc., etc.

173. But today the liberator of humanity, the man who, through his martyrdom, that is, through his passion and death, liberated the innocent Abel, also liberated all the others who died in God's grace during the first stone age. I should finish up, deepen, and expand this philosophical thought, but now is not the appropriate time, for I should first let the mist of the forest cross from forest to forest, and I have to leave behind my own wool, entangled in the thorns of the bush, wherein every one of us who crosses the prairie of the valley leaves something behind: the sheep its wool, and man his virtue.

174. The record of my thought, or thoughts, does not reach major heights; it is rather like the cloud that hovers over the prairie, and which also remains for some moments over the forest; as when the eagle shakes her thick plumage and combs it, getting ready to soar into the skies. In the same stage remains today the thought of the Indian who was educated in the forests, watching the chicks of my thought which very soon shall fly like a concert of pigeons and whisper out there in the garden of science of civilization.

175. I have said "spiritual manna" because it was from that garden that Noah ate, and also his family, during the time when he sailed on the waters which had swallowed humanity: and that because he was a good Christian.

176. Remember the thoughts of Moses, the hero of the people of Israel; remember the thoughts of Nebuchadnezzar when he tied up the three youths because they had refused to worship the statue; remember the prophet when he was thrown into the lion's den; in the same way I have been the victim since my tender youth of the experts of envy, of usury, and of sophisms; experts who are the staunchest enemies of the Indian Quintín Lame, myself. But they have not been able to destroy me or humiliate me as they have done before to other Indians, according to history, because I have taken refuge in Noah's vessel. And what is Noah's vessel? It is the Immaculate Conception |of Mary| to whom all Christians pray, saying: "Oh Mary, conceived without sin, intercede on behalf of us sinners who come to thee." Because it could be the most corrupt man, but if he is devout to the Virgin, she will lead him to the mansion of bliss!

177. The record of all my campaigns shows that the attacks of those experts of usury and sophisms have been broken against the triumphant and persuasive wall of Mary, conceived without sin; because this is the spiritual manna of the Christian; because Mary conceived without sin is the sanctuary that preserves the mystery of the Most Holy Trinity; and she indicated it to me by giving me two roses for a crown: one rose for life, and the other for death. The flower of life was faith, a very high and lively faith, which taught me the prehistory of my ancestors in the times when they used to sing hymns to the Sun God in the same way that Christians used to offer their holocausts to the God Jehovah, before the coming of Jesus Christ; the Sun God of whom historians hardly mention when they refer to the Bochica of the Tequendama Falls. And I ask why and for what purpose did the Bochica appear? Well, this is a fabrication of thinkers, because redemption took place in another form, that is, the redemption to which the Tequendama Falls refers, from which Bochica appeared. Because, was he born of a woman? Was he not rather the son of the God of the rivers? I do not want to reveal to Spanish science what I know of the domain of the waters, how, why, and for what purpose, because my non-Indian enemies are very treacherous and hate me to death.

178. The flower of death is man's reality in the moment when he is about to exhale his last breath, when he sees the light of immortality which allows him to see the good works of faith and charity, and to take the road to eternity. This is the road which Jesus Christ opened, and all Christians shall live for a long time in that promised land, if we have served and loved those second gods who are our parents, and through them the infinite God of mercy; and as long as that time lasts, man shall remain man.

179. Man's spiritual manna is the Holy Host that is raised at the altars at the time of the celebration of the holy sacrifice of the Mass, so that we may partake in the same way in which the apostles took part in the last supper when the master said to them: "Take, eat, this is my body; take, drink, this is my blood; and all who eat of this bread and drink of this blood shall live forever."

180. Man's aspiration is not only to pile up riches for time but to embellish the crown of immortality which is faith together with good works. The same is true of science: when it is not accompanied by faith, it perishes in the claws of error.

181. I have said before that Ollo was the image of my thought because she was the image of the thought of my sovereign ancestors, who offered holocausts to the Sun God, and this god provided everything, everything for them. Others had faith in the God of the rivers, and still others in the God of the moon, etc. Of these gods, the mightiest one was the Sun God who excelled among them and sent a messenger to redeem the waters. And why? Because the god of the waters had taken possession of innumerable gardens and habitations.

182. Now, let me ask historians how and why did these things happen? Because his thoughts are hidden and misunderstood out there in the cemetery of the prehistory of my Guananí race, before October 12 of 1492.

183. Because the image of my thought was transformed through a mysterious dream under the forests of ignorance and illiteracy in the time when I used to greet others, saying, *auchimga,* and it was not *auchimga,* but *buenos días*; and when I used to say to my grandfather, *cuscachi,* and it was not *cuscachi* but *hasta mañana*. Because my language was transformed, as had happened to my thought, which today is transformed into ideas, but not expressed in proper language studied in a primary school or high school, where my non-Indian enemies have studied for so many years.

Chapter 6
Man's Friend

184. Who is, or could be, man's friend? The history of philosophy says that man's friend is man's heart; but it cannot be! Why? Because it is true that the heart is a good friend, but there are times when it appears wearing a mask! The good thing is that it does not grow old!

185. The civil knowledge that I have of universal history tells me that man's good friends are the dollar and a good intelligence because with these two elements man feels himself happy in any land, in any city, and in all the inhabited fields that one may cross during youth; but he has to have a good or precocious memory to hear the murmur of the waters, and the harmonious melody of human nature over material nature.

186. And what shall I say of the nature of the spiritual world? About it Moses said nothing after his return to his world; the ox said nothing about it after its mooring; about that nature nothing has been said by the poets of the eucharist; that nature was made known only by the one who was born in the Inn of Bethlehem; one needs only to know how to interpret the mysteries of the incarnation, life, passion, and death of the one who died among two thieves, hated by the populace, and sentenced by the Caesar and the Roman Governor.

187. Some say that man's friend is the dog; others say that man's friend is the person who comes to visit when one is sick or in jail; others say that man's friend is one's mother; and still others say that man's friend is a good wife, etc. Which of these shall be the focus of attention according to good reason? Because, what happens when one falls prisoner away from home where only God knows, but not one's friends, or neighbors, or wife, or mother?

188. Well, the true friend is the dollar in the pocket, together with a good intelligence which does not let man fall in the claws of error, and even when accused, God and his good intelligence shall vindicate him because God is the Supreme Judge over all the judges of the world, and above God there is no one. The Holy Spirit said to man, "God is above all things, and man shall be measured by the same rod with which he measures others, and with the same judgments that he judges, he himself shall be judged."

189. It is true that when one is made prisoner near his residence or in the same district, one receives visits; but one is also visited by the lawyers who offer to secure freedom for a handful of money, etc.

190. In regard to what was already said about man's real friend, I need to go to the root of things: because human reality does not last in this world, because everything is transitory, and man is like the soft wind that shakes the flower, and only ice and solitude is left, in whose arms man remains sleeping forever.

191. Because in the human heart there is no [lasting] reality — the mother abandons her son; the wife abandons her husband; the bride her bridegroom; the sister her brother; and the domestic dog bites his own master when he returns in the evening, in spite of having been the companion which, day in and day out, had walked and eaten with him.

192. What shall I say of the many judges who insisted in bringing me to trial with threats, forgeries, and lies? And what about the Superior Court of Popayán in the years from 1907 to 1922? And what to say of Rebollero Joaquín who belonged to that court until the end? In another book I shall report on the briefs presented by Rebollero Joaquín, and on the sentences of that court in defense of the poor little Indian, with the exception of the brief presented by Dr. José Hilario Cuellar, already mentioned in book I of this work.

193. I hope that it will not be said that it is my custom to find fault with juridical persons in charge of administering justice in matters defined by the law, which is the thought of the legislator turned into idea. Take, for example, the resolution given in 1923 by Dr. Sofonias Yacú of the House of Representatives, when he was commissioned by the President of the House to investigate the charges which I presented about the bad administration of justice in regard to the crime in Los Limpios. It was on March 12 of 1922 when Señor Ricardo Perdomo C., together with the chief of police, Señor Luis Solano, of the district of Neiva, department of Huila, cowardly and villainously murdered three defenseless Indian peasants while they were sleeping in their house, to which I already referred above in chapter 8, book I, of this work. But here, and in a future work that this little Indian shall write, I have to unmask the tangle of lies, sophisms, and false logic with which the civilized Spaniards, Ricardo Perdomo C., Luis

Solano, and the official investigator, Dr. Luis Ignacio Andrade, who was at the time secretary of government of Huila, tried to cover up the crime.

194. The same can be said of the judges and of the inspector of police! And what shall I say of the wicked court, that is, of the tribunal of Neiva? Because it has scratched the surface of nature with its equivocal pen, and crossed out the dawn of the destiny and ministry of my race! As had been said by Sinviora, before October 12 of 1492, the Indian race and its wealth would fall prey under *Guagaz,* which means, the white man. God delays, but never forgets!

195. When Sofonias Yacú presented his report to the House about the crime of Los Limpios, Dr. Luis Ignacio Andrade thundered against it, but Dr. Yacú reaffirmed his report. Later, Dr. Luis Ignacio Andrade said to me in the privacy of his room in Bogotá, when the Conservative Party had been reduced to nothing, that he had done all he could to help in my defense, but it was a lie, because that is the way in which the Indian race has been deceived since October 12 of 1492 until today, everywhere, in all the lands inhabited by my forefathers.

196. Prehistory has shown me the cemeteries that the Guananí Planet keep hidden in its bowels, which Spanish civilization has not been able to discover; nor have they been able to discover the large treasures of carved gold which are also deposited in the bowels of the Guananí Planet. And many other treasures are protected by powerful rivers because their owners were devotees of the god of the rivers, whereas those which are hidden in the bowels of the earth belonged to the devotees of the Sun. And what about the devotees of the moon? Those three planets are the only witnesses and owners of the treasure or treasures of my ancestors, treasure of extraordinary dimensions, and carved with extraordinary beauty. Because in them is carved the image of Indian monarchs, in solid gold, surrounded by fetishes carved in gold, and which no civilized Spaniard has been able to discover, not even one of them, because of the selfishness and envy which are like poison that makes those treasures invisible to the sight of civilization.

197. My Indian brethren: Beware of white or mestizo friends! Among that race there are no material friends of ours, the Indians. The white man accepts the Indian as friend only when the Indian humiliates himself and places himself under his orders. Take the example of some priests who have hated the campaigns of the Indian Quintín Lame in Cauca, Valle del Cauca, Huila, Tolima, etc. In another book I shall report the facts and the truth of the events that took place in each department, if God grants me life.

198. The Colombian Indian is the flower of contempt, cultivated by the white man who arrived from Spain on October 12 of 1492. It becomes satanic hate when the Indian claims his right and does not let himself be robbed and cheated, or his property stolen; or when he defends his own kin; or when he is able to give them lessons in practice and in theory for the present and for the future. When the Indian possesses major and minor cattle, or a coffee plot, or a wheat plot, etc., the white man says, "You are my friend, my pal"; but when the Indian lives off his daily work, nobody turns a face towards him; the white man looks down on the wretched poor as he would look at a rotten dog lying on the street; he tightens his nose and says: "Those Indians smell like hell!" But if the same white man knows that the Indian has enough, then the Indian does not smell like hell anymore, and he approaches him with a scoffing smile, offering a miserable cigar or cigarette.

199. This is, my Indian brethren, the mirror that never loses its luster, because what has been said is the truth, and nothing but the truth!

200. Now, what shall I say of politics? It is (hear this, you Indians!) the element that buries us, day by day, in the cemetery of pain and sadness. My intentions are with all my heart to protect the future which still lies asleep in ignorance, so that tomorrow this book can serve as a microscope, to confront the enemy of the Indians, that we may know the Prairie of our great destiny, and do not rush like women in love, abandoning their parents' love, etc., etc., in search of the great society of civilization, because we Indians have a greater memory, and inspiration comes to us faster than lightning when it breaks through the darkness of the night. The Indian strolls with greater poise and faster than the bee among all the flowers of the garden of science.

201. Politics, therefore (hear this, Indian brethren), is like birds of prey having a banquet, because the politician who does the least thunders with words and with his pen, offering to the ignorant Indian peasant what he is lacking, inventing things, as when the seducer deceives with sweet words the woman in love, until the moment when he is satisfied, etc., and the woman is not a virgin anymore, is not a lady anymore, and is despised by everybody. The same happens to the poor Indian peasant during the days of politics, when he comes down to the urns [to vote], because representatives later will not remember the promises made to the poor Indian. Some of them say that, as conservatives, it is necessary to defend the Church and religion. Those are lies because the Church is defended by God; the Church falls into the hands of her enemies for the little faith and misbehavior of her children, as when the tablets of the law which were in the Ark fell in the old times into the hands of the enemies; but it was God's punishment for [Israel's] disorder.

202. In 1930 some priests had disputes over politics: some of them said that one should vote for Dr. Guillermo Valencia and others for Vasquez Cobo. There were "Valencista" bishops and "Cobista" bishops because the moment had arrived when human intelligence was confused in a manner similar to the tower of confusion of ancient times.

Chapter 7
The Spirit of the Poor Little Indian
Who Writes this Work

203. Man has two spirits because he has two souls: a human soul and inside the human soul inhabits another soul that is man's spiritual soul, which is the soul for God. The human soul is known, but the spiritual soul is invisible and nobody knows it. My knowledge of psychology is very little because I learned it, or learned to interpret it, when I was contemplating the Prairies which form the valleys of civilization.

204. And how was that? Watching the rays of the sun which at five thirty in the morning in a place called the Orient announce its arrival with extraordinary beauty coloring the clouds and the infinite in red and blue and lifting up the spirit of the wayfarer who carries his body to the grief and the duty of the day. At the same time the universal choir of harmonious songs that nature has gets ready for the devotees of the sun, bursting each one of them with songs and their special stanzas. And I was contemplating those Prairies, like Jesus Christ was once contemplating the city of Jerusalem where he was going to die, unjustly tried by a wicked court. But Jesus Christ was the divine man, the immortal man, who held his empire in that immortality unknown to us. But he taught man to think how to think. He foresaw the thought of everyone who belonged of his following, the thoughts of the present and of the future. And he said to his men, "Tomorrow some will give me away and others will deny me, etc.," thus revealing that in the human heart there is no reality. Because I would like to express some thoughts against Luther and against Calvin and against Vicente Arenas, the swindler, priests and soldiers of the Church who were defeated by their weakness and vice, together with many others whom I do not mention for the moment.

205. It is the human soul which builds the Palace for the happiness of the immortal soul when she leaves the body. And how does she come out of the body? In the same way that the warrior's sword comes out of its sheath, because the sheath is like the human soul. But if the warrior allows his sword to get rusty, so that when he needs to present it to his higher in command it is stained, he is not considered a good warrior. Likewise with man's spiritual soul: if stained, it cannot be presented before the Court of Divine Justice!

206. And how to get rid of that stain? By doing penance by means of true faith. And how does the human soul wage its combats?

207. First, by offering herself to God, our Lord, that is to say, through the suffering of blows, beatings, robbings, the feet pierced with thorns, etc., etc., bleeding with humility and saying to our Lord, "In your hands I trust my sufferings for satisfaction of all my sins."

208. Secondly, God immediately assuages the pain, etc., because God is present everywhere, penetrating and searching the human heart.

209. Thirdly, take, for example, the history of Isidro, the tiller of the land, and of many other cultivators who now enjoy the fruits of their humility in the Palace of immortality.

210. And when was that Palace built? We cannot know; because before the creation of the raw material, God already existed in himself; and God is the architect of the Palace of immortality as well as the builder of the Palace of wisdom, because wisdom is not for everybody. Because wisdom was granted only to Solomon and even then it escaped from him because of the pleasures of the flesh.

211. There will be geniuses and talents after Solomon, but not wise men, and up to this day the image of the winds and the image of the years have kept silent about a second wise man.

212. The universal history of Christian philosophy speaks only of those who have strolled the gardens of science; gardens that were cultivated by other men who now lie asleep in some corner of the world, abandoned by their friends, by their pleasures, and by the riches of this world. And the same thing happens to the authors of anti-Christian philosophy in spite of being this latter science, prior to the first.

213. But the Indian Quintín Lame, myself, has not known the paths which St. Augustine knew, because he was educated in Carthage, the great African metropolis; take also the example of Virgil; and of the Mute Bull[4] whose shadow is the concern of so many thinkers who wish to know where he did his last bellowing, to descend and enjoy the Palace of immortality; but all these three were educated by teachers. The poor little Indian, however, has not known or enjoyed these principles of knowledge or education; rather, nature educated me under its shade, under its heat and under its frosts; under those shades she showed me the Idyll of Poetry and the three kingdoms, mineral, animal, and vegetable. She taught me to think how to think; she pointed out to me my desk in the desert delivered to me by solitude.

214. And what is solitude? It is a maiden who enjoys nature. And both used their key to open the ministry for this Indian to enter, who has been hated, slandered, chained, jailed, and insulted by word and deed by the descendants of the Spanish who arrived on October 12 of 1492 to this land in search of fortune. But they did not come to civilize the Indians who inhabited these Guananí lands, but to plunder their wealth and to place them under their boots, so that they do not complain even though they hurt, and willingly walk like sheep to the slaughterhouse; for this reason the white and the mestizo hate me to death, but have not been able to make me climb even one step towards the gallows, thanks be to God! And the Supreme God to whom I am grateful is Divine Nature, upon which human nature depends, and who dictated and made known the very laws that regulate human nature, according to the ministry of wisdom and wealth. And this wealth the most famous theologians of the ancient age and of the Middle Ages and of the present age have not been able to foresee or interpret, or to study that marvelous book whose pages are not of gold and whose cover is not made of any of the precious metals; its title reads: "The Book of the World, etc." This is the thought of the one who educated himself under the shade mentioned before.

215. Solomon, the wise man, was the only one who knew that book, but he did not say anything about it in his psalms, or in his sayings, or in his other works. Solomon considered writing a book entitled "La Radiola," dealing with the three kingdoms of human nature, to which this little Indian has given so much thinking in the present book.[5] Unfortunately he was held back by the love of a woman who overwhelmed him with carts of perfumes. If a wise man was held back and dragged by error, what could not happen to an illiterate Indian who was never taught even the roundness of the letter "o"? But that faith of which I have spoken in the thoughts about immortality has allowed me to know some principles, very great, profound, and lofty, which are not yet converted into ideas, but are only thoughts, which I have written in this work.

Chapter 8
The Birth of the Fountain in Darkness

216. What do I mean by "darkness"? I mean the ineptitude of the illiteracy or the savagery of the wild ass, that is, of the Indian who used to greet others saying *auchimga* (hello), *auchimiuy* (walk), *guachimiyu* (run), *cuscahi* (good-bye), etc., etc., in the dialect of the Páez Indians, of the mountain chain known as *Tierradentro* (hinterland). And why are they called "Paéces"? Because in the heart of the immense mountain chain a river is born called the Páez River, of which for the moment I do not say any more, nor about the history of the Indian sovereigns, nor of the sages who lived in the area before October 12 of 1492.

217. The fountain with great slowness built its own riverbed to flow and to water the rose gardens whose stems have been broken by the envy of the Spanish civilization which arrived on October 12 of 1492. But today all those groups of civilized men, non-Indian men, are buried with their capes on, biting their lips, etc.

218. That fountain was born in darkness breaking through the sardonix rock, very near the house of the Indian who was studying the spirit of the book of human life in the garden of science; and the fountain did not spring from human nature, but from the mystery of Divine Nature, which has preserved my life to this day.

219. Many have wished my death, have made attempts on my life, have resorted to the witch goddess, but today find themselves curbed to the ground, lying spread underground; others robbed all my possessions and burnt to the ground my place of residence, and still others stole my cultivations, against the law and against all justice; the municipal authorities of Ortega denied my right, violating the law and the charter of rights, and put justice in jail so that it could not be commutative, distributive, and legal in my favor. In Ortega I have been looked upon and still am looked upon as a wild beast because I don't allow my Indian brothers who occupy *resguardo* lands to be robbed and cheated, because Ortega is a den of dishonest, deceitful, and perjurious men.

220. Sirs, would you ask me why? History has been and still is the deposit of my actions, and it will answer.

221. The mysterious shadow of Jehovah was transformed into a ray of light to point out to me the fountain produced by the breaking of the sardonix rock, making me understand that savagery and ineptitude did not exist anymore, and that I was not any longer the wild ass, but the devoted Indian (*el indio aficionado*) who would come to know the human destinies wherein the mystery of human life is hidden.

222. But it is the thought of a mountaineer who received his inspiration on the mountain, educated himself on the mountain, and learned to think how to think on the mountain. He also went deep into the forest and climbed to the treetop of a proud cedar of Lebanon, to scatter his thoughts over the prairies of civilization; if they appear in this work limping, in the future they will surprise universal history because they are not the work of a fool. All the authors of ancient times and of the Middle Ages and of the present age refer to the schools where they were educated. For this reason I also should speak of the classrooms where I was educated by nature, the college of my education!

223. The first book: to watch the blowing of the four winds of the earth.

The second: to gaze at the Mansion of the four winds of Heaven.

The third: to observe the rise of the solar star in the East, and to watch when it dies in the twilight, and to realize that man, born of a woman, dies also in the same way.

The fourth book: to contemplate the smile of all gardens sown and tended by the Young Lady who dresses in blue and who crowns herself with flowers, and perfumes herself at her interminable dresser, etc., etc.

The fifth book: the unending choir of songs.

The sixth book: the beautiful garden of forest zoology.

The seventh book: to listen carefully to the conversation of the streams in the forest, which seemed to me like a concert of children passing from ecstasy to ecstasy.

The eighth book: the Idyll.

The ninth book: the book of true love, because it is not the lovers' secretary.

The tenth book: to study the harmonious rules of that lady by the name of Nature, in the Palace of her three kingdoms.

The eleventh book: on agriculture and on who are the owners, that is to say, the users.

The twelveth: the book of wild husbandry.

The thirteenth: the book of hygiene.

The fourteenth: the Metaphysics of the supreme reasons of this world, which are found in this book.

The fifteenth: Ontology, which points out and looks after being in general and its immediate attributes, etc.

224. And what shall I say of that book entitled "Logic," what was the key of my knowledge?

225. Under the shade of ancient oak trees and cedars of Lebanon I contemplated once the proud treetops which towered over the forests; I am similarly crowned among my people after 447 years of ineptitude and illiteracy, that is, since October 12 of 1492.

226. And these fifteen books which I have cited, who, do you think, could have shown them to me? I will reveal to you the secret: all of them have their origen in Theodicy, and they have been my consolation and in the future they shall be the virtues in the Palace of bliss. And the Idyll which I cited does not belong to poets who interpret the human heart; it is rather the Idyll of songs of the spiritual soul, which the prophet Isaiah heard in heaven and wrote them down.

Chapter 9
The Three Mansions that Support the Bird of Human Immortality

227. What are these three mansions? They are the three temples: firstly, the inexorable Court of Divine Judgment; secondly, the temple where the soul is purified; and thirdly, the temple where the soul enjoys the cooling shade of the immortal palm tree.

228. Coming to the end of the present book of thoughts, I should say something about the bird of human immortality because it is the human soul which becomes a dove, whiter than snow, purer than the brightness of the sun when it rises in the East to illuminate all humanity. And what is the origin of this thought? It is born of the interpretation of the Lord's ascension into the heavens, in body and soul, which is a mystery.

229. The man who knows how to suffer knows how to live, and he who does not know how to suffer does not know how to live. Because the liberator of humanity suffered to ensure the continuation of the Gospel in the holy sacrifice of the Mass inside his house called the Militant Church where we the great military go to wage war against the devil and to chase him out of our hearts; because if a man does not fear God, it is because the devil dwells in his heart, and the devil is God's enemy.

230. The flight of the soul was made known by the Condor of Immortality that flew over accompanied by a choir of pigeons which surrounded him in the heights; the first one was Abel the Innocent, and then Noah the Just, Abraham the generous, the faithful Moses, Joseph the chaste, etc., etc. This concert of pigeons had lived for four thousand years in the second mansion, getting ready to soar into heaven together with the Condor of Divinity. These birds were the souls of the righteous who had died in God's grace, and had been awaiting his holy arrival, to go with him to sing under the shade of the palm tree.

231. This mystery, as well as the others, was revealed so that the wild jackass, or the wild wolf, mentioned before in book II, chapter 8, hit by a ray of light, could become a student of the three powerful books kept by the forest and by the rugged mountains: Metaphysics (Ontology, Theodicy), Psychology, or the science of the human soul, and Cosmology, or the science of the world. These have been the grounds of my knowledge. These books which I have studied, mentioned in the last chapter, are not all, because there are thousands and thousands of them that have not been even perused by those men who have burnt their eyelashes during fifteen, twenty, or thirty years of study, etc. History calls some of them thinkers, others geniuses, other ingenious men, and others crooks or bandits, such as Nero!

232. What will historians call the little Indian Quintín Lame? Perhaps I will be called the Indian of the riverbanks, or the wolf educated in the Colombian forests by Nature, which presented him with those thousands of books to be able to talk about the inner recesses of the bird of human immortality. Because the Condor that flew over, accompanied by the pigeons, taught us that tomorrow we also shall fly, having been rewarded for the untiring perseverance of our good works; and we will fly surrounded by them, which will be the impulse of our own virtue, in the same manner in which the son of the old carpenter, called Jesus of Nazareth, who flew over from immortal eternity to this world and incarnated himself in the womb of a woman to vindicate or redeem humanity, or to pay on the cross for the error of the old Adam, as the woman who gave birth in the Inn of Bethlehem had also to pay at the bottom of the cross for the whim of the old Eve.

233. The mysteries of human nature have not been revealed as have been those of divine nature, thanks to which I have been able to transform my savagery into desire for learning, and thus to give birth to a book of thoughts, not written in proper language or with a fine calligraphy. Therefore, when the Spanish civilization which arrived on October 12 of 1492 will know my work, [its adherents] will gnash their teeth, muttering "*Cras, cras, cras.*" However, I stand by what I say, as the Roman governor who said, "What is written, is written."

234. Some Christian thinkers have spoken and still speak of the road to heaven, but they have not developed this thought as to how, why, and in what form. The human soul is the one that has a road, but the spiritual soul is spiritual. Now, let me point out to them that the breeze that crossed the mother forest, which is the perfumed fan of the young maiden, was felt by me, but I could not see it. It is likewise with the spiritual soul when it leaves the body, and no Christian thinker can be sure of having known the road to heaven. Because the flight to heaven is prepared by man himself with his good works, because faith that is not accompanied by good works is dead, as the sciences that are not accompanied by faith are dragged away by errors.

235. What shall I say of those unbelievers who do not believe in baptism, which was taught by the child born in the Inn of Bethlehem, who was baptized by St. John who ever after has been called St. John the Baptist? That baptism took place in the Jordan River, and the child was the one who had been worshiped by the wild ass and by other animals, who rendered him tribute at the place where he had been born, because men had despised him, following the proud aristocracy. The music was prepared by human nature which ordered those musicians to repeat their untiring stanzas; like those choirs which had sung in the highest, the choirs possessed by Divine Nature.

236. Christian thinkers have not developed the thought of the road to heaven; but the spiritual soul is a breath of the Divinity, because the divine breeze penetrated the human body to give impulse to that human soul referred to so many times. It was the eternal architecture which made the human armature, both the visible and the invisible, because man has two armatures.

237. A priest was talking to me about the road to heaven and how it was very narrow but covered with flowers; this is true of the flight towards heaven which was made known by the son of God the day that he ascended into heaven, having vindicated humanity, that is, having liberated the bird of immortality which had been kept in jail by the devil who was chained by one of the daughters of Israel with the name of Mary, conceived without sin.

238. The Indian Quintín Lame, "the wild jackass," "the savage Indian," "the brute," has been transformed, not into a jurist or a pedagogue, but into the wild jackass who renders homage to the newly born surrounded by poverty in the Inn of Bethlehem; because he did not need a cradle of gold or crystal, like the aristocrats who have persecuted and hated to death the treetop of science, which had smiled at the Indian from the riverbank when he was climbing the Cedar of Lebanon, in the shade of solitude; this solitude was the image of my mind, which showed me where to find the perfumed garden of the logic of Nature; the precious garden of human nature; the beautiful and perfumed garden which has filled all my thoughts which have been and are oriented towards a chimera. In solitude I knew the Idyll that has been praised and interpreted by poets other than the aristocratic and envious poets like the one who wrote *Anarcos*; in solitude is where the true book of philosophy is found, where the tick-tock of thought never stops, like the thoughts of Quintín Lame; where the thinker is not afraid of any event engendered by the civilization which arrived on October 12 of 1492 to murder, cowardly and villainously, my ancestors who had been born and raised in this Guananí land before October 12. That garden of human nature has told me not to be afraid of saying the truth to anyone, regardless of how white he might be, like those who threw me in the dungeon of Popayán for an entire year incommunicado with iron shackles, without having been heard or convicted in a trial. This was done by a gang of aristocrats from Popayán, for which reason Popayán is today in ruins, because of the injustice against the Indian councils! The Law of Compensation is drawing near, gentlemen!

239. The day shall come when a handful of Indians shall form a column to reclaim their rights as God reclaimed humanity, that is, as God rescued it from the tyranny of the devil; in the same way the Indian race shall rescue its rights in Colombia, and the white man shall become the tenant of the Indian, of those Indians who are still asleep in the mind of God, due to the hate, the evil administration of justice, and the envy of the white man against the Indian.

240. The white man will say about my book, "Those are beastlike things of the Indian Quintín Lame," because the white man has hated me and still hates me to death; has slandered me; has sworn falsely against me before God and men; has laughed at me and made mockery of me, making faces of hate as the devil does when he is unable to snatch away a man's soul.

241. These are, gentlemen, the thoughts of the knight of the sad countenance!

Manuel Quintín Lame

The book is completed the 29th of December of the year 1939.

NOTES

The following abbreviations are used in the Notes and Select Bibliography:

CDI, Comité de Defensa del Indio
CIDOC, Centro Intercultural de Documentaciòn (Cuernavaca, Mexico)
PUF, Presses Universitaires de France (Paris)

CHAPTER 1

1. The older members of the group, referred to as "old fighters" (*antiguos luchadores*), preferred to call Lame "General."
2. *Acta No. 72*, October 1967 (Tolima: Archivo del Cabildo Indígena de Ortega). Spanish Original: *"Aquí duerme el cacique Indio Manuel Quintín Lame Chantre, que no se dejó humillar de ninguna de las autoridades departamentales, ordinarias, municipales, ni de los ricos, acaparadores, archmillonarios, oligarcas, aristocratas, que le ofrecieron pagarle sumas de dinero para que abandonara el pleito del resguardo nacional de la tribu de Indígenas de Ortega, y el contestó: 'yo soy un defensor a pleno sol ante Dios y los hombres, que defiendo las tribus y huestes Indígenas de mi raza de la tierra Guananí: muerta, desposeída, débil, ignorante, analfabeta, abandonada triste y lamentablemente por la civilización.'"*
3. English translation: see Appendix. According to Abel Tique, president of the Lamista Indian Council of Ortega, Tolima, in 1970, the content of this work was dictated by Lame to Florentino Moreno B., a literate Indian who was gifted with beautiful penmanship. Tique become one of Lame's "secretaries" during his Tolima campaign through the 1930s and 40s, and was recognized by the Indians of the area as the oral "historian" of the movement. The manuscript was finished on December 29, 1939, and was jealously kept from strangers. However, it was used intensively by the most intimate of Lame's disciples, who could recite long paragraphs by heart on appropriate occasions. After Lame's death, the manuscript remained in the custody of the *cabildo*, especially its president, Abel Tique. It was Tique who lent the manuscript to me in 1970. Later, with the approval of the *cabildo*, the manuscript was published in a limited edition (1,000 copies) under the title *En Defensa de mi Raza* (Bogotá: Comité de Defensa del Indio, 1971), with an introduction by me. In this published form Lame's work is 133 pages long, divided into three sections: Prologue, pp. 1-10; Book I (eleven chapters), pp. 11-72; and Book II (nine chapters), pp. 73-133. For the sake of convenience to the reader, all references to Lame's manuscript quote the original Spanish title given by Lame himself, but shortened to "Pensamientos," indicating the paragraph where the quotation appears. For this purpose the paragraphs have been numbered consecutively from 1 to 241.
4. "Pensamientos," par. 222.
5. Ibid., par. 14.
6. The term "prophetic" is here used in the biblical sense to indicate a kind of theology marked by a paramount concern with justice as the criterion of genuine faith, in the light of a certain eschatological view of history. (See below, pp. 24ff.

The specific nature of Lame's theology will be analyzed in chapters 3 and 4.)

7. "Pensamientos," par. 239.

8. See full exposition and interpretation below, chapters 3 and 4.

9. "Pensamientos," par. 22, 47ff.

10. Ibid., par. 40.

11. Ibid., par. 22, 183.

12. Ibid., par. 222.

13. Ibid., par. 6. Besides "Pensamientos," two shorter manuscripts have been preserved. The first one, published in 1927, carries the title "El Derecho de la Mujer Indígena en Colombia" ["the right of indigenous women in Colombia"], 10 pages. It first appeared as a broadside endorsed by hundreds of Indian women whose names appear at the bottom of the leaflet. The original is said to have been signed by 14,000 Indian women. The second one is even shorter. It was written by Lame in the last years of his life. It is dated 1963, when his public activity had been reduced to a minimum, four years before his death. It is entitled "La Bola que Rodó en el Desierto" ["the ball that rolled in the desert"], 6 pages. Neither of these minor writings adds any new ideas or information not already contained in "Pensamientos." Both of them have been published in one booklet under my editorial responsibility with the title *Las Luchas del Indio que Bajó de la Montaña al Valle de la Civilización* (Bogotá: CDI, 1973).

14. I refer here to the view that sees theological activity as the bailiwick of a small number of qualified professionals whose credentials must include at the most basic level evidence of having had assimilated (or been assimilated by) the Western intellectual tradition. In this sense, "theology" has been regarded as one dimension of Western consciousness, sharing with the Western philosophical tradition its tendency to identify "being" with "thinking," as expressed, for example, by Hegel.

15. This attitude is revealed, for example, in certain interpretations of the *Popul Vuh* which Americanists have regarded for a long time as the most important single native-language text in the New World. One of the main reasons for this high regard is the pre-Columbian nature of its contents. However, the *Popul Vuh* has also here and there, particularly in its opening sections, material that clearly reflects the experience of the European conquest, a fact that many Americanists see with embarrassment and disappointment. Adolf E. Bandelier, for example, wrote a century ago that the *Popul Vuh* "appears to be, for the first chapters, an evident fabrication . . . a pious fraud" ("On the Distribution and Tenure of Lands and the Customs with Respect to Inheritance Among the Ancient Indians," *Annual Report 11*, Peabody Museum, 1878, pp. 385-448). More recent scholars have referred to the same passages as "syncretistic" or simple "paraphrases" of Genesis (see Munro S. Edmonson, "Narrative Folklore," in *Handbook of Middle American Indians,* vol. 6, Manning Nash, ed. [Austin: University of Texas Press, 1967], pp. 357-68).

16. This same attitude has detracted from interpretive studies made of the "cargo cults" of Melanesia, according to Jean Guiart: "Up to now, few anthropologists have troubled to analyze Christianity in the area as it has evolved over nearly two centuries. We talk of missionization (only) as an external factor which plays havoc with traditional society." Guiart suggests that "cargo cults" are best understood as creative responses to the specific forms in which Christianity was introduced in the area, as "the reinterpretation of occidental traditional religious ideas and structures by people who have chosen to make use of them as their own" ("The Millenarian Aspect of Conversion to Christianity in the South Pacific," in Sylvia L. Thrupp, ed., *Millennial Dreams in Action, Comparative Studies in Society and History* [The Hague: Mouton and Company, 1962], pp. 122-37).

17. This perspective has a long tradition. Francisco Ximénez, for example, the

Dominican friar who discovered the manuscript of the *Popul Vuh*, warned readers that even though the Indian text alluded to some truths " known to us through revelation," these allusions were, however, "wrapped in a thousand lies and tales" authored by "the father of all lies, Satan" (quoted by Dennis Tedlock, *The Spoken Word and the Work of Interpretation* [Philadelphia: University of Pennsylvania Press, 1983], p. 262). The same prejudice is evident today, for example, in the negative value judgment attached to the popular religiosity of Indian communities of Latin America when it is labeled "syncretism," "a distortion of Christian theology" or "christopaganism" (see Alan R. Tippett, "Christopaganism or Indigenous Christianity," in *Christopaganism or Indigenous Christianity?*, Tetsunao Yamamori and Charles R. Taber, eds. [Pasadena: William Carey Library, 1975], pp. 13-34).

18. It should be remembered that Lame — though far from lacking in intellectual capacity, as his manuscript abundantly shows — completely lacked any kind of formal schooling and was regarded by his immediate antagonists as a beastlike Indian (*Indio extra-bruto*) of which Lame himself complained bitterly (see "Pensamientos," par. 238, 240). Even the progressive intellectuals who offered him occasional support and verbal praise did so in a paternalistic and condescending way; see Diego Castrillón-Arboleda, *El Indio Quintín Lame* (Bogotá: Ediciones Tercer Mundo, 1973), pp. 172ff.

19. A number of Latin American scholars have suggested hermeneutical models and methodological paths to help overcome the totalitarian tendencies of Western rationalistic tradition. Among others, José Severino Croatto, *Liberación y libertad: Pautas hermeneúticas* (Buenos Aires: Ediciones Mundo Nuevo, 1973); Clodovis Boff, *Teologia e prática: Teologia do político e suas mediações* (Petrópolis: Vozes, 1982); Raúl Vidales, *Cuestiones en torno al método en la teología de la liberción* (Lima: Secretariado Latinoamericano, 1974); and Juan Carlos Scannone, *Teología de la liberación y praxis popular* (Salamanca: Sígueme, 1976). However, in Latin America the most developed critique has been proposed by Enrique Dussel in his *Método para una filosofía de la liberación: Superación analéctica de la dialéctica hegeliana* (Salamanca: Sígueme, 1974). For a short summary and analysis of this book in English, see Roberto S. Goizueta, "Liberation and Method: the Analectical Method of Enrique Dussel," in *The Pedagogy of God's Image,* Robert Masson, ed. (Chico, California: Scholars Press, 1981), pp. 113-34. Beginning with Aristotle, Dussel shows that the dialectical method is "a method or primary path which, originating in everyday reality, opens itself to the fundamental: to being" (*Método,* p. 30). By focusing attention on the everyday, dialectics leads to the demonstration of the basic scientific axioms, the primary one being that of the impossibility of self-contradiction: that something cannot be and not be simultaneously. Dialectical thinking affirms the oneness of reality, its *totality*. What lies outside this oneness is nonbeing. Thus, for Dussel, the early identification of reality with *being* points towards the definition of the *other* (i.e., that which lies outside the *totality* of being) as unreality or nonbeing. Later, this dialectical tradition becomes increasingly ego-centered to the point that in modern Western thought the dialectical method takes as its starting point not the everyday, or objective reality, but the rejection of it in order to turn inward to consciousness-as-subjectivity (ibid., p. 33). Dussel shows this development as it moves from Descartes (*ego cogito*), Kant, Fichte, and the young Schelling, to Hegel, Feuerbach, and Marx (*Ich arbeite*). For Hegel the task of dialectics is to discover the absolute, the fundamental unity which underlies the apparent contradictions projected onto it by our understanding, and which through its dialectical movement will ultimately eliminate those contradictions. The dialectical process is thus "a progressive involution of an initial and final *totality* which is, nevertheless, always *becoming totalized* intrasubjectively" (ibid., pp. 80, 93). Thus, this dialectical movement is not merely a method, but "the real process of

consciousness, of the spirit of humanity: God as subject" (ibid., p. 84). Thus, for Dussel, Hegelian dialectics run the risk of reducing reality to thinking or, as the mature Schelling would argue, of confusing ontology with logic, reality with mere possibility. It is the mature Schelling in fact who suggests a "beyond-being," an opening up of dialectic, thus initiating, according to Dussel, a new philosophical era in which the idea-as-God is challenged. Beyond the idea there is the person! "The person seeks out the person" (Schelling, in Dussel, ibid., p. 125). Beyond the rational *logos* there is the exteriority experienced, for example, in mythology, as positive revelation. Dussel traces the development of Schelling's critique through Feuerbach to Marx and finds that Marx's dialectic, though inspired by the Hegelian dialectical form, gives that form a new content: the dialectical movement does not take place in the human consciousness (in the head) but in the history of the forces of production. Yet, Dussel rightly calls attention to the fact that, despite the Marxian transformation of the Hegelian dialectics, the ontological category of the "totalized totality" remains intact. In other words, in Marx the bourgeois totality already contains within itself its own negation, the proletariat. Thus, the dialectical future continues to be simply "a development of the potentiality *internal* to the bourgeois totality" (ibid., p. 148). As a corollary, Marx is unable to supersede the category of "the nation" as his analytical horizon, and hence to provide a conceptual framework for adequately appreciating "the Third World" (as it is called now) as a reality that exists *outside* European cultures.

20. Dussel, *Método*, p. 183. Attempts to develop an adequate methodology grounded on these three premises are already under way in the Latin American context. One of them is represented by the work of Enrique Dussel himself who suggests the "analectical method" as the only alternative to the dialectical method characteristic of Western philosophical tradition. Dussel incorporates in his formulation the critique of the dialectical method represented by Kierkegaard, the phenomenological school of Husserl and Heidegger, Sartre and Levinas. It is especially Levinas who, according to Dussel, contributed the most by proposing a key alteration to the dialectics with his threefold discovery: (1) that underlying the entire European philosophical tradition is the Greek notion of being as "what-is-seen" (*idein* = to see); (2) that the I-Thou relationship, where the Thou is the *absolutely* Other, is based on language; and (3) that, therefore, reality is "what-is-heard" from afar, issuing from a being not embraced in *my* totality but revealed in its *word* (ibid., pp. 171-72). Dussel's method is an attempt to discover "the Other," not as Kierkegaard's "wholly Other" or Levinas' "absolute Other," but as "the Other" represented in the poor of the Third World, in Latin America with respect to the European, in the Latin American poor and oppressed with respect to the dominant oligarchies (ibid., pp. 181-82). Dussel's "analectical method" goes beyond and further than (*ana-*) the dialectical method. It challenges the dialectical totality and affirms the freedom of the other, taking as its starting point the other's *word* (as in the Hebrew *dabar*) which carries the sense of dialogue and "revelation." Thus, *the other* is not assimilated into "my" totality, but allowed to say its word as an *ana-logos* to me.

21. In the debate Sepúlveda's position was that the Indians "are barbaric, uninstructed in letters and the arts or government, and completely ignorant, unreasoning, and totally incapable of learning anything but the mechanical arts; that they are sunk in vice, are cruel, and are of such character that, as nature teaches, they are to be governed by the will of others" (quoted by Las Casas, *In Defense of the Indians* [De Kalb: Northern Illinois University Press, 1974], p. 11). Against this view, which denied human dignity to the inhabitants of the New World, Las Casas emphatically protested that, on the contrary, not only were the Indians, like all the other populations of the world, "men" (i.e., human beings), but that

their societies possessed all the expressions of human culture and civilization ("they had properly organized states, wisely ordered by excellent laws, religion and custom; [they] cultivated friendship and, bound together in common fellowship, lived in populous cities" [ibid., p. 43]), and that their social relations "in many points surpass" that of Europeans, "and could have won the admiration of the sages of Athens" [ibid.]. Similar concepts are expressed also in Las Casas, *Brevisima Relación* (English edition, pp. 41-42, 137-38).

22. One of the earliest missiologists of the Spanish church, José de Acosta, published in 1577 his work *De Procuranda Indorum Salute,* in which he suggested a typology of "barbarians," referring to the natives of the New World. "After long and careful considerations," he concluded, "all barbarian nations can be reduced to three different classes or categories." First, there were "barbarians in the general sense," which meant "those who reject true reason and the way of life commonly accepted among men, and who thus display barbarian roughness [in the Spanish translation, *rudeza*] and barbarian savagery." A second kind of "barbarian" consisted of those such as the Aztecs or the Incas who, although they "have not attained the use of writing or the knowledge of philosophy, do possess, however, political, social and religious institutions." These are, for Acosta, somewhere between the first and third group. Finally, the third category of barbarians "is composed of savages resembling wild beasts. . . ." Acosta warned that in the New World "there were countless of them" and consequently, that "it was necessary to teach these people who are hardly men, or who are half men, how to become men, and to instruct them like children." And he added, "they must be held by force, even against their will; they must be compelled to enter the Kingdom of heaven" (*Obras del Padre José de Acosta* [Madrid: BAE, 1954], pp. 392ff.) It is against this ideological background that Pierre Chaunu has said that "the sixteenth century brought about the greatest mutation in the human species" (*Conquête et exploitation de nouveaux mondes* [Paris: PUF, 1969], p. 7), because, from that century on, the citizen (who had been for Aristotle "the political man") became the one who inhabited the European city: the *civis,* the civilized person, one who displayed *civilitas,* civilization. For this reason it could be considered that Gonzalo Fernández de Oviedo (1478-1557) was representing the whole of Europe when he wrote in his *Historia General y Natural de las Indias*: "these people of the Indies, though they are rational and descended from the same stock that came out of Noah's Ark, have become irrational and beastlike by reason of their idolatries, sacrifices, and infernal ceremonies" (Madrid: BAE, 1959, III, p. 60). In more recent times Jean-Paul Sartre aptly described the European perspective of the world, which saw the earth populated by a small minority of "men" surrounded by a vast majority of "natives" (Preface to Frantz Fanon's *The Wretched of the Earth* [New York: Grove Press, 1963], p. 7).

23. This point is documented historically on a global scale in Eric R. Wolf, *Europe and the People Without History* (Berkeley and London: University of California Press, 1982).

24. One such myth is implicit in the fictional generic term that was applied to the native population: "Indian" or "Indians." It is part of the ideology that postulates a radical dualism between the European and the authocthonous population: one civilized, rational, Christian, and powerful; the other uncivilized, natural, pagan, and weak.

25. The concept of "Indian peasant areas" shall be used in the present study to draw attention to the cultural instability implicit in the eclectic accumulation of more than one cultural ethos — that of the indigenous ("primitive") population and that of the peasant culture first introduced by the European conquest. See Robert Redfield, *The Primitive World and its Transformations,* 2nd edition (New York: Dover Publications, 1947), pp. 44-46. Also, Orlando Fals-Borda, *Peasant*

Society in the Colombian Andes (Gainesville: University of Florida Press, 1955), pp. 195, 231; and Sutti Ortiz, "Reflections on the Concepts of Peasant Culture and Peasant Cognitive Systems," in Teodor Shanin, ed., *Peasants and Peasant Societies: Selected Readings* (Harmondsworth, Middlesex, England: Penguin Books, 1971).

26. This concept has been developed by the Brazilian educator and philosopher Paulo Freire to define a condition that derives from the interplay of structural relationships between the dominated and the dominators in the social system. In such a culture "...to exist is only to live. The body carries orders from above. Thinking is difficult, speaking the word, forbidden." *Cultural Action for Freedom*, (Cambridge, Mass.: Center for the Study of Development and Social Change), p. 22.

27. Enrique Dussel calls attention to the fact that "the Israelites themselves (in the Old Testament) whether as a result of ideological contamination from the neighboring nations and empires, or as a development occurring during the period of the monarchy, used the category of *goyim* to indicate those people who were barbarian, foreign, inferior" ("Modern Christianity in Face of the Other," in *The Dignity of the Despised of the Earth*, Jacques Pohier and Dietmar Mieth, eds. [New York: Seabury Press, 1979], p. 51).

28. "The Status of Those Without Dignity in the Old Testament," in Pohier and Mieth, *Dignity*, pp. 4ff.

29. See Hans Walter Wolff, *Anthropology of the Old Testament* (Philadelphia: Fortess Press, 1974), p. 225.

30. This major theological development can be illustrated in the Old Testament by the core of messianic announcements of Deutero-Isaiah around the theme: "I have put my spirit upon him; and he will bring forth justice to the nations (goyim) (Isa. 42:1); and in the New Testament by the announcements about "the end" in Matthew 25: "When the son of man comes in his glory...he will sit on his glorious throne, and before him will be gathered all the nations (*ethne*)." Thus, according to Wolff, "with the message of Jesus Christ, the promise is realized that men of all nations shall partake in the process of becoming truly men" (*Anthropology*, p. 222).

31. Both the concern with justice and the eschatological expectation associated with shalom are characteristics of a special kind of Hebrew prophets who appeared in the history of Israel in times of national crisis. Max Weber names them "ethical prophets" (*The Sociology of Religion* [Boston: Beacon Press, 1963]). According to the Old Testament, such prophets spoke out of an insight or revelation into the nature of God as shalom (justice and peace) and, as a consequence, developed a keen awareness of social conditions, not as impartial observers or analysts, but as partisans who thundered: "Woe to those who decree iniquitous decrees, and the writers who keep writing oppression; to turn aside the needy from justice, to rob the poor of their right, that widows may be their spoils, and that make the orphan their prey" (Isa. 10:1-2). Besides, the "ethical prophets" of the Old Testament were eschatological figures, not in the sense of predicting the future but in announcing God's intentions for the future which involved a vision of the ultimate end of history and of its transformation. In Joachim Wach's terms, "the prophet views the things of the world in the light of their final destiny" (*Sociology of Religion* [University of Chicago Press, 1944], p. 349).

32. Along the same lines of theological reflection, some contemporaneous theologians analyze the meaning of the Christian faith for today in Latin America. Gustavo Gutiérrez, for example, writes: "It is only through concrete deeds of love and solidarity that our encounter with the poor person, with the exploited human being, will be effective, and in that person our encounter with Christ ("for you did it to me," Matt. 25:40) will be valid as well. Our denial of love and solidarity

will be a rejection of Christ ("you neglected to do it to me," Matt. 25:45). "The poor person, the other, becomes the revealer of the Utterly Other [God]" (*The Power of the Poor in History* [Maryknoll, N.Y.: Orbis, 1983], p. 52). Both the recognition of God in the oppressed and the commitment to the struggle for justice and liberation, in view of an estchatological reading of history, are characteristics of current liberation theology in Latin America. It is an understanding of the Christian faith along the lines of the prophetic tradition of the Bible, interpreted in the following terms: "The prophets announce a kingdom of peace. But peace presupposes the establishment of justice: 'Righteousness shall yield peace and its fruit shall be quietness and confidence forever' (Isa. 32:17; cf. also Ps. 85). It presupposes the defense of the rights of the poor, punishment of the oppressors, a life free from fear of being enslaved by others, the liberation of the oppressed. Peace, justice, love, and freedom are not private realities; they are not internal attitudes. They are social realities, implying a historical liberation. A poorly understood spiritualization has often made us forget the human consequences of the eschatological promises and the power to transform unjust social structures which they imply. The elimination of misery and exploitation is a sign of the coming of the Kingdom" (Gustavo Gutiérrez, *A Theology of Liberation: History Politics, and Salvation* [Maryknoll, N.Y.: Orbis, 1973], p. 167).

CHAPTER 2

1. See Ernesto Guhl, *Colombia: Bosquejo de su Geografía Tropical* (Bogotá: Instituto Colombiano de Cultura, 1976), II, pp. 147ff.

2. The limits and definitions of temperature zones (*pisos térmicos*) of tropical America are not standardized. In Colombia the *tierra templada,* or temperate zone, goes from 1,000 to 2,000 meters altitude with an annual average temperature of 18 degrees centrigrade. Below this level lies the *tierra caliente,* or hot lands, and above it the cool uplands, or *tierra fría.* Still higher there is a fourth zone, the *páramo,* generally above the tree line, roughly 3,000 meters and higher. Higher than the *páramos* only the solid rocky peaks stand out covered with perennial snow, called *nevados* (see *Atlas de Colombia,* Instituto Geográfico Agustín Codazzi, 2nd ed., 1969, pp. 87ff.).

3. Tierradentro as a cultural zone has been studied by the archeologist José Pérez de Barradas (*Arqueología y Antropología Precolombinas de Tierradentro,* Ministerio de Educación Pública, Publicaciones de la Sección de Arqueología no. 1, Bogotá, 1937). The earliest ethnographic description of the area is that by the priest Eugenio Del Castillo I Orozco, a linguist, who wrote a most valuable grammar and vocabulary of the Páez language, with important observations on the christianization process carried on among the Indians in the eighteenth century (*Vocabulario Páez-Castellano, Catecismo y Nociones Gramaticales y Dos Pláticas; con adiciones y correcciones y un vocabulario castellano-Páez, por Ezequiel Uricochea* [Paris: Maison Neuve, 1878]). More recently the Colombian ethnologist José María Otero has contributed a fuller description of the various ethnic communities of the region, with special emphasis on their religious world (*Etnología Caucana* [Popayán: Editorial Universidad del Cauca, 1952]). Among current anthropological studies, especially on the Páez economy, and modes of relation to the land, see Elias Sevilla-Casas, "Atraso y Desarrollo Indígena en Tierradentro" (Bogotá: Universidad de los Andes, 1976); and "Estudios Antropológicos sobre Tierradentro" (Cali: Fundación para la Educación Superior, 1979).

4. Otero, *Etnología Caucana,* pp. 227ff. According to Otero's observations, made in the 1930s and 40s, the Páez and the Paniquitá were by far the largest linguistic groups, each one comprising around 20,000 speakers, whereas the Guambiano group was formed by 5,441 Indians.

5. The Indians did not hold these reserved lands in fee simple, for the crown retained the ownership as part of its regalian rights, and in theory could increase or diminish the size of the *resguardos*. Nor were the Indians allowed to lease their community lands to Spaniards, *criollos*, or mestizos. The Indians, however, did enjoy usufruct. One of the best studies of the *resguardo* institution, especially in its relation to the land tenure problem and to the history of the Indian communities of the Colombian southwest, is Juan Friede, *El Indio en Lucha por la Tierra* (Bogotá, 1944), which is also the first to highlight its ideological dimensions, especially its legal and religious aspects. Also important is Guillermo Hernández Rodríguez, *De los Chibchas a la Colonia y a la República* (Bogotá, 1949), pp. 300-324, where the study of the Indian *resguardos* is set in the larger context of the evolution of private property in the Colombian countryside since colonial times. Magnus Mörner, in his paper "Las Comunidades Indígenas y la Legislación Segregacionista en el Nuevo Reino de Granada," *Anuario Colombiano de Historia y de la Cultura* (no. 1, vol. 1, Bogotá, 1963), has underlined the aspect of racial segregation, to a large extent neglected by previous studies. More recently the following studies deal competently with the subject, adding precision and clarifying other dimensions of the question: Orlando Fals-Borda, *El Hombre y la Tierra en Boyacá* (Bogotá, 1957), pp. 72-105; idem, *Historia de la Cuestión Agraria en Colombia* (Bogotá, 1975); Indalecio Liévano Aguirre, *Los Grandes Conflictos Sociales y Económicos de Nuestra Historia* (Bogotá, 1968), pp. 419-23, 517, 519; Juan Friede, "De la Encomienda Indiana a la Propiedad Territorial y su Influencia en el Mestizaje," *Anuario Colombiano de Historia Social y de la Cultura* (no. 4, Bogotá, 1969); and Margarita González, *El Resguardo en el Nuevo Reino de Granada* (Bogotá, 1970), dealing with the nature and role of the *resguardo* institution in the earlier stages of its creation in the region around Bogotá.

6. William Paul McGreevey, *An Economic History of Colombia, 1845-1930* (Boston, 1971), pp. 51ff.

7. Name given to Spanish descendants born in America.

8. See Friede, "Encomienda Indiana," pp. 58-61.

9. Jorge Ulloa and Juan y Santacilla, *Noticias Secretas de América,* 1748. English translation by John J. TePaske, *Discourse and Political Reflections on the Kingdoms of Peru* (University of Oklahoma Press, 1978), pp. 69ff.

10. Bolivar himself decreed the division of all *resguardos* on May 20 of 1820, a determination reiterated on October 11 of the following year. The enforcement of this decree, however, was never seriously attempted, because of local Indian resistance, political instability, and the lack of effective mechanisms for law enforcement in the new republic. See Hernández-Rodríguez, *Chibchas,* pp. 311ff.

11. Fals-Borda, *Hombre y Tierra,* pp. 72-105.

12. Friede, *Indio en Lucha,* pp. 120ff.

13. Otero, *Etnología Caucana,* pp. 199ff.

14. Ordenanza No. 47 of 1898, in Marino Balcázar Pardo, *Disposiciones sobre Indígenas, Adjudicación de Baldíos, y Represión de Estados Antisociales* (Popayán, 1954), p. 166. This work contains a complete collection of all national and Departmental legislation concerning Indians, with particular reference to the Department of Cauca, from 1820 to 1953.

15. Ordenanza No. 10 of 1922, in Balcázar Pardo, *Disposiciones,* pp. 193ff.

16. The *resguardo* of Timbío, for example, in the district of Popayán, was declared "inexistent" by Law 13 of 1903 on the basis that the Indians had already achieved "a measure of instruction and progress" at variance with the condition of "savages," which the legislators of 1890 had in mind in issuing Law 89 recognizing the *resguardo* institution. See Balcázar Pardo, *Disposiciones,* pp. 167ff.

17. For more on *terrazguero* Indians, see above, pp. 26ff.

18. This name was given in colonial times to white or mestizo settlers who —

against the official segregationist legislation intended to "protect" the Indians from pernicious influences — found their way into Indian towns and *resguardos*, and established themselves there, sometimes paying rent to the *resguardo* officers, other times arbitrarily invading Indian lands, forcing the *resguardo* officers to initiate complicated lawsuits that most of the time had no resolution favorable to the Indians. See Friede, "Encomienda Indiana," pp. 59ff.

19. See Charles W. Berquist, *Coffee and Conflict in Colombia, 1886-1910* (Durham, N.C.: Duke University Press, 1978), pp. 77ff.

20. McGreevey, *Economic History*, pp. 201ff.

21. J. Fred Rippy, *The Capitalists and Colombia* (New York, 1931), pp. 54ff.

22. Joaquín Ospina, *Diccionario Biográfico y Bibliográfico de Colombia* (Bogotá: Editorial Aguila, 1939).

23. Alvaro Pio Valencia, Muñoz's grandson. Interview recorded in Popayán, on Thursday, July 15, 1971. Archives of the Comité de Defensa del Indio (hereafter CDI), Bogotá.

24. Michael Taussig, "The Genesis of Capitalism Among a South American Peasantry," *Comparative Studies in Society and History,* vol. 19, no. 2 (Cambridge |Mass.| University Press, April 1977).

25. Article 15, Law 89 of 1890, in Balcázar-Pardo, *Disposiciones*, pp. 100ff.

26. The title reads: "Law 89 establishing the manner in which those savages in process of being reduced to civilized life shall be governed." The Spanish title reads: "*Por la cual se determina la manera como deben gobernarse los salvajes que vayan reduciendose a la vida civilizada*." See the full text in Balcázar-Pardo, *Disposiciones*, pp. 100ff.

27. G. Castillo-Cárdenas, "The Indian Struggle for Freedom in Colombia," in *The Situation of South American Indians* (Geneva, 1972), pp. 86ff.

28. Article 1 of Law 89 reads: "The general legislation of the Republic shall not apply among the savages in process of being reduced to civilized life through Missions." See Balcázar-Pardo, *Disposiciones*, pp. 100ff.

29. In the Department of Cauca this special role assigned to the church was first spelled out in Decree 74 of 1898 in which the regional government delegated a large measure of its responsibilities for the Indian population in the fields of education, land tenure policies, political organization, judicial and police matters, to the Catholic authorities. See Balcázar-Pardo, *Disposiciones*, pp. 110ff.

30. Article 1 of the law reads: *La Nación ratifica y confirma las declaratorias judicial y legalmente hechas de estar vacantes globos de terrenos conocidos como resguardos de indígenas, asi como tambien las ventas de ellas efectuadas en pública subasta, y reconoce como título legal de propiedad de esos terrenos el adquirido por sus rematadores.* See Fabián Díaz-Aristizabal, *El Resguardo Indígena, su Realidad y la Ley* (Bogotá, Ministerio de Gobierno, vol. 1, pp. 28ff.).

31. Victor Lame (Quintín Lame's nephew). Interview on July 16, 1971. Spanish original reads as follows: *"A uno le cobraban hasta veinte dias de terraje por sólo tener un arrendito, unas poquitas cabecitas de ganado en unos rastrojos pu'alla. Eso era mensual. Así como algunos eran más considerados cobraban tres dias cada semana. Así era en todas lad haciendas; y decían los patrones que el arrendatario que no saliera cada semana a descontar ese terraje . . . pues que se vaya! A unos les ponían la obligación de ir a dejar a Popayán a la espalda un bulto de cinco arrobas de papa, sin bestia, sino a cargueo a la espalda. Asi tenian que llevarlo por cuenta de descontar arrendamiento. A los que estaban enfermos el terraje no se lo perdonaban, sino que si habia durao dos meses enfermo, pues tenia que pagar arrendamiento do los meses que habia estao enfermo. Y si alguno se resistía, pues a picarle los cercos, a echarle ganado en las sementeras, y hasta prenderle candela al rancho!"* (The rural Spanish spoken by Indians of the area has been preserved.)

32. Gregorio Arcila Robledo, *Las Misiones Franciscanas en Colombia* (Bogotá: Imprenta Nacional, 1950), pp. 398ff. See also Segundo Eleazar Bernal, "Religious Life of the Paez Indians of Colombia," M.A. thesis, Faculty of Political Science, Columbia University, 1956, pp. 46ff.

33. Eugenio Del Castillo I Orozco, *Vocabulario Páez-Castellano, Catecismo, Nociones Gramaticales, y Dos Pláticas, Con Adiciones, correcciones y un Vocabulario Castellano-Páez, por Ezequiel Uricochea*. Collection Linguistique Américaine, vol. 2 (Paris: Maison Neuve, 1877).

34. Manuel Rodríguez, *El Marañon y Amazonas* (Madrid, 1684), p. 73.

35. Ibid., italics added.

36. Castillo I Orozco, *Vocabulario*, p. 84. Spanish original: *"una natural aversión a aprender la doctrina cristiana."*

37. Carlos Cuervo Márquez, *Estudios Arqueológicos y Etnográficos* (Madrid, 1920), vol. 2, p. 191.

38. Bernal, "Religious Life," pp. 54ff.; Otero, *Etnología Caucana*, pp. 15ff.

39. The archeologist José Pérez de Barradas, who visited the Páez in 1936, wrote about their religious life: "In the major events of their life, in their religious festivals, they mix Christian ceremonies with ancestral practices. There are still remnants of witchcraft, worship of stones, and superstitious practices without end," *Arqueología y Antropología Precolombinas de Tierradentro* (Bogotá: 1937), p. 8. Similar judgments have been expressed by Gregorio Hernández de Alba, "The Highland Tribes of Southern Colombia," in *Handbook of South American Indians*, Julian H. Steward, ed., vol. 2 (Washington, 1946), and Jesús María Otero (*Etnología Caucana*, pp. 36-42). Segundo Eleazar Bernal, who studied the religious life of the Páez during the 1950s, reached a similar conclusion ("La fiesta de San Juan en Calderas, Tierradentro," *Revista Colombiana de Folklore*, no. 2, segunda epoca, 1953, pp. 177-221.

40. See Hermann Trimborn, "South Central America and the Andean Civilizations," in Walter Krickeberg et al., *Pre-Columbian American Religions*, History of Religion Series (New York: Holt, Rinehart and Winston, 1968), pp. 96-97.

41. Castillo I Orozco, *Vocabulario*, pp. 109-10. Spanish original: *"Ayudándome Dios quiero predicar lo que es el infierno... porque sabed que sí hay infierno para los que no guardan la ley de Dios... Y si morís sin pedir perdón a Dios, sin confesaros de todos vuestros pecados, ni arrepentiros de ellos, iréis sin remedio al infierno, de donde no vuelve a salir el que llega a caer, mientras Dios fuere Dios!... El Infierno es una caverna muy grande, que está en el centro de la tierra, cerrada por todas partes, oscurísima, sin que pueda entrar el aire ni un rayo de luz. Allí no se oye otra cosa sino aullidos, y griteria de los demonios, que estan atormentando a las almas que estan alli condenadas. Estas estan gritando, maldiciendo, aullando como perros rabiosos; gritan, estan temblando y crujiendo los dientes."*

42. Ibid., p. 114. Spanish original: *"Y por eso quered vosotros mucho a la Santisima Virgen, para que le pida a su Hijo que no os eche a los calabozos del infierno."*

43. Ibid., p. 115.

44. Ibid., p. 116. Spanish original: *"Ahora os quiero predicar lo que es la gloria y las cosas que Dios tiene en el cielo para premiar a los buenos. "*

45. Ibid.

46. Ibid., pp. 120-22.

47. Ibid., p. 122.

48. See Trimborn, "South Central America," pp. 95-105; Otero, *Etnología*, pp. 38ff.; and Bernal, "Religious Life," pp. 81ff.

49. See Segundo Bernal, "Medicina y Magia entre los Páeces," in *Revista Colombiana de Antropología*, vol. 2, 1954, pp. 221-63. The German archeologist

and ethnologist Horst Nachtigal also emphasized "the nominal Christianity" of the Páez and devoted special attention to the magical practices that persisted in the communities during the 1940s and 50s ("Shamanismo entre los Indios Páeces," *Revista Colombiana del Folklore*, no. 3, segunda epoca, June 1953, pp. 223-41).

50. David González, *Los Páeces. Genocidio y Luchas Indígenas en Colombia* (Popayán: Editorial Rueda Suelta, n.d.), p. 124. Spanish original: *"Los gobiernos consentian en el absurdo de que los indios se creyeran y obraran como dueños de inmensidades de tierra....Por eso mismo dejaron a la raza Páez entregada a su natural indolencia, a su pereza racial, dejaron que vegetara en su carencia de sentimientos de dignidad, en la ausencia de todo anhelo de superacion, ya que el indígena por natural inclinación quiere permanecer en su estado primitivo."*

51. Ibid., p. 125.

52. See, e.g., Luis López de Mesa: *"Sobre estas materias de la civilización de los aborígenes americanos, la historia y la sociología tienen una palabra que añadir: y es que sólo el cruzamiento con las razas superiores saca al indígena de su postración cultural y fisiológica....De ahi que el esfuerzo catequista de varios siglos este representado por nada"* (*De Como se ha Formado la Nación Colombiana* [Medellín: Editorial Bedout, 1970], p. 113; italics added). English translation: "On the subject of the civilization of the aborigines, history and sociology have something to add: that *only mixture with superior races* can lift up the Indian from his cultural and physiological prostration....It is for this reason that the catechetical endeavors of several centuries have resulted in nothing." Also, Miguel Antonio Arroyo, who praises the Indians of Cauca Indígena for their ancestral solidarity, but charges them with *"una indole retardataria, indiferente a todo lo que sea novedad y progreso, como si carecieran de curiosidad y emoción....Ello determina el estancamiento"* (*El Cauca es Así* [Popayán: Editorial Universidad, 1953], p. 102). English translation: "a lagging indolence, indifference to progress, as if they lacked curiosity and emotion, which is the reason for their stagnation."

53. Fals-Borda, for example, observed that among the peasants of Saucío, in the Eastern range of the Colombian Andes, the priest as an *alter Christus* exerted an effective control over believers, not only through his preaching but also through the fear of possible sanctions. In fact, the fear of infringing the obligatory commands of the church was considered to be an essential factor for the people's participation in religious services. For the peasants, therefore, Christianity "means mainly the fulfillment of the requirements of the Church and obedience to the dictates of the priest" (*Peasant Society in the Colombian Andes* [Gainesville: University Press of Florida, 1955], p. 220). Victor Daniel Bonilla, who studied intensively the work of the Capuchin missionaries in the neighboring Indian communities of Sibundoy towards the south of Cauca Indígena, reached a more radical conclusion: the mission not only controlled the religious life of the Indians but also dominated completely their economy, as well as the administration of the community (*Servants of God, or Masters of Men?* The Pelican Latin American Library [Harmondsworth: Penguin Books, 1972], pp. 252ff.). Gerardo Reichel-Dolmatoff also, who has studied attentively the work of missions in a number of Indian communities of Colombia, reaches the same conclusion: not only through religious innovation but mainly through the introduction of cultural change in education, clothing, housing, time schedules, etc., the missionary creates a condition of dependence and control in the process of "integrating" the Indian into civilized life (Gerardo Reichel-Dolmatoff and Roberto Jualin, eds., *El Etnocidio a traves de las Américas* [Mexico City: Siglo Veintiuno Editores, 1916], pp. 290ff.). Also, Father Humberto Restrepo in his study of popular religion in the Antioquía province as it is expressed in the literary work of Tomás Carrasquilla, finds that the Church appeared to the peasant as a "sacred power...

to excommunicate, to prohibit books, to force the conscience, to dictate commandments...and [he adds] before this sacred power the faithful trembled!" (*La Religión de la Antigua Antioquía* [Medellín: Editorial Bedout, 1972], p.100).

54. Article 1 of the Concordat states that: "The Roman Catholic Apostolic Religion is the religion of Colombia; the public powers recognize it as an essential element of the social order, and they are bound to protect it and to enforce respect for it and for its ministers, while leaving to it at the same time the full enjoyment of its rights and prerogatives." See Angelo Mercati, *Raccolta di Concordati su Materie Ecclesiastiche tra la Santa Sede e la Autorità Civili* (Tipografia Poliglotta Vaticana, 1954), II, pp. 1051-61. For Catholic exegetes this article means not only that the State professes the Catholic faith, but also that it vows to protect and enforce respect for the Catholic Church as "an essential element of the social order." See Gonzalo Castillo-Cárdenas, *The Colombian Concordat, In the Light of Recent Trends in Catholic Thought Concerning Church-State Relations and Religious Liberty.* Colección Sondeos no. 22 (Cuernavaca: Centro Intercultural de Documentación [CIDOC], 1968).

55. By means of revisions and adaptations in 1892, 1928, and 1953, the text of the Agreement became the Convention on Missions, additional to the Concordat. In this convention Indian regions are called "national territories" in which the authority of the church became virtually supreme. Specific clauses grant the missions "the direction of public schools" and the right to "the quantity of land required for the service and benefit of the missions; the guarantee that the nomination of public officials will fall on persons recommendable from every point of view and known to be favorable to the missions and to the members of missionary orders," it being "a sufficient ground for removal of the government employees that the head of the mission present a complaint against them, provided this is based on proven facts"; and finally, that the state has the obligation "to provide invariably and uninterruptedly the said missions with the means necessary and sufficient for their life and growth" (Mercati, *Raccolta,* II, pp. 79-83).

56. Law 89 of 1890.

57. Law 79 of 1892.

58. Bernal, "Religious Life," pp. 42ff. Father David González registers the main lines of development of the christianization process from 1905 to the present: it includes the building of churches, schools, and above all, catechization campaigns aimed at baptizing the largest number possible and uniting in holy marriage those who were living together "in sin" (*Páeces,* pp. 109ff.). Another brief historical record of missionary activity under the administration of the Lazarist fathers is given in Ricardo Quintero Nieto, *Territorio Ignoto* (Popayán: n.d.), pp. 48ff.

59. González, *Paéces,* pp. 107ff.; Quintero Nieto, *Territorio,* pp. 31ff.

60. Such was the conclusion, for example, of the governor of Cauca, Carlos Vernaza, the first political leader of such high investiture to personally visit Tierradentro (in 1927). In his report to the president he wrote: "It has been only the selfless, persistent, and solicitous action of the children of the Angel of Charity [the Lazarist missionaries] who, using all kinds of means of attraction, have been able, little by little, to erase from the Indians their barbarian characteristics, thanks to preaching, personal example, and the foundation of schools" (report to the president of the republic on a visit to Tierradentro, March 1, 1927, in *Informe del Gobernador del Cauca a la Asamblea del Departamento* (Popayán: Imprenta del Departamento, Archivo Departamental, 1927). Ricardo Quintero Nieto (a mestizo born in the Cauca Indígena region himself) agrees with the governor. To his own question: "Who subjugated the Páeces?" he answers proudly: "The Lazarist fathers: with meekness and true evangelical spirit they occupied foot by foot the entire territory, and with goodness they conquered the heart of

these wild (*arizcos*) Indians" (*Territorio*, pp. 47-48). These evangelical qualities notwithstanding, the "subjugation" was real. In the areas where missionaries achieved greater success, according to Quintero-Nieto, baptism and Christian marriage became obligatory to the point of being imposed by force with the help of authorities of the Indian Cabildo (ibid., pp. 58ff.), and in matters of morality, according to the same author, a woman's conduct was watched with much greater rigor to the point of not allowing her "even to talk with any man other than her husband or her father" (ibid., p. 58).

61. Bernal, "Religious Life," pp. 46ff.

62. Hernández de Alba refers to this cult briefly ("Highland Tribes," p. 955), and Bernal provides further details from oral tradition of the region ("Religious Life," pp. 47ff.), but without analysis. Recently, a much fuller description of this movement has been provided by Joanne Rappaport on the basis of documentary research in the Archivo Histórico de Tierradentro. Rappaport analyzes this movement and other similar ones in the context of the messianic religious traditions of the Andean world (see "Mesianismos y las Transformaciones de Símbolos Mesiánicos en Tierradentro," in *Revista Colombiana de Antropología,* v. 20, 1980-81: pp. 367-413).

63. Cuervo Márquez, *Estudios,* p. 195.

64. Ibid., pp. 193ff. Bernal reports that during the time he did his research in the area, he found out there was a widespread belief in a "spectre" which some identified with the devil, who appeared on dark nights carrying on his left knee a "malignant child" who never grew, because "if the child were to grow, it would mean the end of all Christians" ("Religious Life," pp. 63ff.).

CHAPTER 3

1. The primary sources on Lame's life and thought are of five kinds. First and the most valuable is Lame's major work, "Los Pensamientos." Secondly, the official records kept in public notaries and judicial courts in the Colombian departments of Cauca, Tolima, and Huila, where Lame was active most of his life. Thirdly, the public statements by Lame himself and a number of interviews about his activities which appeared in Colombian newspapers from 1910 to 1940. Fourthly, the internal records of the *Cabildo Indígena* (Indian council) of Ortega with which Lame was intimately associated during his Tolima campaign until the last days of his life. This source shall be referred to as: Archives, Cabildo Indígena, Ortega. And finally, the collective memory — as expressed in several units of oral tradition — of the Indian communities of the areas where Lame was active. Between 1969 and 1973, when the main body of this research was carried out, some of Lame's relatives were still alive, as well as several of his original followers in Cauca and Tolima. Relevant testimonies from these informants were recorded and have been used in this study. The only secondary source on Lame's life is Diego Castrillón-Arboleda, *El Indio Quintín Lame* (Bogotá: Ediciones Tercer Mundo, 1973). Castrillón-Arboleda, curator of the Archivo Central del Cauca and himself a member of one of the aristocratic families of Popayán, has produced in this book more a historical novel than a biography, in the sense that he uses some accurate historical information and combines it with anecdotes and literary narratives, often reflecting the traditional attitudes of the Colombian upper classes towards the Indians. Before the completion of his book, however, he did have the opportunity to read Lame's manuscript "Los Pensamientos," whose text had been published in its original form, under my own editorial responsibility, with the title *En Defensa de mi Raza* (Bogotá: CDI, 1971), on which Castrillón relies for most of his biographical data.

2. This date is given by Lame himself ("Pensamientos," par. 2). However, in the Cathoic parish of Puracé, forty-five kilometers north of his place of birth, in the Book of Baptisms No. 13, there is the entry of a child named Juan Quintín, born October 26, 1880, the son of Mariano Lame and Dolores Chantre, the same parents of Manuel Quintín. It is very likely that it refers to the same person, although the reason for the Juan to Manuel change is never explained in any of Lame's manuscripts. According to Ezequiel Uricochea, changing names was an ancestral practice among the Páez Indians as part of the transition from childhood to adolescence (Castillo I Orozco, *Vocabulario,* p. xxii). The discrepancy between dates of birth is not very important: such discrepancies are very common among the peasant groups.

3. "Pensamientos," par. 150.

4. It is quite likely therefore that most communication between the Lames was carried on partly in Páez (the father's native language) and partly in Spanish. But it seems that Quintín regarded Páez as his native language (see "Pensamientos," par. 183, 216).

5. This attitude might be explained by the fact that his father, who seemed to have been at the time making a strenuous effort to achieve a measure of economic independence, and had just bought a small plot of land in the rural neighborhood (*vereda*) of San Alfonso, needed very badly the labor of his six children (see Castrillón-Arboleda, *El Indio Quintín Lame,* pp. 34ff.). "Going to school" for the child of a *terrazguero* Indian would probably have meant to send him to Popayán as the servant of some white family. This early confrontation with his father was registered by Quintín himself in a dramatized form: "'Do you want school?' (my father asked me twice). Then he handed over to me a machete, an ax, a sickle, a shovel, and a bar, saying: 'This is the real school of the Indian! Get going with your brothers to clear up the forest!'" ("Pensamientos," par. 153).

6. Gregorio Hernández de Alba, "Segunda Entrevista con Quintín Lame. Encuestas Realizadas por el Jefe de Resguardos Indígenas, Noviembre, 1958, Coyaima, Tolima." Report to the Ministry of Agriculture (Bogotá: Archivo del Ministerio de Gobierno, División de Asuntos Indígenas, 1958).

7. "Pensamientos," par. 11. According to his nephew, "learning came to him" (*a Quintín le vino el estudio*) due to a number of coincidences. Once he had learned to read and write, thanks to the moral support of his maternal uncle Leonardo Chantre who occasionally visited the Lames in San Isidro and who provided him with the first reading materials, Quintín befriended a small landholder of the area, Don Manuel María Puyo, who on his deathbed asked him to be the executor of his estate (*su albacea*). Problems that ensued in the distribution of the small inheritance put him in contact with Francisco de Paula Perez Esparza, a well-known lawyer of Popayán, who liked the young Indian (*le cogió voluntad*) and introduced him to some books from his own library, especially practical legal books about proceedings and legal forms to follow when addressing a magistrate or a judge, in initiating a lawsuit, and so on. Quintín enjoyed this so much that the lawyer made him his "assistant" (most likely his office boy or *mandadero*, information provided by Pedro Lame, still living in the town of Puracé on July 5, 1971, Archives, CDI, Bogotá). This helps to explain the surprising fact that later on in his embattled life Manuel Quintín Lame shows acquaintance with the Colombian civil code and with aspects of Colombian legislation on Indians, and that in " Los Pensamientos," he often makes references to scattered but not insignificant pieces of history from different periods, all related to the struggles and sufferings of his own people.

8. "Pensamientos," par. 12.

9. See Eleazar Bernal, "Religious Life," pp. 54ff.; Castrillón-Arboleda, *El Indio,* p. 36.

10. Information provided by Alvaro Pio Valencia, Munoz's grandson, interviewed in Popayán, July 10, 1971.

11. The extent to which the Christianity of the Catholic missions was blended with the religious tradition of the Páez Indians, with their worldview and ideology, and how this blend came to provide Lame with the elements to articulate his "doctrine and discipline," will be taken up in the following chapter, on the basis of an exegesis and exposition of "Los Pensamientos," and other documents.

12. Par. 117. It was in fact the practice of most landowners not only in Cauca but throughout the Colombian countryside to draft their *terrazgueros* and peons to fight the internecine wars of the various factions ruling the country. According to this own testimony, Lame was drafted by the government forces, whose rhetoric at the time was one of intense nationalism, and sent south to the border with Ecuador where severe fighting was taking place against guerrilla groups organized by liberal *caudillos*. However, there is no information on how long or where the young Lame was involved in battle.

13. The turn of the century was a time of permanent convulsion in Panama, due to separatist movements instigated by international interests related to the construction and control of the canal. Again, it is not known how long Lame was involved in this expedition.

14. Soon after his return from Panama Quintín married Benilda León, an Indian of the area, and settled down in San Isidro as *terrazguero* attached to the hacienda of Ignacio Muñoz, his father's *patrón*. Benilda died during the birth of their first child and months later the baby also died. The same year Quintín married Pioquinta León, who would bear him three children: Hermelinda, Angelina, and Roberto. Hermelinda Lame León was still alive in 1971 in the rural neighborhood of Agua Colorada, not far from San Isidro (see Castrillón-Arboleda, *El Indio*, pp. 55ff.).

15. An ironic label stressing the peculiar stamp impressed on the movement by Quintín's personality, not necessarily representative of the Indian community as a whole.

16. Interview published by *El Espectador* (Bogotá, July 12, 1924, p. 1). The Indian *cabildos* that would have taken the initiative were those of Pitayó, Puracé, Pandiguando, Poblazón, Cajibío, "and some others." There is no independent record of this "election," but Lame will play this role ever since that date. A portrait done in canvas and still preserved by the "Lamista" Indian Council of Ortega, Tolima, carries the date October 1912, with the inscription at the bottom: "Manuel Quintín Lame, Chief of all Indian tribes of Colombia."

17. In his old age Quintín Lame described to the representatives of the Ministry of Agriculture the specific event which set him on the road to open rebellion. Once when he returned to his father's house in the hacienda of San Isidro, he found "his father, his brother, and two others" hanging by their wrists from the ceiling because they had refused to pay "six days of *terraje*" (land rent). Lame set them loose and burst into angry rebellion: "I had the lines of the telegraph cut, gathered 600 Indians, and resolved myself to defend the Indian race" (Hernández de Alba, "Segunda Entrevista," p. 9).

18. Pedro Lame, Quintín's nephew, still remembered in 1971 the intense activity displayed by this uncle sixty some years before, as well as some of his favorite agitational themes: "He roamed around this area many times. He traveled to Dinde, Poblazón, Belalcazar, San Antonio, Inza. He gave speeches in favor of the Indians. He taught us how to handle ourselves. He said that the lands did not belong to the *hacendados* but to the Indian communities . . . that all the lands from Popayán upwards belong to the Indians, that the rich had seized them because they preyed on our ignorance" (taped testimony, Puracé, July 1971. Archives, CDI, Bogotá). Spanish original: "*El voltio mucho por aqui. Anduvó mucho por Dinde, Poblazón,*

Belalcazar, San Antonio, Inza. Daba conferencias a favor de los Indios. Nos ensenaba como debiamos manejarnos. Que estas tierras no eran de los hacendados sino de parcialidad. Que de Popayán pa'rriba todo era de los Indios, pero que los ricos habian abarcado todo porque nos habian cogido muy ignorantes."

19. See "Pensamientos," par. 238. For an analysis of Lame's critique of civilization," see above, pp. 57ff. and 88ff.

20. One of the militants of those days reported: "Quintín said to us that we needed to arm each other until the entire population of the *parcialidad* was armed to the last man, to oppose the division of the *resguardos*. He told the women to guard respect for ourselves, resorting if necessary to kitchen knives! I have never seen or heard any man like him!" (Carmen Mazabuel, taped testimony, July 1971. Archives, CDI, Bogotá). The Spanish text says: "*Nos decía que debíamos armarnos los unos a los otros, y armarse toda la parcialidad como un solo hombre para no aceptar las divisiones de los resguardos. A las mujeres nos decía que aunque fuera con el cuchillo de guisar nos hiciéramos respetar. Nunca he visto ni oído ningun hombre como él.*"

21. All these accusations, probably exaggerated, appear in the annual reports of the secretary of government presented to the governor, during the years 1915 through 1918. Each report covers events of the previous year, and always includes sections on *Indígenas* and *orden público* (public order). In the report corresponding to 1915, for example, the secretary writes that Lame had been preparing "a general Indian uprising" to take place in 1916; that the Indian leader had been instigating and organizing all the way from Bogotá (where he had traveled to search for land titles) to Tierradentro; that fortunately Lame had been denounced by "the Indian governor of Julumito" ("a wise Indian, respectful of legitimate authority") and apprehended, together with his brother Gregorio Nacianceno Lame, and five other *edecanes* (assistants) by the Junín police batallion, under the command of Lieutenant Diago (*Informe del Secretario de Gobierno del Cauca, Leandro Medina, al Governador, año 1915* [Popayán: Imprenta Departamental, Archivo Departamental, Año 1915], pp. 38-42. According to Secretary Medina, Lame's purpose would have been "to separate the Indians from the whites and to reclaim their lands" (ibid., p. 40).

22. This seems to have been one of the favorite insults thrown at Lame by his urban enemies; he refers to it several times in "Los Pensamientos," e.g., par. 43, 221.

23. *Governor's decree no. 261,* of May 28, 1911 (Popayán: Archivo Departamental, Año 1911).

24. *Informe sobre Orden Público, Secretaría de Gobierno* (Popayán: Archivo Departamental, 1916), pp. 33-35.

25. Ibid., p. 35.

26. Lame denounced the direct participation of priests in his persecution and of having, at least in one occasion, encouraged the torture and killing of Indians suspected of protecting him ("Por mi Desventurada Raza" [message of Manuel Quintín Lame to the civil authorities]), *El Espectador,* January 23, 1922, p. 1. See also "Las Crueldades de los Misioneros Españoles en Tierradentro" (interview of Quintín Lame by Mario Ibero), *El Espectador,* July 12, 1924, p. 1.

27. *Informe sobre Orden Público, Secretaría de Gobierno* (Popayán: Archivo Departamental, 1917), pp. 35-38.

28. Interview with Victor Lame (Quintín's nephew) in the hacienda San Alfonso, near San Isidro, July 16, 1971 (Archives, CDI, Bogotá).

29. "Pensamientos," par. 22. Years later Lame recalled: "I had been held incommunicado since the day I was captured on the Bridge El Cofre because of a treason on May 9 of 1915. And on May 9 of 1916 the blacksmith came in hastily, armed with hammer and chisel, and said: 'Señor Lame, I have come to take off

the bar between your feet. Congratulations!'" (ibid., par. 23).

30. Par. 22. For an analysis of this experience, see above, pp. 48ff.

31. The secretary of government reported the following year that "The Indians cover up |Lame's activities| and render him an effective espionage system, while at the same time they propagate false rumors and misleading reports about his whereabouts" (*Informe*, p. 38).

32. Ibid.

33. *Informe*, p. 37. This event became nationally known with several versions of what actually happened. Father David González has gathered the most common version prevailing among the white population: *"En 1916 sucedió en Tierradentro la Quintinada, movimiento subversivo racial encabezado por Manuel Quintín Lame, de raza Páez, nacido en la hacienda San Isidro de Popayán. Congregó una multitud de raza Páez, avanzó hacia Tierradentro a exigir de manera violenta el éxodo de todo elemento que no fuera indígena de la región. Desde su cuartel de Guanacas envió un ultimatum al alcalde Benjamín Nieto Guzman. Le daba 24 horas a él y a todos los blancos para salir de tierra Páez. El alcalde contestó al fin del papel: 'te doy doce horas para que te entregues incondicionalmente.' Avanzaron los indios contra Inzá. El alcalde ocultó seis hombres armados a la vera del camino, él, armado de un machete esperó sólo en el centro de la vía. Llegó el tropel indígena, arrebató el alcalde la bandera, dió un machetazo al indio, dió orden de fuego, seis rindieron la vida, hubo heridos; huyó la multitud en desbandada, por Yaquivá, San Andrés y Tumbichuque. Guió Quintín sus montoneras al municipio de Páez. Los revoltosos cogieron mucha fuerza. La ilusión del triunfo de la raza engrosó las huestes de Quintín, el Gobierno nacional envió al general Enrique Palacios, quien no dió cuartel a los revoltosos, muchos cayeron, otros fueron a dar al panóptico o a la cárcel"* (*Los Páeces*, pp. 104-5).

34. "Por mi Desventurada Raza," p. 1.

35. "Las Crueldades de las Misioneros," p. 1.

36. In a telegram to Bogotá requesting reinforcements, the governor stressed the urgency of the crisis: "The moment has arrived for the political authorities to act with energy to regain public tranquility and to guarantee the rights of peaceful citizens |and| the interests of the white race which is under threat!" (telegram addressed to the ministers of state and war, November 1916). *Informe del Secretario Gobierno al Gobernador del Cauca, Orden Público, 1917* (Popayán: Archivo Departamental).

37. The capture took place near the Palacé River while he attended a "secret appointment" (*una cita secreta*) at the house of José María López, the one mestizo peasant who had been able to gain Quintín's absolute confidence (personal testimony of his daughter Tulia López, in Cali, July 17, 1971. Archives, CDI, Bogotá). Tulia López explained the reasons for the betrayal: "Lame wanted the rich to disappear; |he| wanted to eat their cattle, take away their lands . . . the rich of Popayán were in despair and all of them (the Arboledas, the Angulos, the Valencias) offered to give my father money . . . but you know that if the money is not received first, afterwards one gets nothing. They did not give anything . . . instead my father earned for himself the hatred of the Indians and, with his ten children, had to flee the area because the Indians threatened to burn his house."

38. Report on public order, 1917 (Popayán: Archivo Departamental). Spanish original: *"A Don Pio Collo, Indígena de prestigio en Tierradentro y que no apoyaba a Lame, interesó la Gobernación avida de restablecer la tranquilidad para que contribuyera al mantenimiento del orden, y a infundir en los indígenas el respeto y acatamiento a las autoridades legitimas. Otro tanto se hizo con los Reverendos Padres Misioneros de esas regiones."*

39. Lame wrote about this period: "My campaign began in April 1922 and ended on December 31, 1938"("Pensamientos," par. 57). However, this period

may be said to have lasted until December 31, 1939, when Lame finished his manuscript, or it might even be extended through April, 1942, when the registry of the newly reconstituted *resguardo* of Ortega-Chaparral was declared formally closed. Even though Lame spent the rest of his life in Tolima, only during the 1920s and 30s did he follow the kind of concerted pattern of activity towards a discernible goal that would qualify as a "campaign." Later, Lame's activities were dictated by the survival needs imposed on the entire peasant population by "La Violencia," an explosion of social and political violence which battered most of the country during the 1940s and 50s.

40. Lame seems to have left the Popayán prison with a renewed sense of destiny, even of predestination. On his way to Tolima he traveled first to Bogotá with the intention of delivering a "message to the high powers," which the national press published in part. The "message" was couched in messianic language. Lame introduced himself thus: "Having passed almost five centuries [since the Spanish invasion of America] there makes its appearance someone in the shape of a pilgrim, breaking through the shadows of the night; in the same way in the midst of the darkness of ignorance I have been able to catch a glimpse of the valley of justice, and before the end of my days I have considered presenting myself privately and publicly before the societies that guard this valuable treasure [justice] so that they may be able to examine in detail all the vexations and crimes committed violently and villainously against the Indian race, and punish the guilty and grant each of us the rights that are rightly our own" ("Por mi Desventurada Raza. Mensaje de Quintín Lame a los Altos Poderes," *El Espectador*, January 23, 1922) [Bogotá: Archivo de la Biblioteca Nacional, Sala de Periódicos]. Despite his high hopes, Lame was unable to meet with the "high powers" and instead found himself temporarily detained by the police as part of the investigation of certain crimes which had just taken place in Huila, and which involved his sympathizers of that area ("El Cacique Quintín Lame ha sido detenido por causa de los disturbios del Caguan," *El Espectador,* March 17, 1922) [Bogotá: Archivo de la Biblioteca Nacional, Sala de Periódicos].

41. This has been the position of the authorities of the department of Tolima from the 19th century to this day (see Pedro Labrador Rivera, "Estudio del Problema de Indígenas de Ortega," *Informe Rendido al Gobierno del Tolima,* November 18, 1953) [Ibague: Archivo de la Gobernación, 1953].

42. In spite of these obvious signs of assimilation, racial and ethnic identity had not been fully lost, as indicated by the fact that in the 1920s and 30s the official studies of the area registered that as many as 90 percent of the rural population were "Indians" and reported that they were concentrated in the municipalities of Purificación, Natagaima, Coyaima, and Ortega (see Gonzalo Paris-Lozano, *Geografía Económica de Colombia*, VII, Tolima [Bogotá: Publicaciones de la Contraloria, Editorial Santa Fe, 1946], pp. 81ff.

43. See Absalon Machado C., *El Café: de la Aparcería al Capitalismo* (Bogotá: Editorial Punta de Lanza, 1977), pp. 245ff. Also, Paris-Lozano, *Geografía*, pp. 171ff. See also Gloria Gaitan, *La Lucha por la Tierra en la Década del Treinta* (Bogotá: Ediciones Tercer Mundo, 1976). pp. 63ff.

44. On the social and political dynamics of the period, see Gaitan, *Lucha;* Alvaro Tirado Mejía, *Aspectos Políticos del Primer Gobierno de Alfonso López Pumarejo, 1934-1938* (Bogotá: Instituto Colombiano de Cultura, 1981); Dario Mesa, "El Problema Agrario en Colombia, 1920-1960," in *La Agricultura en Colombia en el Siglo XX,* Mario Arrubla, ed. (Bogotá: Instituto Colombiano de Cultura, 1976), pp. 83-147; Gonzalo Sánchez G., *Las Ligas Campesinas en Colombia* (Bogotá: Ediciones Tiempo Presente, 1977); and Hermes Tovar, *El Movimiento Campesino en Colombia durante los Siglos XIX y XX,* 2nd edition (Bogotá: Ediciones Libres, n.d.).

45. (See the full analysis and interpretation of Lame's ideology above, pp. 47ff.) During the early years of his Cauca campaign, Lame seemed to have belonged to the Conservative Party and conservative politicians tried to capture his popular base, without success. In Tolima both liberals and conservatives courted Lame's allegiance but the charismatic leader rejected them both when he realized that both followed the policy of deception and self-enrichment (*la política de negocio*) ("Pensamientos," par. 201). Lame was also courted by socialist intellectuals in the 1920s and by some communist leaders in the 1930s. About these contacts he wrote: "I wish to refer... to a number of non-Indians who have asked me to walk in their paths, to follow their teachings, to develop their doctrines, in favor and in defense of my people. But I offered them all the flower of contempt and went on with a very high faith searching the road of the good" (ibid., par. 51). Lame's apparent rejection of the socialist doctrine was not shared by a good number of Indian leaders from Cauca and Tolima who became nationally known for their intelligence and political capacity in the early stages of the socialist movement of Colombia. Among these leaders were José Gonzalo Sánchez and Eutiquio Timoté. In his history of the popular struggles of the Colombian masses the socialist intellectual Ignacio Torres Giraldo wrote: "Quintín Lame was the Indian representative to a Workers National Congress in 1925 and the following year led an uprising of the natives against the system of absentee ownership of land (*latifundismo*) in Tolima. [However] that courageous leader [Lame] who distinguished himself by his long hair and his respectable hieroglyphic signature was finally converted [to the Catholic faith] in the jail of Ibagué, in 1930, and relegated to live his senility as a convert in the town of Ortega, Tolima" (*La Cuestión Indígena en Colombia* [Bogotá: Publicaciones de la Rosca, 1975], p. 96). This summary indictment, however, does not do justice to the reality of Lame's profound religious faith before 1930 or to his untiring political activity from 1930 until the end of his life in 1967.

46. A short account of these activities and of their relation to the wider social process going on in the area during the 20s and 30s is given in G. Castillo-Cárdenas, "Estudio Introductorio. Manuel Quintín Lame: Luchador e Intelectual Indígena del Siglo XX." In Manuel Quintín Lame, *En Defensa de Mi Raza* (Bogotá: Comité de Defensa del Indio, 1971), pp. xi-xiv.

47. The appointment was made through a legal document (*poder general*), registered in the Public Notary of Purificación. The family heads who signed the document were among the most traditional Indian families of the region: Totena, Sogamoso, Capera, Tique, Bocanegra, Asencio, Yate, Rada, Oyola, Tapiero, Chilatra, Ducuara, Alape, Maceto, Luna, Cerquera, Vinche, Aguja, Vaquiro, Montiel, Yara, Caleno, etc. Through this document both Indian leaders were recognized as "the Chiefs of the Indigenous Tribes of Colombia," and charged with the following responsibilities: (1) to establish an Indian settlement (*una población indígena*) with school, church, and other houses, and to make collections to that end; (2) to initiate the necessary lawsuits to reclaim the lands of the old *resguardo* "which have been snatched off from us through violence by the civilized white and mestizo who now possess them"; (3) to do everything within their capacity "for the general good of the Indian race as well as for the education of our children"; (4) to reorganize the government of the *resguardo* according to Law 89 of 1890; and (5) "to assure that our *resguardo* is respected!" (*Escritura No. 165*, May 15, 1924, Tomo 3 [Purificación, Tolima: Notaría del Circuito, 1924], folios 874-83).

48. Information provided by the old Lamista militants Abel Tique and Lisandro Pérez, who were interviewed several times from 1970 to 1973 at the house of the *cabildo* in Ortega, Tolima.

49. These same holidays, without the nativistic features added by Lame, have been celebrated in the Huila-Tolima area since colonial times as *fiestas reales*

with the supervision of the local priests and the official sponsorship of the civil authorities (see Cesareo Rocha-Castilla, *Prehistoria y Folclor del Tolima,* pp. 10ff.).

50. The original manuscript is kept in the Archives of the Cabildo Indígena, Ortega, Tolima. A copy has been published in *Manuel Quintín Lame, El Indio que Bajó de la Montaña al Valle de la Civilización* (Bogotá: Editorial La Rosca, 1971), pp. 20-36.

51. The regional and national press vented these fears and magnified the threat of the movement as reflected in the following headlines: "Mas de Mil Indios de Tierradentro se han Alzado en Armas y han declarado en Estado de Sitio a Ortega," *El Espectador,* July 28, 1923; "Se han Sublevado las Tribus Indígenas en el Huila y en el Sur del Tolima: Las Gobernaciones de Neiva y de Ibagué concentran tropas para defender las propiedades; los sublevados intentan apoderarse de las haciendas" (report from Girardot), *El Espectador,* May 5, 1923, p. 1; "El Cacique Lame y sus Secuaces Amenazan con Atacar a Ibagué" (report from Ibagué), *El Espectador,* September 7, 1923, p. 5; "Se Tomarán Enérgicas Medidas en Ibague para Dominar la Rebelión de los Indios en Ortega" (report from Ibagué), *El Espectador,* September 9, 1923, p. 5 [Bogotá: Archivo de la Biblioteca Nacional, Sección Periódicos].

52. Besides Lame's own memories of these events scattered throughout "Los Pensiamientos," and the testimonies of old Lamista militants who were still alive in 1973, various non-Indian citizens of Ortega who took part in the repression of the movement were also interviewed the same year. Among them, Ramón Rivera, local politician of the Liberal Party, and Jesús Abraham Ramírez, landowner and businessman of the Conservative Party. Both sides coincide in the basic facts of the fateful events of 1931: (1) it was an attack planned and carried out by influential citizens of Ortega; (2) it took place in the late afternoon of a Saturday, the day before a crucial municipal election; (3) several Indians were killed and many wounded; (4) the Indian hamlet was burned to the ground; (5) Lame escaped the attack without injury, a fact which, according to the Lamista informants, was due to his supernatural power to become "invisible."

53. "Pensamientos," par. 59.

54. It is not known how many persons participated in the assembly. The minutes of the *cabildo* say simply that it was "an extraordinary number of natives" (*Acta No. 1,* January 22, 1940, registered as *Escritura No. 162,* October 2, 1941, folio 2934. Purificación, Tolima: Notaría del Distrito, 1941). The Lamista Indians emphasized the risk involved: "Whenever we met in a certain place to deliberate about the ways of putting into practice Law 89 of 1890, the mayor of Ortega, the municipal judge, and the inspector of police would show up and have us arrested and put in jail, sometimes in groups of up to 100 natives, and then punished us with forced labor in the streets of Ortega" (Leoncio Maceto, Delfin Suarez, Pastor Bocanegra, "Declaración extrajuicio" [declaration under oath], registered in *Escritura No. 93,* folios 1609ff. Purificación, Tolima: Notaría del Distrito, 1942). In spite of the formality of the assembly, of which Lame sent prior notification to the municipal authorities, as required by Law 89 (*Acta No. 1,* January 22, 1940), the decision to reconstitute the *resguardo* and the election of the *cabildo* never achieved official recognition, because the mayor of Ortega refused to attend, and his presence and signature were required by Law 89. Lame realized this obstacle and sought validation from the national government in Bogotá, but when this came, it was vague and general. (The letter from the minister of state, Dr. Juan Lozano y Lozano, is transcribed in *Acta No. 1,* January 22, 1940).

55. "Pensamientos," par. 57.

56. The registry or census (*El Libro Padrón*) was formally closed on April 20, 1942, at a special meeting of the council called for that purpose. An impressive

number of family heads (562, representing almost 5,000 persons) had their names registered and their genealogies recorded, going back sometimes to ancestors "who paid tribute to the king of Spain" (*Escritura No. 93*, Notaría de Purificación, Tolima, 1942: folio 1605). However, the profound divisions that had plagued the movement surfaced in the very same meeting. There were Indians "who refused to register in the *Libro Padrón*," or who asked that their names be withdrawn. Among the latter there were two who had belonged since 1938 to the original 12 members of the *cabildo*. Among the reasons given were: "that [the idea] would not work; that [if it worked] it would be a robbery; that they already had their right [by possession], and that the businesses of Ortega had promised to open their doors to them if they kept out of the council" (*Acta No. 8*, April 20, 1942; *Escritura No. 93*, folios 1605ff.). One Indian peasant, Manuel Tapiero, asked that his name be withdrawn because "if the Indians should win, a war would develop!" (ibid.). Lame was deeply moved by those who did sign because it was "a sign of patriotism," considering that the *Libro Padrón* was "sprinkled with tears, pain, and sadness, shed in the dungeons of the Tolima Department." At the close of the session Lame addressed the group, saying: "I have been and I am the cry of a race hated by civilization; but God, who is man's creator, has allowed [our race] to continue up to this day, and that the members of this legislation be ready to defend it, by God's power before men" (ibid.).

57. "Pensamientos," par. 57; italics added.

58. Among the first decisions taken by the *cabildo* were the following: (1) to reject the contention of the civil authorities that in Ortega there are no Indians, and to declare that all those who signed the *Libro Padrón* are legitimate Indians; (2) to declare "null and void" any sales that Indians might have made in the past, unless anyone who alleges to have land titles is able to show "either at the head or at the tail of his title" the judicial certification proving that the requisites imposed by Law 89 have been fulfilled (i.e., that Indians were granted judicial permission to sell and that sales were done in public auction); and (3) in consequence, that all properties which are not thus legally protected become the legal property of the *cabildo*, which shall have the right to distribute them among the Indians registered in the *Libro Padrón* (*Acto No. 4*, November 10, 1941. Ortega, Tolima; Archives of the Cabildo Indígena). The actual implementation of these decisions, to the extent that it happened, is described by Gregorio Hernández de Alba, the head of the Division of Indian Resguardos, of the Ministry of Agriculture: "*Ya en los ultimos años, posiblemente apoyados por Quintín Lame, los descendientes de los Indígenas vendedores (i.e., que habían vendido terrenos en el pasado) comenzaron a apoderarse de pequeñas parcelas en lo que fuera propiedad de sus abuelos, levantando sus ranchos de bahareque, haciendo cercados de una hasta mas o menos quince hectáreas, estableciendo cultivos, en tanto que el resto de las haciendas permanecía y permanece por la mayor parte como 'tierra en soltura,' a la manera de las tierras en los llanos orientales*" ("Informe Comisión Tolima," December 12, 1958. Bogotá: Archives of the Ministry of Agriculture, 1958).

59. An impressive testimony of Lame's authority over his Indian peasant constituency is provided by the eminent historian and anthropologist Juan Friede, who at Lame's invitation attended one of his gatherings in July 1943 in the mountains around Ortega. According to Friede, Lame spoke to the audience scattered among banana trees, thundering with accusations of the white authorities, complaining and criticizing the Indians themselves, his own followers, for their lack of discipline; and after every sentence the entire crowd answered: "That is the truth, Quintín Lame!" Friede comments: "This dialogue between a man who looked like a bronze statue standing on the sandy floor and a multitude scattered around the banana field, all of them bathed by the reddish light of the bonfire under the tropical sky full of stars, produced a lasting impression in my mind. It is one revela-

tion of the grandeur of American primitivism: Lame embodied a principle of authority that did not rely either on bayonets or money" (Letter to Javier Arango Ferrer, San Agustin, September 5, 1943. Bogotá: personal archives of the author). There is also the moving testimony of one of the members of the recently reconstituted *cabildo*: "I am but an ignorant Indian, but watching the perseverance of this Caucano Indian who is our chief, many times I have cried in hiding, and only God knows it; because I had heard from my forebears that an Indian would arise to defend the right of the illiterates that have been in slavery under the non-Indian foreigner, according to the prediction of my aged mother who lived 142 years!" (Placido Timotee, *Acta No. 7*, October 10, 1950. Ortega, Tolima: Archives of the Cabildo). Considering Lame's sufferings, another member of the *cabildo* said: "Our representative and advocate [Manuel Quintín Lame] has been as Jesus of Nazareth when he was taken before the judges of Judea to be tried without justice" (Nicolas Chilatra, Cabildo Indígena de Ortega, *Acta No. 30*, November 11, 1950, registered as *Escritura No. 276*, Tomo 8, folios 2686ff. Purificación: Notaría del Circuito, 1950).

60. See Mons. German Guzmán-Campos, et al., *La Violencia en Colombia*, 2 vols., 2nd ed. (Bogotá: Ediciones Tercer Mundo, 1962); Dario Fajardo, *Violencia y Desarrollo*, Colección Historia (Bogotá: Fondo Editorial Suramérica, 1979); Orlando Fals-Borda, "The Role of Violence in the Break with Traditionalism: The Colombian Case," in *Transactions of the Fifth World Congress of Sociology*, vol. 3 (Washington, D.C.: September 2-8, 1962), pp. 21-31.

61. In 1950 Lame called the Indian peasants to a new registration to update the *Libro Padrón*, but only nine families came forward to sign up (*Acta No. 30*, November 11, 1950).

62. Bogotá: Archives of the Ministry of Agriculture, 1967.

63. The reference here is to the organization of the Consejo Regional Indígena del Cauca, CRIC, in February of 1971. (See CRIC, *Nuestras Luchas De Ayer y De Hoy*, Cartilla, No. 1, Feb. de 1973.)

64. "Pensamientos," par. 50.
65. Ibid., par. 157.
66. Ibid.
67. Ibid., par. 158.
68. Ibid., par. 160.
69. Ibid., par. 44.
70. Ibid., par. 157.
71. Ibid., par. 205.
72. Ibid., par. 206.
73. Ibid., par. 209.
74. Ibid., par. 65, 131.
75. Ibid., par. 176.
76. Ibid., par. 46.
77. Ibid., par. 129.
78. Ibid., par. 92.
79. See above, chap. 2.
80. "Pensamientos," par. 172.
81. See ibid., par. 30
82. Ibid., par. 31
83. Ibid., par. 33.
84. For an analysis of Lame's eschatological ideas, see below, chap. 4.
85. "Pensamientos," par. 32, 48, etc.
86. See above, pp. 48ff.
87. "Pensamientos," par. 22.

88. Ibid., par. 47.
89. Ibid., par. 136.
90. Ibid., par. 4.
91. Ibid., par. 90.
92. Ibid., par. 30.
93. Ibid., par. 28.
94. Ibid., par. 31.
95. Ibid.
96. Ibid., par. 201.
97. Ibid., par. 168.
98. Ibid., par. 171.
99. Ibid.
100. Ibid., par. 197.
101. Ibid., par. 116, 197.
102. Ibid., par. 82.
103. "Las crueldades de los Misioneros Españoles en Tierradentro." Interview of Quintín Lame by Mario Ibero, *El Espectador,* July 12, 1924, p. 1 [Archivo Nacional, Bogotá, Sala Periódicos].
104. Father Luis Alberto Lombo "used the confessionary to impose penance on the Indians to force them to stop making petitions to the authorities, and to abandon Quintín Lame who was the Anti-Christ" (*Acta No. 1*, Cabildo Indígena de Ortega-Chaparral, December 31, 1953) [Archivo, Cabildo Indígena, Ortega].
105. See Rudolf Otto, *The Idea of the Holy* (New York: Oxford University Press, 1958).
106. "Pensamientos," par. 22.
107. Probably in April 1916; see ibid., par. 22.
108. Ibid.
109. Ibid., par. 40.
110. Ibid., italics added.
111. Ibid., par. 221.
112. Ibid., par. 40.
113. Ibid., par. 120.
114. Ibid., par. 221; italics added. This insistence in the "hominization" process achieved through his religious experience acquires its full significance in view of the historical experience of the Indian population, because as Lame himself denounced: the Spanish "treated us as beasts of burden, and still continue to do so" (ibid., par. 27).
115. Ibid., par. 41, 78, etc.
116. Ibid., par. 78, 96.
117. Ibid., par. 238.
118. Ibid., par. 41.
119. Ibid., par. 96.
120. See n. 17 above.
121. "Pensamientos," par. 47.
122. Ibid., par. 162.
123. Ibid., par. 69.
124. Ibid., par. 96.
125. Ibid., par. 150.
126. Ibid., par. 120.
127. See n. 17, above.
128. "Pensamientos," par. 240.
129. Ibid., par. 198.
130. Ibid., par. 20.

131. Ibid., par. 45.
132. Ibid., par. 115.
133. Ibid., par. 51. For this reason the non-Indian will also be referred to as the "white-mestizo" in my interpretation of Lame's thought.
134. See ibid., par. 105.
135. Ibid., par. 72.
136. Sometimes Lame uses also the expression *los indiecitos* (the poor little Indians) to refer to Indians as a people, and in several passages he uses it in the singular (*el indiecito*) referring to himself (see ibid., 17, 27, 167). The same expression is commonly used by the white mestizo population to refer to the Indians who stroll down from the surrounding countryside into the towns on market days. It is a condescending, paternalistic, and benign way of showing pity for the Indians who are considered powerless, harmless, and resigned. Lame's use of the term, therefore, is not without sarcasm.
137. Ibid., par. 96.
138. Ibid., par. 214, 238.
139. Ibid., par. 58.
140. Ibid., par. 21, 78.
141. "Por mi Desventurada Raza," p. 1.
142. "Pensamientos," par. 115.
143. Ibid., par. 105, 196.
144. Ibid., par. 115.
145. Ibid., par. 27; italics added.
146. Ibid., par. 60.
147. Ibid., par. 71.
148. Ibid., par. 198.
149. Ibid., par. 73.
150. Ibid., par. 61.
151. Ibid., par. 45.
152. Ibid., par. 73.
153. Ibid., par. 4. This self-image was shared by his closest Indian followers, judging from the epitaph that they placed on his grave: "Here sleeps Manuel Quintín Lame Chantre: the man who did not humiliate himself before Justice" ("Minutes, No. 72" [Tolima: Archivo, Cabildo Indígena de Ortega], October 7, 1967).
154. Ibid., par. 6.
155. Ibid., par. 80.
156. Ibid., par. 20, 71, 120, etc.
157. Ibid., par. 112, 197.
158. Ibid., par. 163, 198.
159. Ibid., par. 33.
160. Ibid., par. 154. "Spanish blood" stands here for "non-Indian blood."
161. Ibid., par. 31.
162. Ibid., par. 104.
163. Ibid., par. 105.
164. Ibid.
165. Ibid., par. 105.
166. Ibid., par. 146.
167. Ibid.
168. Ibid., par. 238. Throughout "Los Pensamientos" expressions such as "the Spanish civilization," "the white man's civilization," and "the Colombian civilization" (white and mestizo) are used interchangeably.
169. Ibid., par. 144, 146; italics added.
170. Ibid., par. 151.
171. Ibid.

172. Ibid., par. 10.
173. Ibid., par. 16.
174. Ibid., par. 112.
175. Ibid.
176. Ibid., par. 16.
177. Ibid.
178. Ibid., par. 112, 113; italics added.
179. Ibid., par. 19.
180. Ibid., par. 213.
181. Ibid., par. 145.
182. Ibid., par. 239.
183. Ibid., par. 33.
184. Ibid., par. 239.
185. Ibid.
186. Ibid.
187. Ibid., par. 120, etc.
188. Ibid., par. 79, 96, 120, 145, 217, 238, etc.
189. Ibid., par. 167.
190. Ibid., par. 86, 87.
191. Ibid., par. 2, 3; italics added.
192. Ibid., par. 38; italics added.
193. Ibid., par. 62. Lame has in mind the *tinterillos de pueblo* or local practitioners, whose only "title" is that of being friends with the local authorities, and who sooner or later fall into disgrace, sink into poverty, and suffer "hunger, misery, and ruin."
194. Ibid., par. 171.
195. Ibid., par. 145.
196. Ibid., par. 38.
197. Ibid., par. 150.
198. Ibid., par. 35.
199. Ibid., par. 37.
200. See Otero, *Etnología Caucana,* pp. 99ff.; Bernal, "Religious Life," pp. 98-105. The Juan Tama legend is also reported by Trimborn ("South Central America," p. 96).
201. On this historical core there is agreement among ethnohistorians. See Bernal, "Religious Life," pp. 100-105.
202. This summary is based on Bernal's account ("Religious Life," pp. 98ff.) who based his information on direct field research, as well as on the studies made by Hernández de Alba, "The Highland Tribes of Southern Colombia," pp. 953ff.; Pérez de Barradas, *Arqueología,* pp. 8ff.; and Otero, *Etnología Caucana,* pp. 99ff.
203. "Pensamientos," par. 22.
204. Ibid., par. 176.
205. Ibid., par. 167.
206. Ibid., par. 10.
207. Ibid., par. 167.
208. Ibid., par. 204.
209. Ibid., par. 167.
210. Ibid., par. 93.
211. Ibid., par. 96.
212. Ibid., par. 8, 9.
213. "Slowly I have come to see in the midst of such darkness what the Indian is called to become in the future" (ibid., par. 165).
214. This is a widespread popular saying among the Colombian poor.
215. "Pensamientos," par. 167.

178

Notes

216. Ibid., par. 214.
217. Ibid., par. 88.
218. Ibid., par. 115.
219. Ibid., par. 84.
220. See above, pp. 50ff.
221. "Pensamientos," par. 4.
222. Ibid., par. 70.
223. Ibid., par. 5.
224. Ibid., par. 96, 100, 102.
225. Ibid., par. 117.
226. Ibid., par. 116.
227. The understanding that "unjust laws" are invalid, for example, was a well-established ethical criterion coming from the colonial times, based on Thomistic and Suarezian moral theology. The criterion of justice had been in fact wielded every time that an insurrection had taken place in Colombian history. See John Leddy Phelan, *The People and the King: The Comunero Revolution in Colombia, 1781* (Madison: University of Wisconsin Press, 1978), pp. 134-35.
228. "Pensamientos," par. 43.
229. Ibid., par. 183. Lame describes here the process of becoming bilingual, moving from the Páez language of his tribe to the Spanish of the national society.
230. Ibid., par. 12; italics added.
231. Ibid., par. 34; see also above, pp. 37ff.
232. Ibid., par. 57.
233. Ibid., par. 60, 197.
234. Ibid., par. 61, etc.
235. Ibid., par. 68.
236. Ibid., par. 200.
237. Ibid., par. 38.
238. Ibid., par. 90.
239. Ibid., par. 46.
240. Ibid., par. 29.
241. See above, pp. 67ff.
242. "Pensamientos," par. 99, 104, etc.
243. Unfortunately, the colonial period had produced in the *resguardo* Indians a sort of legalist deformation evident in the blind confidence they placed in the letter of the law, as though this in itself were an effective guarantee of their rights in practice, independently of those who control the system. Researchers into the social history of Indian areas have come across the pathetic experience of communities following for generations the deceptive method of "juridical struggle," in which their Indian chiefs exhausted themselves physically and economically paying barristers and presenting thousands of petitions, appeals, and affidavits of every kind, to prove what everybody knew — namely, that the land belongs to the Indians, whereas the white landgrabbers (usually the great patriots and patricians of the region) took possession of Indian lands by force, deceit, or coercion. In this way entire communities were wiped out in Cauca, Huila, Tolima, Caldas, and Cundinamarca, in the Colombian Andes. One scholar explains Indian legalism as follows: "It is understandable that a weak and unarmed Indian, standing in the margin of the political and social life of the country, should look on the law as his only source of protection. Without weapons or resources, at the mercy of social forces which he does not understand, harassed on every side, the Indian becomes the victim of the judicial system which postpones his lawsuits, does not carry out decisions when they are in his favor, and obstructs the course of justice. With time he becomes convinced that he has the law on his side but that it is 'the government' which is responsible for his misfortunes" (Juan

Friede, *El Indio en Lucha por la Tierra* [Bogotá: Ediciones Espiral, 1944], pp. 37-38).

CHAPTER 4

1. See chap. 3 above; also, Diego Castrillón-Arboleda, *De la Colonia al Sub-desarrollo* (Popayán: Editorial Universidad, 1970).
2. This appellative was used time and again in reference to Lame and his closest followers by the Lamista Indians themselves during my field research from 1970 to 1973.
3. See chap. 3, n. 17. On one occasion a reporter from Bogotá asked Lame about the point in time when he first began to fight for his people, and Lame answered: "Ever since I was aware of myself." The reporter kept searching for a date and then Lame became more precise: "Ever since I started wearing trousers" (interview with Quintín Lame, *El Espectador*, July 12, 1924, p. 1). However, though it may be true that Lame's rebellious *spirit* could be traced back to his childhood, it seems that his first open act of rebellion which took the form of an "uprising" was in fact ignited by the incident to which he referred in his inter-view with Hernández de Alba (chap. 3, n. 17). The precise date of this occurrence has not been identified, but it probably took place in 1910.
4. "Pensamientos," par. 10, 214, 51.
5. The title "prophet" is less ideologically bound or theologically confined than is the concept "messiah" in both Jewish and Christian traditions. In the vast literature about "prophets" arising in colonial situations, the works of E. E. Evans-Pritchard (*Neuer Religion* [Oxford, 1956], pp. 287-310) and Dorothy Emmett ("Prophets and Their Societies," *Journal of the Royal Anthropological Institute,* 86 [1956] 13-23) are most helpful. More recently, with emphasis on the effects in the political field of prophetic activities and movements, the work of Michael Adas, *Prophets of Rebellion: Millenarian Protest Movements Against the Euro-pean Colonial Order* (Chapel Hill: University of North Carolina Press, 1970) is illustrative of the universality of the religious phenomenon associated with the category of prophet.
6. See above, pp. 34-35.
7. "Pensamientos," par. 166.
8. Kenelm Burridge attaches importance to the role of interpreter as a means of gaining recognition and authority in the case of "oceanic prophets" (*New Heaven, New Earth: A Study of Millenarian Activities* [New York: Schocken Books, 1969], pp. 153ff.).
9. See above, pp. 14ff.
10. See above, p. 6.
11. "Pensamientos," par. 239.
12. Ibid., par. 226.
13. Genesis 18:27.
14. Rudolf Otto, *The Idea of the Holy,* p. 50. Otto suggests that this attitude is related to the "creature-feeling" that according to him is inherent in human nature.
15. "Pensamientos," par. 214.
16. Ibid., par. 22.
17. Ibid., par. 31, 154.
18. According to Enrique Dussel, "The rural population [of Latin America] is weighed down by the traditions of the 'mediations' instilled by the practices of Catholicism — the 'fiestas,' the 'prayers,' the 'devotions' and the pilgrimages to holy places — many times associated with the superstition and magic of folk Ca-tholicism" (*A History of the Church in Latin America* [Grand Rapids: Eerdmans, 1981], p. 120). This lack of integration is, rather than syncretism, the major char-

acteristic of the popular religiosity of the Latin American countryside. The Christianity of the masses has been traditionally charged by some with being simply "external" and not internalized; and by others with being a juxtaposition of two religions: the religion of the missionaries and the pre-Columbian religion of the Indians. Neither of these seems to be the case. According to Dussel what appears to have taken place is "an accumulation of Hispanic Catholic liturgy with its many gestures, symbols, and attitudes that were rooted in the prehispanic religions: not so much a *mixed* religion as an *eclectic* accumulation" (ibid., p. 68).

19. "Pensamientos," par. 6.
20. Ibid., par. 42.
21. Ibid., par. 20.
22. Ibid., par. 134.
23. Ibid., par. 135.
24. In a related passage Lame called the creation story a "legend," somewhat "improbable" (*inverosímil*), and spoke rather of "the creation of the world" which could have taken place "in great epochs," where "the world" seems to stand for "human history" (ibid., par. 123, 124).
25. Ibid., par. 36.
26. Ibid., par. 49.
27. Ibid., par. 47.
28. Ibid., par. 139, 141.
29. Ibid., par. 214.
30. Ibid., par. 44, 46.
31. Ibid., par. 148.
32. Ibid., par. 32.
33. The plurality of the divinity is one of the characteristics of the pre-Columbian religions of the Andes, both before and after the Inca empire. See José Imbelloni, *Religiosidad Indígena Americana* (Buenos Aires: Ediciones Castañeda, 1981), pp. 133ff. In south central America and the northern Andes, between the advanced civilizations of Mesoamerica in the north and the Inca empire in the south, Chibcha religious traditions were also characterized by plurality. See Herman Trimborn, "South Central America and the Andean Civilizations," in Walter Krickberg, et al., *Pre-Columbian American Religions* (New York: Holt, Rinehart and Winston, 1968), pp. 83ff. Scholars agree that in the preconquest religion of the central Andes the divinity manifested itself in a triad form whose members were variously identified in different periods and regions. According to one tradition the sun (*Apu-Inti*) was the first member; the day (*Churi-Inti*) was the second; and the third was "the brother" (*Inti-Guauqui*) who possessed the virtue of creating. *Guauqui* manifested itself in a triad form also, by lightning (*chuquilla*), thunder (*catuilla*), and lightning-bolt (*inti-illapa*). See R. Kusch, *El Pensamiento Indígena y Popular en América* (Buenos Aires: Hachette, 1973), pp. 98ff., and Jacques Monast, *L'univers religieux des Aymaras de Bolivie,* Sondeos No. 10 (Cuernavaca, Mexico, 1966), pp. 26ff. See also Imbelloni, *Religiosidad Indígena Americana,* pp. 308ff. Plurality seems to have been also the fundamental characteristic of pre-Columbian theology among the Maya. According to the *Popol Vuh,* for example, God was conceived as a duality and sometimes as a trinity or a quaternity. See Miguel León-Portilla, *Time and Reality in the Thought of the Maya* (Boston: Beacon Press, 1973), pp. 35ff.; Dennis Tedlock, *The Spoken Word and the Work of Interpretation* (Philadelphia: University of Pennsylvania Press, 1983), pp. 280ff.
34. "Pensamientos," par. 131.
35. Ibid., par. 55, 78, 147.
36. Ibid., par. 156.
37. Ibid., par. 176.

38. Lame's reference seems to be to Mama Ocllo, the wife of the first Inca emperor, Manco Capac, who himself had been the child of the sun. See Monast, *L'univers,* p. 27. However, in another context Lame refers to a tradition that links Ollo or Ocllo to "the northern coasts of Mexico" ("Pensamientos," par. 127).

39. "Pensamientos," par. 131, 132, 181.

40. "Pensamientos," par. 127: "God, that is to say, Jehovah, the true Muschca, in the language taught by Ollo, the woman who appeared to educate my race three hundred years before October 12 |1492|. But she was not born of a woman, but had been sent by Nature to educate my race . . . she taught some Indian peoples one language and others another."

41. Kusch, *Pensamiento Indígena,* pp. 109ff.

42. The persistence of this feature in the popular religiosity of Indian regions of the Andes has been documented by the empirical studies of Monast, *L'univers,* pp. 60ff.; Manuel Marzal, *Estudios sobre Religión Campesina* (Lima: Pontificia Universidad Católica del Perú, 1977), pp. 43ff.; idem, *El Mundo Religioso de Urcos* (Cuzco: Instituto de Pastoral Andina, 1971), pp. 253ff.

43. "Pensamientos," par. 40.

44. Ibid., par. 22.

45. Ibid., par. 221.

46. Ibid., par. 22.

47. See above, p. 50.

48. "Pensamientos," par. 96.

49. The biblical doctrine of eschatology covers a broad variety of related themes including: expectation of the *eschaton* ("the end"), associated with rewards and punishments; belief in a millennium, a period of earthly felicity presided over by God; tension between "the already" and "the not yet" because of the New Testament belief that in some sense "the end" has already come in Jesus Christ; and belief that the blessings of the present age are the pledge and guarantee of greater blessings to come. But underlying all these there is a peculiar conception of history, with two major features: (1) that history is the working out of God's purposes; and (2) that history is moving towards a goal: the new heavens and the new earth. See Anthony A. Hoekema, *The Bible and the Future* (Grand Rapids: Eerdmans, 1979).

50. "Pensamientos," par. 49.

51. "Pensamientos," par. 35.

52. Ibid.

53. Ibid., par. 105.

54. According to Lame the Indian ancestors were not totally unaware of their prescribed disgrace since it had been predicted that "the Indian sages and sovereigns" were to fall captive to "Guagaz" (the white man) ("Pensamientos," par. 35).

55. See above, p. 60.

56. "Pensamientos," par. 167, 204.

57. Ibid., par. 170.

58. Felipe Guaman Poma de Ayala, born around 1535, finished his 1179-page *La Nueva Corónica y Buen Gobierno* around 1615. He intended to deliver it personally to the king of Spain. According to his own testimony he was a pure Indian, a descendant, on his father's side, of the Yarovillca kings of Huanaco, and on his mother's side of Tupac Yapanqui, the tenth Inca. (The name Ayala had been granted to Felipe's father, Don Martin Guaman Mallqui, by Captain Luis Avalos de Ayala as a reward for having saved his life in the battle of Huarina in 1547.) Having been expropriated of his estates by a *curaca* collaborator of the Spaniards, he lived in a personal way the oppression of the Indian. His chronicle, written in broken Spanish mixed with Quechua, is not simply a memory or account of what was going on; it is also a painful cry: "To write about it," he says, "is to

cry." All along his work he repeats over and over again like a ritual lamentation: *El mal no tiene remedio . . . no hay nada que hacer* ("the damage has no remedy; nothing can be done"). However, his project of addressing the king carried with it the hope of a decisive intervention. For information and analysis of Guaman Poma and his work, I have relied on Juan M. Ossio, "The Idea of History in Felipe Guaman Poma de Ayala" (thesis for B. Litt., Oxford University, 1970). A summary of Ossio's manuscript is included in his *Ideología Mesiánica del Mundo Andino,* pp. 155-213. See also Nathan Wachtel, "Pensamiento salvaje y aculturación: el espacio y el tiempo en Felipe Guaman Poma de Ayala y el Inca Garcilaso de la Vega," in *Sociedad e Ideología,* pp. 165-228.

59. Poma divides Indian history into four periods, or ages, with a fifth added to cover the Inca empire. In the primordial period the land was populated by the *Huari Virococha Runa* (*Huari*: ancient, autocthonous; *Viracocha*: God, the creator and civilizer; *Runa*: men). The second age belonged to the *Huari Runa* (ancient men), who learned to till the land, to build canals and houses. Although still "barbarians" they respected God's commandments, did not have idols, and worshiped only one God, in three persons, symbolized by three forms of lightning. The third age is called *Purum Runa* (desert people, or people of confusion and disorder). At this time Indians multiplied "like the sands of the sea" and spread out to the lowlands. They learned special skills and created the first political institutions. The fourth age belonged to the *Auca Pacha Runa* (*Auca*: war; *Pacha*: epoch). It was the age of wars. The conflicts which started in the previous age were intensified. However, civilization reached high peaks and there was abundance as never before. The fifth age is that of the *Inca Pacha Runa*: the epoch of the Incas. Poma, who belonged to the non-Incan nobility, expresses his dislike of the Incan domination but recognizes that the Incas perfected the political institutions, created the service of the *chasquis* (mail), and achieved unparalleled power. Poma's view of the biblical and Western world is not totally integrated within his vision of history: Adam and Eve and their descendants, up to the flood, constitute the first epoch; the second epoch begins with Noah whose children repopulate the earth; the third age is inaugurated by Abraham and runs through the time of the judges; the fourth is initiated by David and corresponds to the time of the kings; finally the fifth age begins with Jesus Christ whose birth is placed by the author at the time of the second Incan emperor, Inca Sinchi Roca. During the reign of that same ruler, the Apostle St. Bartholomew came to the (West) Indies and evangelized the Indians.

60. "Pensamientos," par. 21; italics added.

61. Ibid., par. 33; italics added.

62. Ibid., par. 196.

63. Ibid., par. 18, 21.

64. One of the most widespread forms of this popular lore is known in the Andes as the *Mito de Inkarri* (the myth of the Inca king), which conceives of the body of the Inkarri actually living in the underworld (the *Uku Pacha*), together with his guard. His body would be in the process of reintegrating itself and growing underground until it would encompass the entire extension of the *tawantinsuyo* (the sacred territory of the Inca empire). When the Inca's body would reach these limits, he would reappear above ground to restore the right order of the world, a restoration which would take place by means of the symmetrical reversal of the present historical condition of Indians and whites. See J.M. Arguedas and Josafat R. Pineda, "Tres Versiones del Mito de Inkarri"; Onorio Ferreiro, "Significado e Implicaciones Universales de un Mito Peruano," in Ossio, *Ideología,* pp. 219-36 and 417-38. One investigator reports that a certain Indian, Juan Coleto, of the community of Vicos, Peru, answered the question "How do the dead live in heaven?" in the following way: "Only the soul . . . . The body ends

in the grave. What does the soul do? It is said that it works with God. As we do here tilling the land, it is sure that the same is there. The rich are there with the head covered, full of shame, and we who are poor here will enjoy all the best there. Here we work with the yoke, there it is the rich who will work like that. There the Indians make the *mistis* and the *señores* work with the whip. As they make us work here, so shall we make them work there" (Alejandro Ortiz, "En Torno a los Mitos Andinos," dissertation, Lima, Universidad de San Marcos, 1971, quoted by Ossio, *Ideología,* p. 211). The hope in a symmetrical reversal of conditions is a common feature of most millennial ideologies arising in Third World situations: see Vittorio Lanternari, *The Religions of the Oppressed* (New York: Mentor, 1965), pp. 240ff.; Peter Worsley, *The Trumpet Shall Sound* (London: McGibbon and Kee, 1957), pp. 44, 47, 96, 115, 135, and passim; Roger Bastide, "Messianisme et développement économique et social," *Cahiers Internationaux de Sociologie,* 30 (1961) 235.

65. "Pensamientos," par. 6.

66. Ibid., par. 10, 11; italics added.

67. Ibid., par. 3, 103, 150, 173, 229, 237.

68. Ibid., par. 3, 103.

69. Ibid., par. 132.

70. Lame probably borrowed the concept of liberation from the nationalistic and patriotic rhetoric of Colombia where the title is profusely used in relation to Simon Bolivar, the "liberator" of five republics. Lame most likely became acquainted with this usage while serving in the army.

71. Ibid., par. 239.

72. Ibid., par. 234, 236.

73. Ibid., par. 229.

74. Ibid., par. 232.

75. The Páez distinguish two kinds of souls: one they call *us* (heart) which animates the body. This is the soul that the shaman is able to treat to keep a sick person alive. The other kind of soul they call *tafi,* which is the one that leaves the body at the moment of death and goes to heaven, purgatory, or hell. See Bernal, "Religious Life," pp. 14-16 and 159.

76. "Pensamientos," par. 3.

77. Ibid., par. 120.

78. Ibid., par. 115. This reflects Lame's own personal experience. Because of his rebellion, he was "hated by the white man, persecuted by the white man, slandered by the white man, and falsely indicted by the white man" (ibid., par. 106).

79. Ibid., par. 33.

80. Ibid., par. 239.

81. Ibid., par. 43.

82. Ibid., par. 57.

83. Ibid., par. 166.

84. Ibid., par. 204.

85. In effect, what seems to fascinate Lame the most about Jesus is his humanity, not in philosophical but in sociological terms: the fact the Jesus was poor, born of poor and persecuted parents, whose father worked as a carpenter, whose condition in life was so much like that of the Indians (ibid., par. 150, 232).

86. The expression "the wretched poor" (*los pobres infelices*) is the descriptive term that Lame uses to identify Indians in their condition of captivity under white-mestizo domination.

87. "Pensamientos," par. 150: "The liberator of Humanity was rocked as a child in a cradle of straw in the same way that the chicks of the fowl are raised, swung by the four winds of the earth, like children of the Indian marriage, in the same way that the author of this work was born."

88. Ibid., par. 16.
89. "Jesus, born in the Inn of Bethlehem, baptized in the river by John the Baptist, worshiped by a wild ass and by other animals, *because men had despised him, following the proud aristocracy* "(ibid., par. 235; italics added).
90. Ibid., par. 103.
91. Ibid., par. 168; italics added.
92. Ibid., par. 239.
93. Ibid.
94. Ibid., par. 57.
95. "From a wild wolf...into a man" (ibid., par. 120); "from savagery and ineptitude into a devoted Indian" (par. 221); from "a savage Indian" into one who renders homage to Christ" (par. 238).
96. Ibid., par. 41.
97. Ibid., par. 78.
98. Ibid., par. 22.
99. Ibid., par. 7.
100. Ibid., par. 7, 120, 162 (title), 222.
101. See above, pp. 57ff.
102. "Pensamientos," par. 15-21. The expression elicits a profound resonance in certain ideological traditions of the Andean world, which seem to have conceived in dual categories the entire order of the universe. This ontological tension would be expressed, for example, in the Quechua concepts of *Hanán* and *Hurín* ("upper" and "lower"), which were maintained in equilibrium thanks to a unitary principle which was the order of the universe (*pacha*). This cosmological vision was reflected in the social order to the point that Incan society was thought to be organized as an equilibrium between the *Hanán* and the *Hurín* sides of the community whose stability rested on the principle of order represented by the Incan king. According to Guaman Poma, the Indian intellectual of the seventeenth century, the right order of the world could be restored only when the Indians recovered their *Hanán* position with respect to the Spaniards. See "Guaman Poma: Nueva Corónica y Buen Gobierno. Un Intento de Aproximación a las Categorías del Pensamiento del Mundo Andino," in Ossio, *Ideología,* pp. 153ff.
103. In this context it is possible to understand his "message" of 1922 "to the high powers," in which he described himself as a "pilgrim" who had come down from the mountains "in the midst of the darkness of the night," with the messianic purpose of defending his race "before the tribunals of civilization" ("Por mi Desventurada Raza, Mensaje de Quintín Lame a los Altos Poderes," *El Espectador,* January 23, 1922, p. 1).
104. Ibid., par. 95.
105. Ibid., par. 213.
106. Ibid., par. 95.
107. Ibid., par. 16.
108. See chap. 2, above.
109. Intersubjectivity as a concept expressing the Indian's special quality of relation to nature does not necessarily mean that objectification of natural forces cannot take place at the same time. In other words, the special quality of relation to the natural environment does not indicate the absence of the subject/object split which is supposed to take place early in human life and history, and should not, therefore, be subjected to the pejorative treatment often given to the concepts of "animism" or "primitive mind," understood in a psychological or evolutionary way.
110. "Pensamientos," par. 226. Lame was particularly impressed by the "order" and "harmony" which he observed in the three natural kingdoms and by the "laws" that regulate the natural environment. He lays special emphasis on the "secrets"

of the vegetable kingdom which Indians learned to use in medicine and which are hidden from the white man because of the latter's predatory attitude towards nature. Lame refused to accept the traditional belief characteristic of "folk Catholicism" that "original sin" is associated with sexual relations between the first woman and the first man, because such relations according to Lame were "natural" (ibid., par. 132). The inference from these reflections seems to be that Lame exempted nature from any form of evil, recognizing in it only positive attributes.

111. Ibid., par. 223, 224.

112. Sevilla-Casas, *Atraso y Desarrollo Indígena en Tierradentro*, p. 123, quoted by Sutti Ortiz in "Models, Reasoning and Economic Behaviour," in L. Holy and M. Stuchlik, eds., *The Structure of Folk Models* (London: Academic Press, A.S.A. Monograph 20, 1981), p.162.

113. The Lamista Indian Gabriel Yaima, who was also the secretary of the Indian *cabildo* of Ortega-Chaparral which Quintín Lame had declared reconstituted in 1939, expressed his revulsion against the sale of land thus: "The Indian who sells land is like Judas Iscariot who sold Jesus Christ our Lord!" (taped interview, October 17, 1970. Archives, CDI, Bogotá). Against this background it is possible to understand how the legal formula used by public notaries to formalize the sale of land must have sounded to Indian ears like a sentence of death. The transaction was called "real sale and perpetual alienation." It read: "*Venta real y enajenación perpetua. Los vendedores (presentes delante del Notario, previamente identificados, etc.), . . . declaran que desde esta fecha se desapoderan, desisten, quitan y apartan de la posesión, propiedad y dominio que a lo vendido tenian adquirido. Y todo lo ceden, renuncian y transpasan a favor del comprador, con las acciones consiguientes, reconociendole como suficiente título de propiedad al efecto, la presente escritura debidamente registrada de la cual le dara copia el suscrito Notario. . . ." Ademas (declaran) "Que la venta la verificaron por la suma o cantidad de ($) papel moneda, que confiesan tener recibidos de mano del comprador, a su entera satisfacción, como asi lo manifestaron en presencia del suscrito Notario y testigos instrumentales*" (*Instrumento No. 156*, May 5, 1917, Oficina de Registro del Guamo, Tolima). English translation: "The persons doing the sale in the presence of the Public Notary, properly identified according to the law, declare that from this moment on they surrender, desist, leave, and separate themselves from the possession, property, and dominion which they previously had over that which is now sold, and everything they give away, renounce, and transfer over in favor of the buyer, with the consequential effects, recognizing as sufficient title of property the present deed, duly signed and registered, of which the Notary Public shall give a copy. . . . They further declare that the sale is made for the amount of . . . |money| which they confess having received to their complete satisfaction from the hands of the buyer, to which they testify before the present Notary and other witnesses."

114. See above, pp. 58ff. The cultural value that Lame is praising here is not resignation but rather what the anthropologist George M. Foster has called "the limited good" concept characteristic of Indian communities. For Foster, the concept of "limited good" is better understood by way of contrast with that of "unlimited good" value that prevails among middle and upper-middle classes of industrial societies and which he summarizes as follows: it is the belief that "if science and technology, together with the appropriate managerial skills, are applied to the exploitation of natural resources, the end result will benefit everyone; and if population growth is rationally controlled, the goods produced will grow at a higher rate, thus assuring that each new generation will have more of the good things in life than did their predecessors." Conversely, "the limited good" concept recognizes that all resources are limited and non-expandable, and suggests that sudden "success" or advancement in the amount of "good things" acquired by one

person can only come at the expense of others. In this latter view, one finds, therefore, according to Foster, "a much greater concern for distributional equity" coupled with distrust and rejection of "the individual entrepreneur" (*Applied Anthropology* [Boston: Little, Brown and Company, 1969], pp. 82-84).

115. The crucial importance of *money* as the symbolic agent of an unknown and uncontrollable power has been underscored by several authors, especially by Kenelm Burridge, as one of the clues to interpret the development of millenarian doctrines and movements within indigenous societies being exposed to monetary economies. For Burridge, even though the advent of money does not necessarily trigger a millenarian movement, nevertheless "money seems to be the most frequent and convenient axis on which millenarian movements turn. Money points out the difference between qualitative and quantitative measures of man in relation to this moral stature. [Thus] money is significant in the colonial situation and in the collision between a subsistence and a complex economy" (*New Heaven, New Earth,* pp. 146ff.).

116. "Pensamientos," par. 185.

117. Ibid., par. 143.

118. Ibid.

119. Ibid., par. 180.

120. See above, pp. 39ff.

121. "Pensamientos," par. 200. Lame's awareness of the threat to survival inherent in the process of Western penetration of Indian regions has been independently recognized and analyzed by a growing number of modern anthropologists. See, e.g., John H. Bodley, "Alternatives to Ethnocide: Human Zoos, Living Museums, and Real People," and Teodoro Binder, "The Right of the Third World to Develop in its Own Way, and Remarks on the Idea of 'Change,'" in Elias Sevilla-Casas, ed., *Western Expansion and Indigenous Peoples* (The Hague and Paris: Mouton Publishers, 1973).

CONCLUSIONS

1. Christian Lalive D'Epiny, *El Refugio de las Masas: Estudio sobre el Pentecostalismo en Chile* (Santiago de Chile, 1966). Aldo Buntig (*El Catolicismo Popular en la Argentina*) reaches similar conclusions. Segundo Galilea, a Catholic scholar who believes in the possibility of "evangelizing popular religiosity" and thus transforming it into a factor of social change, recognizes, however, that there are forms of popular Catholicism "which reinforce a dualist view of reality and therefore a religious attitude that is alienated from the world." He adds: "This popular Catholicism reinforces the social system of Latin America, with all its injustices, contradictions, and oppressions" ("La fe como principio crítico de promoción de la religiosidad popular," in *Fe Cristiana y Cambio Social en América Latina* [Salamanca: Ediciones Sígueme, 1973], p. 152).

2. Thus, for example, Emile Pin and Fernán E. Gonzáles, "Religion y Sociedad en Conflicto," *Ecclesiastica Xaveriana,* 22/1 (1972) 2-75.

3. These conclusions are common to a variety of empirical studies, such as: Benjamin E. Haddox, *Sociedad y Religión en Colombia* (Bogotá: Coedición de Ediciones Tercer Mundo y Facultad de Sociología de la Universidad Nacional, 1965); Orlando Fals-Borda, *Peasant Society in the Colombian Andes* (Gainesville: University of Florida Press, 1955). Fals-Borda has focused his attention on the "passivity" of the Indian-peasant communities of the Andes, but has attributed it not so much to the indigenous worldview that would have persisted, but rather to the very conditions created by the conquest and colonization. One of the social consequences of these historical facts would have been a kind of religion that was imposed, based on obedience and subordination, in which transcendental

decisions about life and death were delegated to the proper authorities, secular or religious. (See "El Campesino Cundi-Boyacence: Conceptos sobre su pasividad," *Revista de Psicología,* 1/1, pp. 74-83.)

4. Further evidence of this same potentiality is being provided currently by certain developments inside Latin American Catholicism, especially at the popular level, where a similar transformation has been observed in the traditional forms of religiosity. The reference here is to the dynamization of "basic Christian communities" and their political involvement, the emergence of a radicalized lower clergy, as well as to the active participation of Christians in revolutionary movements throughout the continent. See Michael Dodson, "The Christian Left in Latin American Politics," in D.H. Levine, ed., *Churches and Politics in Latin America* (Beverly Hills and London: Sage Publications, 1980), pp. 111ff.; Penny Lernoux, *Cry of the People* (Garden City, New York: Doubleday, 1980); Phillip Berryman, *The Religious Roots of Rebellion* (Maryknoll, New York: Orbis, 1984); F. Houtart and E. Pin, *Los Cristianos en la Revolución de América Latina* (Buenos Aires: Editorial Guadalupe, 1966); *Signos de Liberación. Testimonios de la Iglesia en América Latina, 1969-1973* (Lima: CEP, 1973).

5. Lame's theology belongs, therefore, to the genre of religious reflection that has been called "the interpretation of the faith that arises among the poor" and therefore a truly popular theology, about which Gustavo Gutiérrez has written: "Here is truly an 'oppressed theology,' a theology rejected by the powers that be, in complicity with powerful elements in the church.... [It] is generally fragmentary and oral, as manifested in customs, rites, and the like. Only rarely, until now, have their interpretation [i.e., that of the poor] reached the surface of intellectual consciousness" (*The Power of the Poor in History* [Maryknoll, New York: Orbis Books, 1983], p. 94). The same author calls attention to the fact that this kind of theology has always existed among the poor, on "the underside of history" (ibid., pp. 169ff.).

6. See above, pp. 14ff. and 74ff.

7. According to E. Dussel, these religious traditions of the poor become "dynamized" (*se hacen fecundos*) in historical conjuctures of liberation: "*La Virgen de Guadalupe, para dar un ejemplo, mestiza e india (que venerada por los indios y mestizos solo podía ser interpretada simbolicamente por ellos...) madre sin esposo: no era Malinche (la india que traiciono a su pueblo) ni necesitaba a Cortes (el padre del mestizo, conquistador dominador Europeo), siendo virgen y madre del pueblo pudo transformarse en el estandarte de los ejércitos de liberación de Hidalgo y Morelos (1810-1815) y de Pancho Villa y Emiliano Zapata (1910-1917)*" (*Filosofía Etica Latinoamericana,* vol. 5, p. 121).

8. See Sergio Torres and John Eagleson, eds., *The Challenge of Basic Christian Communities* (Maryknoll, N.Y.: Orbis Books, 1981).

9. See José Comblin, *The Church and the National Security State* (Maryknoll, N.Y.: Orbis Books, 1979).

10. See A.A. Hoekema, *The Bible and the Future* (Grand Rapids, Eerdmans, 1979).

11. See J.L. Phelan, *The Millennial Kingdom of the Franciscans in the New World* (Berkeley: University of California Press, 1970).

12. See George V. Pixley, "Divine Judgment in History," in Pablo Richard, et al., *The Idols of Death and the God of Life* (Maryknoll, New York: Orbis, 1983), pp. 46ff.

13. Attention has already been called to the close alliance with the dominant powers that had characterized the history of the Catholic Church in Latin America. This association was loosened but not dissolved under the pressure of the various anticlerical movements that swept the continent after the wars of independence. Even where separation of church and state was achieved at the political level,

this did not affect the deeper alliance of the church with the social and economic establishments of the different countries. As has been shown, this alliance was particularly overt and institutionalized in Indian areas of Colombia, known as "Mission territories." The ethics of domination implicit in the relation began to be questioned in the early decades of the twentieth century under the influence of the moderate wing of Catholic liberalism, some ideas of French social Catholicism, and the church's social doctrine, particularly as conceived by Pope Leo XIII. It was an attempt to open up the church, moderately, to the values of the modern world, especially to the ideals of democracy and freedom. The international economic crisis of the 1930s opened the door for the introduction of political and economic changes in several countries, including Colombia, and the first steps were then taken towards industrialization and the development of the countryside through rural capitalism. The new questions raised by these changes concerning social injustice provided the opportunity for the transfer to Latin America of the Christian social movement that had played a major role in awakening the social consciousness of certain Christian groups in Europe. The poor of Latin America began to be viewed not only as the "underprivileged" members of the social order with a claim to the charity of the rich, but also as the victims of social injustice, which was recognized as the basic cause of misery. However, the fact that society as a whole and its system of values were being questioned at the roots was not seen clearly. Rather, it was thought that to create a more just and humane society was to transform it into something better, by integrating the marginalized and taking care of the most blatant injustices. The vision of the Christian social movements within the church (especially Catholic Action and Christian Democracy) reached only that far. For this reason, despite their good intentions, these movements did not provide in the final instance anything else than a vague general defense of the "dignity" of the human person. (On this historical summary, see E. Dussel, *A History of the Church in Latin America: Colonialism to Liberation, 1492-1979,* pp. 306ff.; J. Catillo, *Las Fuentes de la Democracia Cristiana en Chile* [Santiago de Chile, 1968]; Marie-Dominique Chenu, "The Church's 'Social Doctrine,'" in Pohier and Mieth, *Christian Ethics and Economics: The North-South Conflict,* p. 71ff.).

14. Besides the authors and major works mentioned in chap. 1 (n.19 pp. 158-159 and n. 32 pp. 162-163, above), the following studies are representative: G. Gutierrez, *A Theology of Liberation: History, Politics and Salvation* (Maryknoll, New York: Orbis, 1973); idem, *The Power of the Poor in History* (Orbis, 1983); Sergio Arce, " Hacia una Teología de la Liberación" (Havana: *Jornada Homenaje a Camilo Torres,* 1971); R. Alves, *Religión: ¿Opio o Instrumento de Liberación?* (Montevideo: Tierra Nueva, 1970); J. Míguez-Bonino, "Teología y Liberación," *Fichas de ISAL,* 26/3 (Montevideo, 1971); E. Dussel, *Para una Etica de la Liberación Latinoamericana* (Buenos Aires: Siglo Veintiuno Editores, 1973); A. Morelli, "Man Liberated from Sin and Oppression. A Theology of Liberation," in T. Quigley, ed., *Freedom in the Americas* (New York, 1971); J.L. Segundo. *The Liberation of Theology* (Orbis, 1976); L.E. Sendoya, "Teología y Proceso de Liberación del Hombre Latinoamericano," *Estudios Ecuménicos,* 9 (1970); P. Richard, et al., *The Idols of Death and the God of Life: A Theology* (Orbis, 1983); H. Assmann, *Theology for a Nomad Church* (Orbis, 1975); idem, *Teología desde la Praxis de la Liberación* (Salamanca: Sígueme, 1974).

15. Samuel Silva Gotay, *El Pensamiento Cristiano Revolucionario en América Latina y el Caribe* (Río Piedras, Puerto Rico: Cordillera/Ediciones Sígueme, 1983), pp. 134-35.

16. See Silva Gotay, *Pensamiento Cristiano,* pp. 135ff.

17. Essential to the political ethic that is being developed by liberation theologians is the need of historical "mediations," especially the idea of a "historical

project" in view of the eschatological vision of the Christian faith (see Silva Gotay, *Pensamiento Cristiano*, pp. 233ff.). Míguez-Bonino, for example, defines the concept of "historical project" by reference, on the one hand, to the "utopian vision," and on the other, to specific plans and programs for the future. The utopian vision has by definition no place or location as a historical mediation; it does not necessarily define coherent structures. On the other extreme, concern for the future may take the form of plans and programs which, given the diversity of goals, determine the means, strategies and tactics. "The idea of historical project" (says Míguez-Bonino) "finds its place somewhere between these two extremes. It is a vision of the future that is sufficiently precise in its political, social and economic contours as to constitute a coherent goal that can be expected to be realized in history. While there is still great flexibility in detail with respect to defining the model to be pursued and determining the technical means for achieving it, the historical project is sufficiently concrete to provide a guide for action and to elicit commitment" (*Toward a Christian Political Ethics* [Philadelphia: Fortress Press, 1983], p. 52).

18. *The Power of the Poor in History* (Maryknoll, N.Y., Orbis, 1983), pp. 65-66.

APPENDIX

1. My translation attempts to reflect the rustic Spanish of its author. The paragraph numbers have been added to the original manuscript.

2. This seems to have been an earlier, provisional title for Lame's book, later discarded and replaced by the current one.

3. The reference is to Guillermo Valencia, famous Colombian poet and politician, who was a candidate for the presidency of the republic in 1914.

4. A reference to St. Thomas Aquinas, called a "dumb ox" by fellow students, because of his size and his reticence. St. Albert the Great, his teacher, said of him: "I tell you that the Dumb Ox will bellow so loud that his bellowing will fill the world."

5. "La Radiola," an old-fashioned record player. Lame seems to be making a reference, serious or jocose, to the cycles of nature, repeating themselves endlessly.

Select Bibliography

PRIMARY SOURCES

Manuscripts

Cabildo Indígena de Ortega. *Actas.* Ortega, Tolima: Archivo del Cabildo (in care of the secretary, Gabriel Yaima).

Hernández de Alba, Gregorio. "Segunda Entrevista con Quintín Lame. Encuestas Realizadas por el Jefe de Resguardos Indígenas, Noviembre 1958, Coyaima, Tolima." Report to the Ministry of Agriculture. Bogotá: Archivo del Ministerio de Gobierno, División de Asuntos Indígenas, 1958.

Informe del Gobernador del Cauca al Presidente de la República (March 1, 1927). Popayán: Imprenta del Departamento, Archivo Departamental, 1927.

Secretaría de Gobierno. *Informe del Secretario de Gobierno del Cauca Leandro Medina al Gobernador.* Popayán: Imprenta del Departamento, Archivo Departamental, 1915.

Secretaría de Gobierno. *Informe sobre Orden Público.* Popayán: Archivo Departamental, 1916.

Secretaría de Gobierno. *Informe sobre Orden Público.* Popayán: Archivo Departamental, 1917.

Published Works

Aguado, Fray Pedro de. *Recopilación Histórica.* Bogotá: Imprenta Nacional, 1906.

Balcázar-Pardo, Marino. *Disposiciones sobre Indígenas, Adjudicación de Baldíos, y Represión de Estados Antisociales.* Popayán: Imprenta Departamental, 1954.

Castellanos, Juan de. *Historia del Nuevo Reino de Granada.* Madrid: A. Pérez Dubrull, 1886.

Castillo I Orozco, Eugenio Del. *Vocabulario Páez-Castellano, Catecismo, Nociones Gramaticales, y Dos Pláticas (Con Adiciones, Correcciones y un Vocabulario Castellano-Páez. Por Ezequiel Uricochea).* Collection Linguistique Américaine. Paris: Maison Neuve, 1877.

Fernández de Oviedo, Gonzalo. *Historia General y Natural de las Indias,* 3 vols. Madrid: BAE, 1959.

Fernández de Piedrahita, Lucas. *Historia General de la Conquista del Nuevo Reino de Granada.* Bogotá: Editorial ABC, 1942.

Ibero, Mario. "Las Crueldades de los Misioneros Españoles en Tierradentro." Interview of Quintín Lame in *El Espectador,* July 12, 1924, p. 1 (Bogotá: Archivo Nacional, Sala Periódicos).

Lame, Manuel Quintín. "Por mi Desventurada Raza. Mensaje de Manuel Quintín Lame a los Altos Poderes." *El Espectador,* January 23, 1922, p. 1 (Bogotá: Archivo Nacional, Sala Periódicos).

Las Casas, Bartolomé de. *Brevísima Relación de la Destrucción de las Indias* (Seville, 1552). English translation, *The Devastation of the Indies, A Brief Account.* New York: Seabury, 1974.

190

————. *Historia de las Indias,* 3 vols. Mexico City and Buenos Aires, 1951.
Simon, Fray Pedro. *Noticias Historiales de la Conquista de Tierra Firma en las Indias Occidentales.* Bogotá: Editorial Kelly, 1953.

Interviews

Lame, Pedro (Quintín Lame's nephew). Interview held in Puracé, Cauca, July 5, 1971.
Lame, Víctor (Quintín Lame's nephew). Interview held in the hacienda San Alfonso (old hacienda San Isidro), Popayán, July 16, 1971.
López, Tulia (daughter of José María López). Interview held in Cali, July 17, 1971.
Mazabuel, Carmen (militant in the Lamista movement). Interview held in Puracé, Cauca, July 5, 1971.
Valencia, Alvaro Pío (grandson of Isaías Muñoz and curator of the Valencia Museum). Interviews held in Popayán, July 10 and 15, 1971.
Yaima, Gabriel (secretary of the Cabildo Indígena of Ortega). Interview held in Ortega, Tolima, October 17, 1970.

SECONDARY SOURCES

Acosta, José de. *De Procuranda Indorum Salute* (1577). Madrid: BAE, 1954.
Adas, Michael. *Prophets of Rebellion: Millenarian Protest Movements Against the European Colonial Order.* Chapel Hill: University of North Carolina Press, 1979.
Aguilera, Miguel; Restrepo Canal, Carlos; and Nieto Caballero, Luis Eduardo. *Marco Fidel Suárez.* Bogotá: Editorial ABC, 1955.
Aguirre-Beltrán, Gonzalo. *Regiones de Refugio.* Mexico City: Instituto Indigenista Interamericano, 1967.
Arcila Robledo, Gregorio. *Las Misiones Franciscanas en Colombia.* Bogotá: Imprenta Nacional, 1950.
Arguedas, J.M., and Pineda, Josafat R. "Tres Versiones del Mito de Inkarri." In Ossio, *Ideología Mesiánica del Mundo Andino,* pp. 219-36.
Balandier, Georges. "La Situation Coloniale: Approche Théorique." *Cahiers Internationaux de Sociologie,* 11 (1951).
Bastide, Roger. *Les Religions Afro-Bresiliennes: Contribution à une Sociologie des Interpenetrations de Civilisations.* Paris: PUF, 1960. English translation, *The African Religions of Brazil: Towards a Sociology of the Interpenetration of Civilizations.* Baltimore and London: Johns Hopkins University Press, 1978.
————. "Messianisme et developpement économique et social." *Cahiers Internationaux de Sociologie,* 30 (1961).
Bernal, Segundo Eleazar. "Religious Life of the Páez Indians of Colombia." M.A. thesis, Faculty of Political Science, Columbia University, 1956.
————. "La fiesta de San Juan en Calderas, Tierradentro." *Revista Colombiana de Folklore,* 2, segunda epoca (1953) 177-221.
————. "Medicina y Magia entre los Páeces." *Revista Colombiana de Antropología,* 2 (1954) 221-63.
————. "Bases para el Estudio de la Organización de los Páez." *Revista Colombiana de Antropología,* 4 (1955).
————. "Economía de los Páez." *Revista Colombiana de Antropología,* 3 (1954).
————. "Mitología y Cuentos de la Parcialidad de Calderas, Tierradentro." *Revista Colombiana de Antropología,* 1 (1953).
Bianchi, Enzo. "The Status of those Without Dignity in the Old Testament." In Pohier and Mieth, *The Dignity of the Despised of the Earth.*
Binder, Teodoro. "The Right of the Third World to Develop Its Own Way, and

Remarks on the Idea of 'Change.'" In Sevilla-Casas, *Western Expansion and Indigenous Peoples, The Heritage of Las Casas,* pp. 51-56.

Bodley, John H. "Alternatives to Ethnocide: Human Zoos, Living Museums, and Real People." In Sevilla-Casas, *Western Expansion and Indigenous Peoples, The Heritage of Las Casas,* pp. 31-50.

Boff, Clodovis. *Teologia e Prática: Teologia do Político e suas Mediações.* Petrópolis: Vozes, 1978. Translated by Robert R. Barr, *Theology and Praxis.* Maryknoll, New York: Orbis Books, 1987.

Boff, Leonardo. *Jesus Christ Liberator. A Critical Christology for our Time.* Maryknoll, New York: Orbis Books, 1979.

Bonilla, Victor Daniel. *Servants of God, or Masters of Men?* Harmondsworth: Penguin, 1972.

Burgos-Guevara, Hugo. *Relaciones Interétnicas en Riobamba.* Mexico City: Instituto Indigenista Interamericano, 1970.

Burridge, Kenelm. *New Heaven, New Earth: A Study of Millenarian Activities.* New York: Schocken Books, 1969.

Castillo-Cárdenas, Gonzalo. *The Colombian Concordat in the Light of Recent Trends in Catholic Thought Concerning Church-State Relations and Religious Liberty.* Cuernavaca, Mexico: CIDOC, Colección Sondeos no. 22, 1968.

———. "The Indian Struggle for Freedom in Colombia." In Dostal, *The Situation of the Indian in South America.*

———. "Estudio Introductorio. Manuel Quintín Lame: Luchador e Intelectual Indígena del Siglo XX." In Manuel Quintín Lame, *En Defensa de Mi Raza* (Bogotá: Comité de Defensa del Indio, 1971), pp. xi-xiv.

Castrillón-Arboleda, Diego. *De la Colonia al Subdesarrollo.* Popayán: Editorial Universidad, 1970.

———. *El Indio Quintín Lame.* Bogotá: Ediciones Tercer Mundo, 1973.

Chaunu, Pierre. *Conquête et exploitation de nouveaux mondes.* Paris: PUF, 1969.

Cobo, Bernabe. *Historia del nuevo mundo,* 2 vols. Madrid, 1956.

Colmenares, German. *Las Haciendas de los Jesuitas en el Nuevo Reino de Granada (Siglo XVIII).* Bogotá: Universidad Nacional de Colombia, 1969.

Colombres, Adolfo, ed. *Por la Liberación del Indígena. Documentos y Testimonios.* Buenos Aires: Ediciones del Sol, 1975.

Comblin, José. "Humanity and the Liberation of the Oppressed." In Jean-Pierre Jossua and Claude Geffré, eds., *Is Being Human a Criterion of Being Christian?* New York: Seabury Press, 1982, pp. 74-80.

Croatto, José Severino. *Liberación y Libertad: Pautas Hermenéuticas.* Buenos Aires: Ediciones Mundo Nuevo, 1973.

Cuervo Márquez, Carlos. *Estudios Arqueológicos y Etnográficos,* vols. 1 and 2. Madrid, 1920.

Della Cava, Ralph. *Miracle at Joaseiro.* New York: Columbia University Press, 1970.

Desroche, Henri. "Les messianismes et la categorie de l'échec." *Cahiers Internationaux de Sociologie,* 35 (1963) 61-84.

———. "Messianismes et Utopies. Note sur les origines du Socialisme occidental." *Socialismes et Sociologie Religieuse,* chap. 2.

———. *Socialismes et Sociologie Religieuse. Textes de F. Engels traduits et présentés avec le concours de G. Dunstheimer et M.L. Letendre.* Paris: Editions Cujas, 1965.

Díaz-Aristizabal, Fabián. *El Resguardo Indígena, su Realidad y la Ley,* 2 vols. Bogotá: Ministerio de Gobierno, n.d.

Dostal, W., ed. *The Situation of the Indian in South America.* Geneva, 1972.

Dussel, Enrique. *A History of the Church in Latin America: Colonialism to Liberation, 1492-1979.* Grand Rapids: Eerdmans Publishing Co., 1981.

————. *Filosofía Etica Latinoamericana. IV: Política; V: Arqueológia*. Bogotá: Universidad Santo Tomás, 1979-1981.

————. *Método para una Filosofía de la Liberación: Superación Analéctica de la Dialéctica Hegeliana*. Salamanca: Sígueme, 1974.

————. "Modern Christianity in Face of the Other." In Pohier and Mieth, *The Dignity of the Despised of the Earth*, pp. 51ff.

Duviols, Pierre. *La Destrucción de las Religiones Andinas durante la Conquista y la Colonia*. Mexico City: Universidad Nacional Autónoma de México, 1977.

Emmett, Dorothy. "Prophets and Their Societies." *Journal of the Royal Anthropological Institute*, 86 (1956) 13-23.

Espinoza R., Gustavo and Malpica S.S., Carlos. *El Problema de la Tierra*. Lima: Biblioteca Amauta, 1970.

Evans-Pritchard, E.E. *Neuer Religion*. Oxford, 1956.

Fajardo, Darío. "La Violencia y las Estructuras Agrárias en Colombia." In F. Leal Buitrago, et al., *El Agro en el Desarrollo Histórico Colombiano*. Bogotá: Ediciones Punta de Lanza, 1977, pp. 265-300.

Fals-Borda, Orlando. *Campesinos de los Andes. Estudio Sociológico de Saucio*. Bogotá: Universidad Nacional de Colombia, 1961.

————. *El Hombre y la Tierra en Boyacá*. Bogotá: Universidad Nacional de Colombia, 1957.

————. *Historia de la Cuestión Agraria en Colombia*. Bogotá: Publicaciones de la Rosca, 1975.

————. *La Teoría y la Realidad del Cambio Sociocultural en Colombia*. Bogotá: Departamento de Sociología, Universidad Nacional de Colombia, 1959.

————. "The Role of Violence in the Break with Traditionalism: the Colombian Case." In *Transactions of the Fifth World Congress of Sociology* (Washington, D.C., September 2-8, 1962), III, 1964.

————. *Peasant Society in the Colombian Andes*. Gainesville, Florida: University Press of Florida, 1955.

Fernández, Ruben Cesar. *Os Cavaleiros do Bom Jesus: Una Introdução as Religioes Populares*. São Paulo: Brasiliense, 1982.

Ferreiro, Onorio. "Significado e Implicaciones Universales de un Mito Peruano." In Ossio, *Ideología Mesiánica del Mundo Andino*, pp. 417-38.

Foster, George. "Peasant Society and the Image of the Limited Good." *American Anthropologist*, 61 (1965) 293-315.

Franco R., Ramón. *Antropogeografía Colombiana*. Manizales: Imprenta del Departamento, 1941.

Freire, Paulo. *Cultural Action for Freedom*. Cambridge, Mass.: Center for the Study of Development and Social Change.

Friede, Juan. *En Indio en Lucha por la Tierra. Historia de los Resguardos del Macizo Central Colombiano*. Bogotá: Instituto Indigenista de Colombia, Ediciones Espiral, 1944.

————. *La Explotación Indígena en Colombia*. Bogotá: Editorial Punta de Lanza, 1973.

————, Friedemann, Nina S. de, and Fajardo, Darío. *Indigenismo y Aniquilamiento de Indígenas en Colombia*. Bogotá: Universidad Nacional, Departamento de Antropología, 1975.

————. *Invasión del País de los Chibchas, Conquista del Nuevo Reino de Granada y Fundación de Santafe de Bogotá (Revaluaciones y Rectificaciones)*. Bogotá: Ediciones Tercer Mundo, 1966.

————. *Los Andaki 1538-1947, Historia de la Aculturación de una Tribu Selvática*. Mexico City and Buenos Aires: Fondo de Cultura Económica, 1953.

————. "De la Encomienda Indiana a la Propiedad Territorial y su Influencia en el Mestizaje." *Anuario Colombiano de Historia Social y de la Cultura*, 4 (1969).

Gaitán, Gloria. *Colombia: La Lucha por la Tierra en la Década del Treinta.* Bogotá: Ediciones Tercer Mundo, 1976.

Galilea, Segundo. "Liberation as an Encounter with Politics and Contemplation." In Gutiérrez and Geffré, *The Mystical and Political Dimensions of the Christian Faith,* pp. 19-33.

Geffré, Claude. "Editorial: A Prophetic Theology." In Gutiérrez and Geffré, *The Mystical and Political Dimensions of the Christian Faith,* pp. 7-15.

Gilhodes, Pierre. "Agrarian Struggles in Colombia." In Rodolfo Stavenhagen, ed., *Agrarian Problems and Peasant Movements in Latin American.* Garden City, N.Y.: Doubleday, 1970, pp. 407-52.

González, David. *Los Páeces. Genocidio y Luchas Indígenas en Colombia.* Popayán: Editorial Rueda Suelta, n.d.

González, Margarita. *El Resguardo en el Nuevo Reino de Granada.* Bogotá: Universidad Nacional, 1970.

Gottwald, Norman K., ed. *The Bible and Liberation: Political and Social Hermeneutics.* Maryknoll, N.Y.: Orbis Books, 1983.

Guhl, Ernesto. *Colombia: Bosquejo de su Geografía Tropical,* 2 vols. Bogotá: Instituto Colombiano de Cultura, 1976.

Gutiérrez, Gustavo. *A Theology of Liberation.* Maryknoll, New York: Orbis Books, 1973.

————. *The Power of the Poor in History.* Orbis Books, 1983.

————, and Geffré, Claude, eds. *The Mystical and Political Dimension of the Christian Faith.* New York: Herder and Herder, *Concilium,* 1974.

Guzman-Böckler, Carlos. *Colonialismo y Revolución.* Mexico City: Siglo Veintiuno Editores, 1975.

———— and Jean-Loup Herbert. *Guatemala: Una Interpretación Historico-Social.* Mexico City: Siglo Veintiuno Editores, 1970.

Guzman Campos, German; Fals-Borda, Orlando; and Umaña Luna, Eduardo. *La Violencia en Colombia, Estudio de un Proceso Social,* II. Bogotá: Ediciones Tercer Mundo, 1964.

Haddox, Benjamin E. *Sociedad y Religión en Colombia, Estudio de las Instituciones Religiosas Colombianas.* Bogotá: Ediciones Tercer Mundo/Facultad de Sociología, Universidad Nacional de Colombia, 1965.

Halbwacks, M. *La Mémoire Collective.* Paris: PUF, 1968.

Hanke, Lewis. *Estudios sobre Fray Bartolomé de Las Casas y sobre la Lucha por la Justicia en la Conquista Española de América.* Caracas: Ediciones de la Biblioteca de la Universidad Central de Venezuela, 1968.

Hegel, G.W.F. *Lectures on the Philosophy of World History.* Cambridge (Mass.) University Press, 1975.

Hernández de Alba, Gregorio. "Etnología de los Andes del Sur de Colombia." *Revista de la Universidad del Cauca,* 5 (1944).

————. "The Highland Tribes of Southern Colombia." In *Handbook of South American Indians,* IV. Julian H. Steward, ed. Washington, D.C., 1948.

————. "Sub-Andean Tribes of the Cauca Valley." In *Handbook of South American Indians,* IV. Julian H. Steward, ed. Washington, D.C., 1948.

Hernández Rodríguez, Guillermo. *De los Chibchas a la Colonia y a la República.* Bogotá: Ediciones Internacionales, 1978.

Hobsbawn, Eric. *Primitive Rebels: Studies in Archaic Forms of Social Movements in the 19th and 20th Centuries.* New York: Frederick Praeger, 1959.

Hoekema, Anthony A. *The Bible and the Future.* Grand Rapids: Eerdmans, 1979.

Huizer, Gerrit. *El Potencial Revolucionario del Campesinado en América Latina.* Mexico City: Siglo Veintiuno Editores, 1973.

Imbelloni, José. "El Génesis de los Pueblos Prehistóricos de América." *Academia Argentina de Letras,* 9 (1941).

————. *Religiosidad Indígena Americana*. Buenos Aires: Ediciones Castañeda, 1981.

Instituto Fe y Secularidad. *Fe Cristiana y Cambio Social en América Latina* (Encuentro de El Escorial, 1972). Salamanca: Ediciones Sígueme, 1973.

Iwánska, Alicja. *Purgatory and Utopia. A Mazahuan Indian Village of Mexico*. Cambridge: Schenkman Publishing Company, 1971.

Jossua, Jean-Pierre, and Metz, Johann Baptist, eds. *Doing Theology in New Places*. New York: Seabury Press, 1979.

Kalmanovitz, Salomón. "Desarrollo Capitalista en el Campo Colombiano." In Mario Arrubla, et al., Colombia Hoy. Bogotá: Siglo Veintiuno Editores de Colombia, 1978, pp. 271-330.

Krickberg, Walter, et al. *Pre-Colombian American Religions*. History of Religions Series. New York: Holt, Rinehart and Winston, 1968.

Kudo, Tokihiro. *Práctica Religiosa y Proyecto Histórico. Estudio sobre la Religiosidad Popular en Dos Barrios de Lima*. Lima: CEP, 1980.

————, and Vidales, Raúl. *Práctica Religiosa y Proyecto Histórico*. Lima: CEP, 1975.

Kusch, Rodolfo. *El Pensamiento Indígena y Popular en América*. Mexico City, 1970.

Lanternari, Vittorio. *The Religions of the Oppressed. A Study of Modern Messianic Cults*. New York: New American Library, 1963.

Las Casas, Bartolomé de. *In Defense of the Indians*. De Kalb: Northern Illinois University Press, 1974.

León-Portilla, Miguel. *Time and Reality in the Thought of the Maya*. Boston: Beacon Press, 1973.

Levine, Daniel H. *Religion and Politics in Latin America: The Catholic Church in Venezuela and Colombia*. Princeton University Press, 1981.

Levine, Daniel H., and Wilde, Alexander W. "The Catholic Church, 'Politics' and Violence: the Colombian Case." *Review of Politics*, 39/2 (April 1977) 220-39.

Liévano Aguirre, Indalecio. *Los Grandes Conflictos Sociales y Económicos de Nuestra Historia*. Bogotá: 1968.

Lopes de Mesa, Luis. *De Como se ha Formado la Nación Colombiana*. Medellín: Editorial Bedout, 1970.

Madsen, William. "Christo-Paganism: A Study of Mexican Religious Syncretism." *Nativism and Syncretism*, 19, Middle American Research Institute, Tulane University, New Orleans, 1960.

Mariátegui, J.C. *Siete Ensayos de Interpretación de la Realidad Peruana*. Lima: Amauta, 1967.

Marx, K., and Engels, F. *On Religion*. New York: Schocken Books, 1964.

Marzal, Manuel. *El Mundo Religioso de Urcos*. Cuzco: Instituto de Pastoral Andina, 1971.

————. *Estudios sobre Religión Campesina*. Lima: Pontifica Universidad Católica del Perú, 1977.

McGreevey, William Paul. *An Economic History of Colombia, 1845-1930*. Boston, 1971.

Mercatti, Angelo. *Raccolta di Concordati su Materie Ecclesiastiche tra la Santa Sede e le Autorità Civili*, 2 vols. Tipografia Poliglotta Vaticana, 1954.

Migúez Bonino, José. *Christians and Marxists. The Mutual Challenge to Revolution*. Grand Rapids: Eerdmans, 1976.

————. "Popular Piety in Latin America." In Gutiérrez and Geffré, *The Mystical and Political Dimensions of the Christian Faith*, pp. 148-57.

Millones, Luis. "Un Movimiento Nativista del Siglo XVI: El Taki Ongoy." In Ossio, *Ideología Mesiánica del Mundo Andino*, pp. 83ff.

Ministerio de Gobierno de Colombia. "Concepto de Parcialidad." *Indigenismo Colombiano,* 1 (January 1974) 9-16.

———. "Indígenas y 'Civilizados.'" *Indigenismo Colombiano,* 2 (April 1974) 33-80.

Monast, Jacques. *L'Univers Religieux des Aymaras de Bolivie.* Sondeos no. 10. Cuernavaca, Mexico, 1966.

Mörner, Magnus. "Las Comunidades Indígenas y la Legislación Segregacionista en el Nuevo Reino de Granada." *Anuario Colombiano de Historia y de la Cultura,* 1/1. Bogotá, 1963.

Mutchler, David E. *The Church as a Political Factor in Latin America, with Particular Reference to Colombia and Chile.* New York: Frederick Praeger, 1971.

Nachtigal, Horst. "Shamanismo entre los Indios Páeces." *Revista Colombiana del Folklore,* 3, segunda epoca (June 1953) 223-41.

———. *Tierradentro. Archäologie und Ethnographie einer kolumbianischen Landschaft.* Zurich: Origo Verlag, 1955.

Neira, Hugo. *Los Andes: Tierra o Muerte.* Santiago and Madrid: Editorial ZYX, 1968.

Norris, William Dale. *The Christian Origins of Social Revolt.* London: George Allen and Unwin, 1949.

Olman, Bertell. *Alienation: Marx's Concept of Man in Capitalist Society.* Cambridge, 1971.

Ortiz, Sutti. "Reflections on the Concept of 'Peasant Culture' and Peasant Cognitive Systems." In *Peasants and Peasant Societies: Selected Readings,* Teodor Shanin, ed. Harmondsworth: Penguin Books, 1971.

Ospina, Joaquín. *Diccionario Biográfico y Bibliográfico de Colombia.* Bogotá: Editorial Aguila, 1939.

Ossio A., María. *Ideología Mesiánica del Mundo Andino.* Lima: Edición de Ignacio Prado Pastor, 1973.

Otero, José María. *Etnología Caucana.* Popayán: Editorial Universidad del Cauca, 1952.

Otto, Rudolf. *The Idea of the Holy.* New York: Oxford University Press, 1958.

Pereira de Queiroz, María Isaura. *Historia y Etnología de los Movimientos Mesiánicos.* Mexico City: Siglo Veintiuno Editores, 1969.

———. *O Messianismo no Brasil e no Mundo.* São Paulo: Dominus Editora, Universidad de São Paulo, 1965.

Pérez de Barradas, José. *Arqueología y Antropología Precolombinas de Tierradentro.* Bogotá: Ministerio de Educación Pública, Publicaciones de la Sección de Arqueología, no. 1, 1937.

Phelan, John Leddy. *The Millennial Kingdom of the Franciscans in the New World,* 2nd edition. Berkeley: University of California Press, 1970.

———. *The People and the King, the Comunero Revolution in Colombia, 1781.* Madison: University of Wisconsin Press, 1978.

Pin, Emile. *Elementos para una Sociología del Catolicismo Latinoamericano.* Bogotá: Centro de Estudios Sociales, 1963.

Pittier de Fábrega, H. "Ethnographic and Linguistic Notes on the Páez Indians of Tierradentro, Cauca, Colombia." In *Memoirs of the American Anthropological Association.* Lancaster, 1907.

Pohier, Jacques, and Mieth, Dietmar, eds. *The Dignity of the Despised of the Earth.* New York: Seabury, 1979.

Posada, Elvira Castro de. *El Pasado Aborígen.* Buenos Aires: Editorial Stilcograf, 1955.

Rappaport, Joanne. "Mesianismos y las Transformaciones de Símbolos Mesiánicos en Tierradentro," in *Revista Colombiana de Antropología,* v. 20, 1980-81: pp. 367-413.

Redfield, Robert. *The Primitive World and its Transformations,* 2nd edition. New York: Dover Publications, 1947.

Reichel-Dolmatoff, Gerardo, and Jualín, Roberto, eds. *El Etnocidio a través de las Américas.* Mexico City: Siglo Veintiuno Editores, 1916, pp. 290ff.

Restrepo, Humberto. *La Religión de la Antigua Antioquía.* Medellín: Editorial Bedout, 1972.

Ribeiro, Darcy. *The Americas and Civilization.* New York: E. P. Dutton and Company, 1972.

Rippy, J. Fred. *The Capitalists and Colombia.* New York, 1931.

Rocha-Castilla, Cesáreo. *Prehistoria y Folclor del Tolima,* 2nd edition. Ibagué, Tolima: Publicaciones de la Dirección de Educación del Departamento, 1968.

Rodríguez, Manuel. *El Marañon y Amazonas.* Madrid, 1684.

Saavedra, Alejandro. *La Cuestión Mapuche.* Instituto de Capacitación e Investigación en Reforma Agraria. Proyecto Gobierno de Chile/Naciones Unidas/ FAO, Santiago de Chile, 1971.

Sánchez, Gonzalo G. *Las Ligas Campesinas en Colombia (Auge y Reflujo).* Bogotá: Ediciones Tiempo Presente, 1977.

Scannone, Juan Carlos. *Teología de la Liberación y Praxis Popular.* Salamanca: Sígueme, 1976.

Schroyer, Trent. *The Critique of Domination: The Origins and Development of Critical Theory.* Boston: Beacon Press, 1975.

Sevilla-Casas, Elias. "Atraso y Desarrollo Indígena en Tierradentro." Bogotá: Universidad de los Andes, 1976.

———. "Estudios Antropológicos sobre Tierradentro." Cali: Fundación para la Educación Superior, 1979.

———. "Lame y el Cauca Indígena." In N.S. Friedemann, ed., *Tierra, Tradición y Poder en Colombia.* Bogotá: Biblioteca Básica Colombiana, Instituto Colombiano de Cultura, 1976, pp. 90-105.

———, ed. *Western Expansion and Indigenous Peoples: The Heritage of Las Casas* (International Congress of Anthropologists, Chicago, 1973). The Hague and Paris: Mouton Publishers, 1973.

Sharot, Stephen. *Messianism, Mysticism, and Magic: A Sociological Analysis of Jewish Religious Movements.* Chapel Hill: University of North Carolina Press, 1982.

Stavenhagen, Rodolfo. "Classes, Colonialism and Acculturation." In Irving Louis Horowitz, ed., *Masses in Latin America.* New York: Oxford University Press, 1978, pp. 235-88.

Steger, Hans-Albert. *El Trasfondo revolucionario del Sincretismo criollo, Aspectos sociales de la transformación clandestina de la religión en Afroamérica colonial y postcolonial.* Sondeos no. 86. Cuernavaca, Mexico: CIDOC, 1972.

Stendal, Chad. *Lenta Aculturación en una Cultura no Materialista, Dirección General de Integración y Desarrollo de la Comunidad.* Bogotá: Ministerio de Gobierno de Colombia, 1971.

Taussig, Michael. *Destrucción y Resistencia Campesina: El Caso del Litoral Pacífico.* Bogotá: Ediciones Punta de Lanza, 1978.

———. *The Devil and Commodity Fetishism in South America.* Chapel Hill: University of North Carolina Press, 1980.

———. "The Evolution of Rural Wage Labour in the Tropical Andes: The Case of the Cauca Valley, Colombia." In *Landlord and Peasant in Latin America and the Carribean,* K. Duncan, ed. Cambridge, England, 1974.

———. "The Genesis of Capitalism Among a South American Peasantry." *Comparative Studies in Society and History,* 19/2. Cambridge University Press, 1977.

Tedlock, Dennis. *The Spoken Word and the Work of Interpretation.* Philadelphia: University of Pennsylvania Press, 1983.

Thrupp, Sylvia, ed. *Millennial Dreams in Action: Comparative Studies in Society and History.* The Hague: Mouton Publishers, 1962.

Torres-Giraldo, Ignacio. *La Cuestión Indígena en Colombia.* Bogotá: Publicaciones de la Rosca, 1975.

——. *Los Inconformes, Resumen de la Historia de los Colombianos,* I. Medellín: Casa de Cultura, 1967.

Tovar, Hermes. *El Movimiento Campesino en Colombia durante los Siglos XIX y XX,* 2nd edition. Bogotá: Ediciones Libres, 1976.

Trimborn, Hermann. "South Central America and the Andean Civilizations." In Krickberg, *Pre-Colombian American Religions,* pp. 96-97.

Ulloa, Jorge, and Juan y Santacilla. *Noticias Secretas de América, 1748.* English translation, *Discourse and Political Reflections on the Kingdoms of Peru.* Oklahoma City: University of Oklahoma Press, 1978.

Vidales, Raúl. *Cristianismo Antiburgués.* San José, Costa Rica: Departamento Ecuménico de Investigaciones, 1978.

——. *Cuestiones en Torno al Método en la Teología de la Liberación.* Lima: Secretariado Latinoamericano, 1974.

Villavicencio-Rivadeneira, Gladys. *Relaciones Interétnicas in Otavalo, Ecuador.* Mexico City: Instituto Indigenista Interamericano, 1973.

Vrijhof, Pieter H., and Waardenburg, Jacques, eds. *Official and Popular Religion: Analysis of a Theme for Religious Studies.* The Hague: Mouton Publishers, 1979.

Wachtel, Nathan. "La Visión de Los Vencidos: La Conquista Española en el Folklore Andino." In Ossio, *Ideología Mesiánica del Mundo Andino,* pp. 35-81.

——. *La Visión des Vaincus.* Paris, 1971.

——. "Pensamiento Salvaje y AcULTURación: el Espacio y el Tiempo en Felipe Guaman Poma de Ayala y el Inca Garcilaso de la Vega." In N. Wachtel, *Sociedad e Ideología.* Lima: Instituto de Estudios Peruanos, 1973.

——. "Rebeliones y Milenarismo." In Ossio, *Ideología Mesiánica del Mundo Andino.* pp. 103ff.

Wallis, Wilson D. *Messiahs, Christian and Pagan.* Boston: Gorham Press, 1918.

Warren, Kay B. *The Symbolism of Subordination. Indian Identity in a Guatemalan Town.* Austin: University of Texas Press, 1978.

Weber, Max. *The Sociology of Religion.* Boston: Beacon Press, 1963.

West, Cornel. *Prophesy Deliverance: An Afro-American Revolutionary Christianity.* Philadelphia: Westminster, 1982.

Whiteford, Andrew H. *An Andean City at Mid-Century, A Traditional Urban Society.* E. Lansing: Michigan State University Press, 1977.

Wilson Bryan. *Magic and the Millennium, Religious Movements of Protest Among Tribal and Third World Peoples.* New York: Harper and Row, 1973.

Wolf, Eric R. *Europe and the People Without History.* Berkeley and Los Angeles: University of California Press, 1982.

Wolff, Hans Walter. *Anthropology of the Old Testament.* Philadelphia: Fortress Press, 1974.

Worsley, Peter. *The Trumpet Shall Sound: A Study of Cargo Cults in Melanesia.* London: McGibbon and Kee, 1957.

Yamamori, Tetsunao, and Taber, Charles R., eds. *Christopaganism or Indigenous Christianity?* Pasadena: William Carey Library, 1975.

Zuidema, T.T. *The Ceque System of Cuzco: The Social Organization of the Capital of the Inca.* Leiden: International Archives of Ethnography, 1964.

——. *A Visit to God.* Bijdrogen, 1968.

Index

Compiled by William H. Schlau